THE LATINA/O PATHWAY TO THE PH.D.

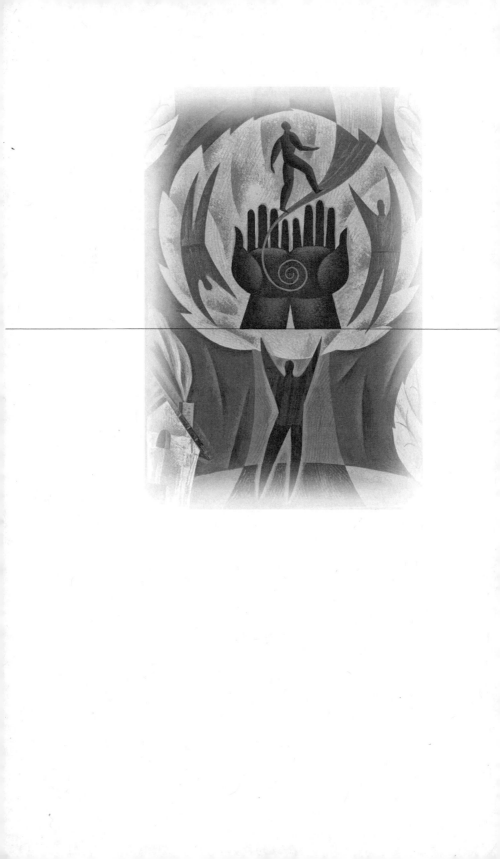

THE LATINA/O PATHWAY

TO THE PH.D.

Abriendo Caminos

Edited by

Jeanett Castellanos, Alberta M. Gloria,
and Mark Kamimura

Forewords by
Melba Vasquez and Hector Garza

Sty/us

STERLING, VIRGINIA

Sty/us

COPYRIGHT © 2006 BY STYLUS PUBLISHING, LLC

Published by Stylus Publishing, LLC
22883 Quicksilver Drive
Sterling, Virginia 20166-2102

Library of Congress Cataloging-in-Publication-Data
The Latina/o pathway to the Ph.D. : abriendo caminos /
edited by Jeanett Castellanos, Alberta M. Gloria and
Mark Kamimura ; forewords by Melba Vasquez and
Hector Garza.— 1st ed.
    p.   cm.
   ISBN 1-57922-106-8 (hardcover : alk. paper) — ISBN
1-57922-107-6 (pbk. : alk. paper)
    1. Hispanic Americans—Education (Higher)
2. Hispanic American children—Education.
3. Academic achievement—Social aspects—United
States.   4. Educational equalization—United States.
I. Title: Abriendo caminos.   II. Castellanos, Jeanett,
1972–   III. Gloria, Alberta M. (Alberta Marie), 1965–
IV. Kamimura, Mark (Mark Allen), 1977–
LC2670.6.L39   2005
378.1′55′08968073—dc22   2005012388

ISBN: 1-57922-106-8 (cloth)
ISBN: 1-57922-107-6 (paper)

Printed in the United States of America

All first editions printed on acid free paper
that meets the American National Standards Institute
Z39-48 Standard.

First Edition, 2006

10 9 8 7 6 5 4 3 2 1

Jeanett Castellanos

To my parents and my grandparents—the inspiration of my life. To my mentors, who taught me about life and academia. To my students, who stimulate me to teach.

A mis padres y abuelitos—la inspiración de mi vida. A mis maestros que me enseñaron de la vida y academia. A mis estudiantes que me dan motivo para enseñar.

Alberta M. Gloria

To my mom, Amelia, and the memory of my father, Albert—may these efforts honor you and our family. To Jeffrey, for your tireless belief that I can.

A mi mamá Amelia y a la memoria de mi padre, Alberto—que estos esfuerzos les traiga orgullo a ustedes y a nuestra familia. Para Jeffrey, por creer interminablemente que puedo.

Mark Kamimura

To my family, Aurora, Marco, and Michio. To the memory of Melody Jiménez Kamimura, my spiritual mentor and mom.

A mi familia, Aurora, Marco, y Michio. A la memoria de Melody Jiménez Kamimura, mi madre y guía espiritual.

CONTENTS

Melba J. T. Vasquez

Dr. Melba J. T. Vasquez is in independent practice in Austin, Texas. She is co-author of *Ethics in Psychotherapy and Counseling: A Practical Guide for Psychologists*, 1998 (2nd ed.), with Ken Pope, and of *How to Survive and Thrive as a Therapist: Information, Ideas, and Resources for Psychologists in Practice*, 2005, also with Ken Pope. She is a past president of APA Division 35, Society for the Psychology of Women, and of Division 17, Society of Counseling Psychology. She was elected to serve as president of the Texas Psychological Association in 2006, and serves on the Council of Representatives for APA Division 42, Psychologists in Independent Practice, for 2004–2007. She has served on numerous boards and committees of the American Psychological Association, Texas Psychological Association, and she is a member of other organizations, including the National Latino Psychological Association.

As part of her presidency of Division 35, she helped to found and co-host the National Multicultural Conference and Summit. She often provides workshops and keynote presentations, and she publishes in areas of women in psychology, ethnic minority psychology, supervision and training, and professional ethics.

She is a Fellow of the American Psychological Association for Divisions 35 and 45 (1989), and also a Fellow of Divisions 1, 9, 17, 35, 42, 45, and 49. She is also a member of APA Divisions 44 and 31, and holds the Diplomate from the American Board of Professional Psychology. She has received numerous awards for her contributions to the profession.

FOREWORD 1

Journey to a PhD: The Latina/o Experience in Higher Education

Melba J. T. Vasquez

"Education is our freedom and freedom should be everybody's business." This is the philosophy and mission of the American G. I. Forum, a veteran's family organization founded in 1948 by Dr. Hector P. Garcia in Texas when Latinos were not welcomed in veteran's organizations. Dr. Garcia and other founders of this organization engaged in civil rights activities, largely through promoting educational opportunities for Latinos (American G. I. Forum, 2004).

This group had a tremendous impact on our family. My father was a veteran and belonged to this group. The only scholarship I received for my education as a first-generation college student was from the local American G.I. Forum group, which considered education very important. My own experience proves that it takes a significant effort on the part of a variety of groups to make education a priority.

Education is considered by many educators to be "a special, deeply political, almost sacred, civic activity" (Loury, 1998, p. xxii). Most U.S. citizens believe that education, at least from pre–K to high school graduation, should be afforded to every American citizen. In addition, a highly educated populace is a symbol of a strong, healthy industrial country. Indeed, the well-being of the country in general is dependent on a well-educated population, and the corporate/business world has long worked to promote a diverse workforce, given the contributions that derive from having richness and variety among employees, managers, and supervisors. Universities that strive to become Hispanic Serving Institutions (25% of the student body population, diverse faculty, etc.) know that attracting and supporting a more diverse faculty, staff, student body, and curriculum enriches the learning and working environments.

Although the educational levels of people of color, including Latina/os, in this country have increased since the 1940s, a very troubling gap still exists between the proportion of students of color and White students in higher education; the proportion of undergraduate Latina/o students relative to the Latina/o proportion in the population is still under-represented as well. The disparities are obvious in the numbers of dropouts, the knowledge gap that increases throughout the school experience, the high school and college graduation rates, and advanced degree attainments. These data are discussed at length in several of the chapters, including one by Contreras and Gándara.

The philosophy that education is a means to civil rights for Latina/os and other disenfranchised groups is more meaningful today than ever before. The fact is that economic power and status are closely related to educational level. Median income by educational level, for example, shows that a person (21–64 years of age) who is not a high school graduate earns $21,332, high school graduates earn $27,351, those with some college earn $31,988, those with a bachelor's degree earn $42,877, and those with advanced degrees earn $55,242 (U. S. Census Bureau, 2000). These educational and economic levels are in turn related to physical and emotional well-being.

The wage gap that divides workers with complex and technological skills from those in manufacturing service and manual jobs has widened, creating a large group of low-wage earners, often referred to as the working poor (American Psychological Association, 2004). Lifelong learning is no longer a luxury, but a necessity, which means that education is very tightly associated with socioeconomic survival.

To improve the educational status of Latina/os, a complex understanding of the multiple issues and challenges that contribute to the educational gap must be identified and analyzed, in order for appropriate strategies to be developed and implemented. For example, which individual and environmental (including family, cultural, school, and community) characteristics and factors impede or facilitate success? What programmatic efforts make a difference? Many themes in the chapters include challenges to stereotypes as well as identification of best practices to effect change. This book is an effort to compile that information, from early childhood education to college and beyond, including lifelong learning. The wealth of information here provides a foundation for a much-needed empirical policy analysis. In addition, the chapters by graduate students and young professionals provide poignant examples of the actual educational experiences that bring to life facts and factors that make a difference. This book provides ample discussion to promote a deeper and broader understanding of the continued changes needed to find ways to tap the full spectrum of human potential among Latina/os.

Progress, though slow, is being made. This volume is a testament to those individuals who have fought long odds in their pursuit of the doctorate; it is cautionary to those who would undertake such pursuit; and it is a challenge to those who are committed to smoothing the pathway for current and future generations of aspiring Latina/o Ph.D.s. Ultimately, students, faculty, university administrators, and those of us who work "from the outside" must heed the message of this book: We must continue to work tirelessly to promote Latina/o access to and progress through the entire education pipeline. We must continue to work to eliminate the barriers—marginalization, lack of access, limited resources, issues of retention, and cultural expectations among them—that restrict access by Latina/os to the Ph.D. Only as we do so will all members of our society reap the benefits of advanced education in equal proportion. This compendium of information could not be more timely, relevant, or useful to students, faculty, and administrators.

References

American G. I. Forum. Retrieved on December 17, 2004, from http://www.agif .org/.

American Psychological Association (2004). *Public policy, work, and families: The report of the APA Presidential Initiative on Work and Families.* Washington, DC: American Psychological Association.

Loury, G. C. (1998). Foreword. In W. G. Bowen & D. Bok (Eds.), *The shape of the river: Long-term consequences of considering race in college and university admissions* (p. xxii). Princeton, NJ: Princeton University Press.

U.S. Census Bureau (2000). Retrieved on December 17, 2004, from http://www .census.gov/hhes/income/earnings/calliusboth.html.

Hector Garza

Hector Garza serves as the founding president of the National Council for Community and Education Partnerships (NCCEP). NCCEP is a national nonprofit organization dedicated to the principle that every child deserves an equal chance at obtaining a quality higher education. NCCEP's goal is to bring together colleges and universities with local schools, parent groups, government agencies, foundations, corporations, and community-based organizations to work collaboratively to improve student achievement and expand educational opportunities for all of America's children.

Prior to founding NCCEP, Dr. Garza served for six years as the vice president for access and equity programs at the American Council on Education (ACE) in Washington, D.C. In this position, Dr. Garza directed the Office of Minorities in Higher Education and also coordinated and supervised the programs and activities of the Office of Women in Higher Education, and the HEATH Resource Center. Through his ACE affiliation, Dr. Garza provided leadership and technical assistance to member college and university presidents in areas of student/faculty recruitment and retention, campus diversity, affirmative action in college admissions, minority affairs, and higher education management.

For the past ten years, he has served as a senior consultant to the Ford Foundation on K–16 initiatives, and during the past three years has served a similar role on behalf of the W. K. Kellogg Foundation. Through this consulting experience, he has gained a wealth of knowledge and field experience in creating and sustaining K–16 educational partnerships and has provided training and technical assistance in areas of educational reform, evaluation of college access programs, partnership building, media relations, community engagement, race relations, and effective strategies for educating low-income and minority students in K–20. Through his work, he has also served on the projects' assessment teams and helped to design, field-test, and implement various assessment strategies, research designs, and evaluation instruments used in the Urban Partnership Project, the Rural Community College Initiative, and the Engaging Latino Communities for Education Initiative.

Prior to his appointment as vice president, Dr. Garza served as the associate graduate dean for academic program development and review at Eastern Michigan University. Other career positions he has held include executive director, Governor's Commission on Spanish-Speaking Affairs, State of Michigan; assistant graduate dean for graduate admissions/records at Eastern Michigan University; and coordinator of experiential education/learning at The University of Michigan.

His long-term service and achievements in academe have earned him many awards and accolades from institutions and organizations such as the University of Michigan, Eastern Michigan University, the U.S. Department of Agriculture, Central Michigan University, the National Hispanic University, George Mason University, the American Association for Higher Education, the Council of Graduate Schools, the State of Michigan, among others.

Dr. Garza holds Baccalaureate, Masters, and Doctorate degrees from the University of Michigan at Ann Arbor.

Hector Garza

More than 15 years have passed since the release of "One-Third of a Nation: Minorities in the United States." Detailing the findings of a joint commission of the American Council on Education and the Education Commission of the States, the 1988 report directed the attention of the education community—and that of the nation at large—to glaring inequities in the educational attainment of ethnic minority groups in the United States. The report inspired the first of a series of national conferences aptly entitled, "Educating One-Third of a Nation" (subsequently "Educating All of a Nation").

These many years later, awareness of the gaps in educational attainment is enhanced, but progress in closing those gaps remains slow. Latina/os' graduation rates from high school through postbaccalaureate education continue to trail those of other ethnic and racial groups. "The continuing lag of Hispanics in high school and college completion rates represents a major challenge to our higher education institutions and to society" (American Council on Education, 2004, p. 6). Indeed, as Frances Contreras and Patricia Gándara point out in this volume, for Latina/os, the problem of few Ph.D.s begins even before kindergarten.

The National Council for Community and Education Partnerships (NCCEP) was founded in 1999 to create and sustain partnerships in support of education reform aimed at increasing low-income students' readiness for and access to college. By building broad-based partnerships, linking schools and communities, developing new initiatives, supporting proven programs, and using research findings to create successful frameworks for action, NCCEP invigorates the principle of equal educational opportunity for all and, in the process, enriches the life of our nation.

Among NCCEP's chief responsibilities is to help direct the federal Gaining Early Awareness and Readiness for Undergraduate Programs (GEAR UP) program and the W. K. Kellogg Foundation's Engaging Latina/o Communities for Education (ENLACE) initiative. Regardless of the particular program or initiative, what matters most are academic achievement and student success for all students—including Latina/os. The critical need is to focus on the teaching and learning functions and to emphasize technological literacy as well as academic proficiency in reading, math, and science. These are the linchpins that facilitate the advancement of all young people along the educational pipeline—even to its very end.

Numerous barriers continue to stand in the way of Latina/o educational attainment and success. Marginalization, lack of access, limited resources, and institutional and cultural factors that collide to limit Latina/os' matriculation and retention once they have enrolled in college all have the effect of severely limiting their graduation and degree completion rates.

Marginalization

Latina/o students continue to be at the periphery of the education enterprise. "Fifty-nine percent of Latina/o students were characterized as not qualified for postsecondary education, compared to 41 percent of white students" (Swail, Cabrera, & Lee, 2004, p. 5). Teachers and guidance counselors tend not to expect Latina/o students to attend college, with the result that far too many of them are enrolled in non-college-preparatory coursework.

In their study of Latina/o youths, Swail, Cabrera, and Lee report that "Among all eighth grade students, 15.2 percent of Latina/o youths earned a BA within 8 years of scheduled high school graduation, compared to 35.7 percent of white students" (p. vii). Marginalization of Latina/o students as early as elementary and middle school clearly takes its toll. Worse, it persists through high school and college. As Solorzano writes in Chapter 7, "Experiences of marginality arise as [Latina doctoral students] confront multiple, intersecting, and ever-shifting power dynamics, including (but not limited to) race, gender, and class, on college campuses."

Apart from the expectation that all students can and should aspire to attend college; receive guidance from teachers and counselors to direct students along the education pathway; and have access to appropriate teaching methods and instructional supports, it is inconceivable that the marginalization of Latina/o students will become any less of a hindrance to their progress toward completion of the Ph.D.

Lack of Access

Lack of access to postsecondary education has long been cited as a factor limiting the progress of Latina/os along the education pipeline. However, lack of access itself is largely symptomatic of deeper, less readily "fixed" issues—for example, the high cost of college, inadequate academic preparation, insufficient guidance, or the lack of information about the college admissions process.

Within the past five years, the public and private sectors have focused increasingly on expanding access to higher education, particularly for low-income students. For example, since its establishment five years ago, the U.S. Department of Education's GEAR UP program has enabled "nearly 1 million low-income middle school students and their families to learn about, plan for, and prepare for college" (Prabhu, Deil-Amen, Terenzini, Lee, & Franklin, 2003, p. 3). State and local GEAR UP grantees determine their own mixes of interventions to help entire cohorts of students graduate from high school and enter college. GEAR UP interventions are targeted at students beginning in middle school (not later than seventh grade), and support remains available through participating students' matriculation at college.

ENLACE is a multiyear W. K. Kellogg Foundation initiative that is strengthening the education pipeline and increasing opportunities for Latina/o students to enter and complete college. (When a Ph.D. is the objective, college is non-negotiable.) ENLACE strengthens partnerships and creates coalitions among Hispanic Serving Institutions and other qualifying higher education institutions, K–12 school districts, communities, businesses, and others who are working to increase opportunities for Latina/os to enter and succeed in college.

ENLACE increases Latina/o access to and success in college by strengthening selected Hispanic Serving Institutions, public schools, and community-based organizations to serve as catalysts and models for systems change in education; supporting higher education/community partnerships that increase community involvement and educational success among Hispanic/Latina/o students; supporting the creation and implementation of education models based on best practices that increase the enrollment, academic performance, and graduation rates of Hispanic/Latina/o high school and college students; facilitating the expansion and sustainability of successful programs through strategic planning, networking, leadership development, and policy efforts; and disseminating information about successful models to stimulate changes in policies and practices related to the education of Hispanic/Latina/o students.

These are just two examples of significant efforts to expand access to postsecondary education for vast segments of the U.S. population. As such efforts continue to increase in number and expand in reach, they are sure to succeed at increasing the number of Latina/os who hold advanced academic degrees.

Technical and community colleges have a crucial role to play in the advancement of Latina/os along the education pipeline. They continue to serve as the primary point of entry for Latina/os into postsecondary education. Their role in partnerships must not be underestimated. (See the chapter by Alfredo de los Santos Jr. and Gerardo de los Santos.)

Limited Resources

"Poverty is a powerful predictor of failing to graduate. . . . Almost 9 of 10 intensely segregated schools also have concentrated poverty" (Orfield et al., 2004, p. 6). It is a deplorable reality that vast numbers of Latina/o students in the United States live in poverty and attend schools that are "intensely segregated." Going to college is rarely an expectation—let alone the norm—at such schools. Instead, students' experience of financial hardship makes college an impossible dream. The dream is even more remote for the approximately 1.4 million undocumented children under the age of 18 who are living in the United States, the vast majority of whom are Latina/o (Fix & Passel, 2003).

It falls to counselors and teachers to clarify for Latina/o students (and their families) the economic benefits of attending and graduating from college. While college can cost a lot, affordable options are available—as are grants and loans to underwrite at least a portion of the cost. Guidance counselors, community colleges, financial aid offices, and college access programs such as those outlined above share responsibility with families and higher education institutions to ensure that Latina/o students are fully informed of the financial resources that may be available to them—resources that can make college a reality.

Matriculation

Latina/o students who do graduate from high school and enroll in college are more likely than any other group to enroll at community and other low-cost colleges. For example, 40% of Latina/o high school graduates enroll at two-year colleges (a higher percentage than any other group), and 83% enroll at public institutions (Swail, Cabrera, & Lee, p. v).

It is not enough to ensure that students graduate from one level of education, be it middle school, high school, or college. What is of increasing importance is that people and pathways are in place to guide graduates to the next point of "academic embarkation"—that is, college or graduate school.

Congress's recent approval of a sixth funding year for GEAR UP programs to support students through the crucial transition from high school to college is significant as it signals a growing awareness of the importance of *next steps*.

Retention

Retention is that critical period of varying length that extends from matriculation to graduation. Only 43% of Latina/o students, compared to 63% of all students and 67% of White students, continue their enrollment in higher education (Swail, Cabrera, & Lee, page vi). Factors such as finances, academic preparedness, career goals, and other, more personal issues all influence whether a student continues his or her enrollment through to graduation. Institutional factors also play an important role. For example, culturally appropriate teaching methodologies may enhance the likelihood that Latina/o students will continue their enrollment in postsecondary education.

It also is important to note that fewer Latina/o students than other students enroll continuously to degree completion. Stopping and/or dropping out because of personal issues (finances, family circumstances) make it less likely that a student will complete a degree. Even at the doctoral level, tensions arising from cultural expectations in conflict with academic demands and even homesickness can tempt students to drop out of their programs. (See Chapter 14 by Segura-Herrera.)

Graduation

Amaury Nora, Libby Barlow, and Gloria Crisp write in this volume that little information is available regarding Hispanic students' persistence to degree completion. Swail, Cabrera, and Lee report elsewhere that almost two-thirds (64%) of Latina/os who entered postsecondary education did not receive a degree [within 8 years after scheduled high school graduation] (2004, p. vi). Clearly, retention and graduation are intricately linked: While it is possible to have retention without graduation, the converse is impossible—whatever the level of education. It also is clear that graduation—from high school, college, and graduate school—is the gateway to successive levels of education.

Projects and programs that succeed in advancing Latina/o youths to subsequent levels of education work both within and outside of schools. Before postsecondary education, they integrate technology and improve classroom instruction in reading, math, and science, and they align their services and activities with a critical student need: academic support. We all must continue to support Latina/o students throughout the education continuum—particularly through completion of advanced academic degrees—and coordinate all that we do to increase their academic achievement and success.

Conclusion

Nationwide, the ambitious plans of state and local education partnerships hold great promise. Hundreds of thousands of students in diverse communities throughout the country are benefiting from tutoring, mentoring, leadership development activities, college tours, cultural programs, and so much more, all in an effort to increase students' academic success.

Public policy and advocacy are key factors in the educational advancement of all of our nation's young people. If we do nothing more than inform our elected officials and the public at large of the arduousness of Latina/os' journey to the Ph.D., then we can expect only minimal improvement. For the greatest gains to be made, we must enlist aid from every corner: government, the private sector, the public, higher as well as K–12 education; business; and the Latina/o community itself. All of these together can help postsecondary education institutions meet the high demand for culturally competent and committed professionals.

Every chapter of *The Latina/o Pathway to the Ph.D.* speaks to the numerous challenges Latina/o students encounter throughout the education system and to the need to narrow the gap in academic achievement and success at every level so that more such students attain the Ph.D. This book is a worthy addition to the arsenal of information that educators and activists for reform should bring to bear as they continue to work to eliminate the barriers that keep the number of Latina/o Ph.D.s to a comparative minimum. From the book's opening chapters, on the status of Latina/os at various points along the education pipeline; to its middle chapters, which broadly describe Latina/o experiences of the doctoral process; to its concluding chapters—personal narratives that variously describe institutional, cultural, and even personal obstacles to success—it is evident that significant work must yet be done to smooth the road to the Ph.D. Among the most important steps may be emphasizing early—not later than middle school, and preferably far sooner—that college is possible for every Latina/o, as well as helping every student succeed academically at each stage of education so that the pipeline remains full of students qualified to continue their studies. Working broadly with the spectrum of institutions charged with educating students in grades K–16 and extending that work to include even those institutions charged with educating Latina/os in grades P–20, we can—we must—level the pathway to the Ph.D. so that vastly greater numbers of students attain a terminal degree.

The National Council for Community and Education Partnerships' (NCCEP) constituency is determined to keep their eyes on what matters most: academic achievement and student success. It is our sincere hope that others will join us as we continue to focus on the teaching and learning functions and to emphasize technological literacy as well as academic proficiency in reading, math, and science. Only as we do so and as we consciously seek to narrow the gap between the traditions of the academy and those of Latina/o culture will all members of our society reap the benefits of advanced education in equal proportion.

References

American Council on Education (2004). *Reflections on 20 years of minorities in higher education and the ACE annual status report.* Washington, DC: ACE.

Cabrera, E. F., Prabhu, R., Deil-Amen, R., Terenzini, P. T., Lee, C., & Franklin, R. E., Jr. (2003). *Increasing the college preparedness of at-risk students.* ED482 155. Washington, D.C.: Department of Education.

Fix, M., & Passel, J. S. (2003). "U.S. immigration—Trends & implications for schools." Presentation at the National Association for Bilingual Education NCLB Implementation Institute. New Orleans, January 28–29.

Orfield, G., Losen, D., Wald, J., & Swanson, C. B. (2004). *Losing our future: How minority youth are being left behind by the graduation rate crisis.* Cambridge, MA: The Civil Rights Project at Harvard University, 6.

Swail, W. S., Cabrera, A. F., & Lee, C. (2004). *Latino youth and the pathway to college.* Washington DC: Educational Policy Institute, Inc.

PREFACE

Entendiendo la Historia de Latina/os en el Camino a la Universidad
(Understanding the History of Latina/os
on the Road to the University)

Education for *la Raza Cósmica*

Alberta M. Gloria, Jeanett Castellanos, and Mark Kamimura

The educational disparity of Latina/os at all educational levels in comparison to other racial and ethnic groups is an issue of great economic, social, and political concern. As the fastest-growing and youngest racial and ethnic minority group in the United States, Latina/os face the likelihood of unemployment and underemployment as a result of the lower educational attainment that fuels the current and ever-increasing economic and social divide (Vernez & Mizell, 2001). At all levels, Latina/os lag behind their educational counterparts, yet they comprise a substantial portion of the population that directly affects the economic structure of the United States. Understanding historical events and cultural considerations of the educational pathway of Latina/os is engendered by the common Latina/o *dicho* (saying), *si no sabes de donde vienes, no sabes a donde vas* (If you don't know from where you come, you don't know where you are going).

Addressing this need, the conceptual framework of this book is presented in three sections. The first section provides a brief overview of Latina/os in the United States, providing information about terminology and general demographic and educational data. The next section provides the historical context of education for Latina/os in the United States. In particular, it addresses the educational entry, integration, and outcome of several historical events and court cases that influenced the educational trajectory for Latina/os. The final section presents the theoretical model and subsequent assumptions that create the structure and rationale for the book. Included here are the data, theories, and stories of Latina/o doctoral students. In particular, eight narratives of current or recent Latina/o doctoral students in various academic fields share their recommendations for students, faculty, and administrators to increase the recruitment and promote retention of Latina/o students on the educational highway to the Ph.D.

Sobre Quien Estamos Hablando (About Whom Are We Speaking): Terminology

Before identifying the historical events central to Latina/o educational issues, a discussion of terminology and differentiation of ethnic subgroups is necessary. Because of varied immigration and generational status, reasons for immigration (e.g., political versus economic), languages, sociopolitical histories, and cultural values and mores, Comas-Díaz (2001), refers to Latina/os as *la raza cósmica* (the cosmic race)—composed of diverse and ever-expanding numbers of individuals with origins in Mexico, Cuba, Puerto Rico, and South and Central America. As such, agreeing on and using a single term to identify millions of racially, ethnically, and culturally diverse individuals has prompted widespread dialogue within academia and local communities to identify a comprehensive yet inoffensive identifier.

Before the 1970 U.S. census, report of a Spanish surname or primary language of Spanish determined an individual as Hispanic (Guzmán, 2001). Government and other public-sector use of the term, Hispanic, however, has colonial implications (Comas-Díaz, 2001) and inappropriately aggregates individuals of different races, languages, and national origins. In contrast, the term, Latina/o, which only appeared on the U.S. census form in 2000, excludes Europeans (e.g., Spaniards), similarly masking between-group differences, fueling the misguided assumption that a "typical Latino" exists (Gloria, 2001). More recently, considerations for classifying Latina/os as White for the 2010 census has prompted the argument that the United States is detaining the browning of America bureaucratically (Gonzales & Rodriguez, 2004).

Choosing a self-reference that reflects personal agency (Gloria & Segura-Herrera, 2004), many individuals choose self-identifiers that affirm national origin (e.g., Mexican, Cuban, Peruvian) or ethnic identity (e.g., Xicano, Boricuas) (Comas-Díaz, 2001). With the ability to connote gender, the terms, Latina (females only), Latino (referring to males only), and Latina/o (both female and male), while acknowledging their sociopolitical limitations, are used throughout this book.

In the United States: *Somos* (We Are)

A statistical overview of Latina/os currently in the United States and their general and educational demographics warrants contextualization. As of

2002, Latina/os comprised 37.4 million or 13.3% of the U.S. population, of whom the largest ethnic subgroup were individuals of Mexican origin (66.9%), followed by Central and South American (14.3%), Puerto Rican (8.6%), Cuban (3.7%), and 6.5% who are identified as "Other Hispanic origins" (Ramirez & de la Cruz, 2003). Accounting for a substantial percentage of the nation's population growth (38%) between 1990 and 2000, Latina/os are estimated to account for 51% of the growth between 2000 and 2050, soon to be the largest minority group by 2005. Estimated at 98 million, Latina/os are projected to represent a quarter of the total U.S. population by 2050 (NCES, 2003).

The proportionate distribution of Latina/os in the United States has changed drastically since 1990. Latina/os who are "Other" classified (e.g., South and Central American, Dominican, individuals who did not identify a specific ethnic background) had almost a 100% population increase (5.1 to 10.0 million), in contrast to Mexicans (59%; 13.5 to 20.6 million), Puerto Ricans (24.9%; 2.7 to 3.4 million), and Cubans (18.9%; 1.0 to 1.2 million; Guzmán, 2001). Of the Latina/os in the United States, approximately 15 million (40.2%) are foreign born, with more than half (52.1%) having entered the United States between 1990 and 2002 (Ramirez & de la Cruz, 2003).

Immigrants (i.e., first-generation individuals) account for almost half (45%) of the growth of U.S. Latina/os between 1970 and 2000, compared to second-generation individuals, who account for 25.7 million (28%). In 2000 first-generation individuals had comprised 40% (14.2 million) of the Latina/o population growth over the last 30 years, while second-generation individuals comprised 9.9 million (28%). Third plus generation Latina/os accounted for 11.3 million (32%) of the Latina/o population (Suro & Passel, 2003). Growth of second-generation Latina/os increased substantially, reaching 63% for the 1990s, compared to 52% in the 1980s. The increase in second-generation Latina/os stems from high levels of immigration during the 1970s and 1980s. Projected estimates reveal that between 2000 and 2020, the number of second-generation Latina/os in U.S. schools will double, and the number in the U.S. labor force will triple. A quarter of the labor force growth will include children of Latina/o immigrants (Suro & Passel, 2003).

Upon entering the United States, Latina/os are represented geographically in every U.S. state; however, more live in the West and South than in the Northeast and Midwest. Specifically, over half of Mexican-origin individuals live in the West (54.6%) and South (34.3%), whereas over half of Puerto Ricans live in the Northeast (58.0%), and three-fourths of Cubans live in the South (75.1%). Individuals of Central and South American heritage are distributed more evenly in the Northeast (31.5%), South (34.0%), and West (29.9%) (Ramirez & de la Cruz, 2003).

Overall the Latina/o population is the youngest and fastest-growing minority group, with Mexican-origin individuals having the highest proportion under the age of 18 (37.1%), and the Cuban-origin population having the lowest (19.6%). With the influx of immigrants, the Latina/o population tends to be younger than the U.S. population average. More specifically, first-generation or immigrant Latina/os had a median age of 33.4 years old in contrast to Whites, who were 38.5 years old (Suro & Passel, 2003). Considering differences in migration patterns of different Latina/o ethnic groups, Mexicans have the lowest proportion (4.0%) and Cuban the highest proportion (22.6%) of individuals age 65 and older (NCES, 2003).

Overview of Latina/o Education

Because each individual chapter specifically addresses status and trends of Latina/os students at various educational levels, this educational overview is brief and broadly focused. Comprising the largest percentage of elementary- and secondary-level children in the United States, Latina/os do not enroll in or graduate from high school and college at proportional rates (NCES, 2000a; 2000b). The cycle of undereducation of Latina/os begins early as Latina/o children enter elementary school with less preschool experience (e.g., having been read to less and having infrequent library visits) than White and Black children. With higher rates of absenteeism, grade retention, and expulsion than their White peers, Latina/os exhibit differences in academic performance by the age of nine (NCES, 1995).

Questioning whether Latina/o families discourage education for their children or whether lower educational attainment equates to intellectual prowess, Valencia and Black (2002) suggest that Latina/os are faced with educational discrimination that perpetuates cycles of segregation and underachievement (Aguirre & Martinez, 1993). Faced with limited educational resources, few bilingual teachers, low academic expectations, mistaken placement into special education programs, educational tracking, and few teachers who integrate culture into curricula (President's Advisory Commission of Educational Excellence for Hispanic Americans, 1996), Latina/o youth often drop out, stop, or in effect are pushed out of education (Secada et al., 1998). The educational disparities and inequalities faced by Latina/os pose economic challenges that are long-lasting and of timely concern given their current and projected population estimates.

Being pushed out as a function of school climate, lack of culturally pertinent and relevant information for students, and educational expectations occurs at all levels of the educational process. From lack of bilingual classrooms to cultural incongruity of institutional and native values of students, the path to social, political, and economic mobility for Latina/os is through educational improvement—a movement beyond high school diplomas or baccalaureate degrees to doctoral degrees.

In effect, the educational journey of Latina/os is similar to a highway in which there are roadblocks (e.g., lack of bilingual teachers), detours (e.g., educational tracking), and traffic jams (e.g., cultural conflicts). As a result, students may exit the educational highway, taking an off-ramp by dropping out, stopping out, or being forced off the road (i.e., pushed out of school). When focusing on the final educational destination, a doctoral degree, understanding the educational road previously traveled is critical. Latina/o prekindergarten children are the pool from which our future doctoral degree earners come.

Maltratados en nuestra propia tierra (Mistreated in Our Own Home)

Understanding how the United States knowingly and willingly misappropriated land from Mexico is to know the beginnings of Latina/o miseducation. With the signing of the Treaty of Guadalupe Hidalgo on February 2, 1848, the Mexican American war ended (1846–1848). With it came the annexation of 525,000 square miles that included what is known today as Arizona, California, western Colorado, Nevada, New Mexico, Texas, and Utah. Losing their civil and property rights, despite explicit assurance by Articles VIII and IX of the treaty, *Mexicanos* became a conquered people overnight (San Miguel & Valencia, 1998). Ultimately, dishonoring the treaty is for many Latina/os, individuals of Mexican descent in particular, a source of the historical oppression and subsequent discrimination encountered today (Rendón, 1971; San Miguel & Valencia, 1998).

Antes de Brown (Before Brown): Segregated Schooling for Latina/os

Considered a major factor impeding the mobility of Latina/os, in particular Mexican Americans, school segregation was an insidious form of discrimination against Spanish-speaking children after the Mexican-American war (San Miguel & Valencia, 1998). In particular, four specific court cases, as identified by San Miguel and Valencia (1998), challenging school desegregation signaled formalized mobilization and action against such discrimination against Mexican Americans. These court cases of substantial relevance to current educational standings of Latina/os (Donato, Menchaca, & Valencia, 1991) are briefly reviewed next.

Independent School District v. Salvatierra *(1930, 1931)*

Mexican American students in the *Independent School District v. Salvatierra* (1930, 1931) argued that they were illegally segregated on the basis of race in Del Rio, Texas. Jesus Salvatierra and other parents argued that their children did not receive academic resources equal to those that White student received, despite the fact that racially, Mexican Americans were considered White. Although the court initially ruled that the school district illegally segregated Mexican American students on the basis of race, the appellate court reversed the verdict, on the grounds that the school district did not intentionally segregate children by race. In that these students needed to learn English, the school district argued its authority to segregate students based on educational needs. Although appealed to the U.S. Supreme Court, the case was dismissed for lack of jurisdiction and was a central impediment in desegregation decisions for many years (Alvarez, 1986; San Miguel & Valencia, 1998).

Alvarez v. Lemon Grove School District *(1931)*

Also challenging the segregation of Latina/o children was the first successful national court case, *Alvarez v. Lemon Grove School District* (1931) (Alvarez, 1986). With directives from the school board, Jerome T. Green, principal of the Lemon Grove Grammar School, blocked Mexican students from entering school. Prompted by growing sentiment against Mexicans in California and throughout the U.S. due to the Great Depression, the school board met approximately six months before barring students to discuss building a separate school. Without the Lemon Grove community's knowledge, a two-room school building was built, commonly referred to as *la caballeriza* (barnyard or stable).

The school board did not believe that Mexican children belonged in school and, further, did not anticipate Mexican families organizing a *Comité de Vecinos de Lemon Grove* (Lemon Grove Neighborhood Committee). The *Comité* sought help from a Mexican diplomat who arranged for two San Diego attorneys to represent the Lemon Grove community (Alvarez, 1986). Ultimately, Superior Court of California Judge Claude Chambers ruled that separate facilities for Mexican American students were not conducive to their "Americanization" and hindered the English proficiency of Spanish-speaking children (San Miguel & Valencia, 1998). Although the first nationally successful desegregation court case, the ruling was considered a local event only (Alvarez, 1986).

Méndez v. Westminister School District *(1946, 1947)*

The first federal court decision concerning desegregation was the California case of *Méndez v. Westminister School District* (1946, 1947). In a class action lawsuit, tenant farmer Gonzalo Méndez and a group of Mexican American World War II *veteranos* in Orange County, California, fought for their children to attend the same schools as White children. Seeking a sanction that would integrate schools, Méndez et al. filed against four Orange County school districts. The Ninth Circuit U.S. Court of Appeals ruled that school districts could not segregate on the basis of national origin or Mexican descent (Mintz, 2003).

Segregation was a violation of state law and denial of equal protection (Meier & Stewart, 1991). A counter to the *Plessy v. Ferguson* doctrine (i.e., separate but equal) resulted in a new interpretation of the Fourteenth Amendment. Ultimately, the school board's actions were considered illegal, and there was no mandate providing California school boards authority to segregate Mexican American students. Judge Paul J. McCormick ruled that no evidence suggested that segregation facilitated language proficiency; instead, language and cultural assimilation were hindered (San Miguel & Valencia, 1998). Despite a landmark case that ended de jure segregation in California, Mexican American segregation remained a common practice and continued to increase in the following decades (Hendrick, 1977; González, 1990).

Delgado et al. v. Bastrop Independent School District of Bastrop County et al. *(1948)*

In another Ninth Circuit Court decision in California, *Delgado et al. v. Bastrop Independent School District of Bastrop County et al.* (1948) found that the separation of races without a specific state law was not illegal. Represented by a group of powerful Mexican Americans and organizations (e.g., League of United Latin American Citizens [LULAC]), Minerva Delgado, along with 20 other Mexican American parents, charged that Mexican Americans could not be segregated in schools from other White students without specific state law. Ultimately, it was hoped that "*Delgado* would do for Texas what *Méndez* did for California—bring an end to school segregation" (San Miguel & Valencia, 1998, p. 376). Although Judge Ben Rice ruled in favor of the plaintiff, the court also ruled that the school district could segregate first-grade Mexican American students who had English-language deficiencies. The deficiencies, however, were revealed only by standardized language tests given to all children. Described as existing in an "era of subterfuge," the Texas school districts did not comply with the *Delgado* decision (San Miguel, 1987; San Miguel & Valencia, 1998).

Each of these court cases is seminal to understanding the educational trajectory for all Latina/os. Despite *Brown v. Board of Education of Topeka* (1954) laying the groundwork for school desegregation, the status of Latina/os in the educational system was not given the same emphasis or historical importance—an example of the manner in which Latina/o education is undervalued.

Trabajando contra la injusticia (Working against Injustice): Dr. George I. Sánchez

Known as the father of Chicano psychology and Chicano studies, Dr. George I. Sánchez was the first psychologist to address Chicano issues (Martinez, 1977; Murillo, 1984), with four of his earliest contributions addressing intelligence testing of Chicano children between 1932 and 1934 (Padilla, 1984). A social justice advocate and activist for Chicanos, Dr. Sánchez argued against the inappropriate use of intelligence testing for Chicano children (Padilla, 1984). Similar to previous educational court rulings for Latina/os, Dr. Sánchez's findings on intelligence testing were disregarded and rarely used within the educational testing literature (Padilla, 1984).

An avid believer that bilingualism was an untapped value and intelligence for Chicano students, Dr. Sánchez contended that social policy was to blame for the stunted educational achievement and social advancement of Chicanos rather than their linguistic abilities or language proficiencies (Murillo, 1984; Padilla, 1984; San Miguel & Valencia, 1998). Challenging the notion of inferior racial intelligence and subsequent low expectations for Spanish-speaking children, Dr. Sánchez advocated that educators not misuse tests by ignoring environmental (e.g., socioeconomic status) and linguistic factors. He argued that innate abilities were not assessed; rather, school performance, coupled with opportunities provided within the home setting, were measured (Getz, 1997). Instead of blaming the child for a lack of success, Dr. Sánchez held schools responsible for inequities (e.g., substandard curriculum and schooling [San Miguel & Valencia, 1998]), advocating that schools provide and make accessible the knowledge and experiences that tests measured (Getz, 1997).

Similar to 50 years ago, Latina/o students contend with attitudes (e.g., blame of student, negative perceptions of students' abilities), approaches (e.g., subtractive schooling), and obstacles (e.g., unwelcoming school and campus climates) that still exist in contemporary educational settings. Although the challenges may appear to be different, the issues of access, information, misperception, and "Americanization" of Latina/o students are fundamentally the same. As a result, the need to contextualize Latina/o students' educational experiences across different educational levels is core to understanding their journey and provides support for advanced educational attainment (e.g., the doctoral degree). The manner in which Latina/os are educated and experience their educational training throughout the school system serves as a beginning point of this book.

Premise and Overview of the Book

Using an approach in which the psychological (P), social (S), and cultural (C) are inextricably intertwined (Gloria & Rodriguez, 2000), this book seeks to provide a contextualized and holistic understanding of the dimensions of Latina/os in higher education. The *psychosociocultural* approach assumes person-environment interactions in which each dimension (i.e., P, S, or C) is equally relevant to and informative about Latina/o educational experiences. Originally developed for counseling Latina/o undergraduates, the psychosociocultural model has been tested regarding academic persistence for Latina/o high school students (Castillo, 1998) and Latina/o undergraduates with success (Gloria, Castellanos, Lopez, & Rosales, 2005). It is our intent therefore, to apply a PSC approach to understanding Latina/o doctoral student training experiences. Using an educational highway metaphor, a pathway that relatively few Latina/os have traveled, the book sets the stage for understanding the psychological, social, and cultural dimensions of Latina/os pursing a doctoral degree.

Section One—*El Camino Recorrido* (The Road Traveled)

The first section provides an educational contextualization—through a synthesis of descriptive data, personal reflections, and integration of research—of the highway or journey on which Latina/o students travel. Beginning with elementary and secondary issues, Patricia D. Quijada and

Leticia Alvarez address current trends and issues for Latina/o children and youth, highlighting the disparities and differential quality of education. Recognizing familial relationships as sources of strength, the chapter provides direction for students', families', and communities' integration into schools. Milton Fuentes discusses educational concerns and the means by which success can be attained for Latina/o high school students. Deconstructing Latina/o student experiences and identifying factors that influence drop out, stop out, and push out, Fuentes discusses a four-dimensional, culturally responsive pedagogy to enhance student learning. Addressing technical colleges and two-year universities, Alfredo and Gerardo de los Santos explore the importance of these institutions in propelling Latina/os on to four-year colleges and universities. Next, Amaury Nora, Libby Barlow, and Gloria Crisp review the undergraduate experiences of Latina/os, providing a preliminary profile of their characteristics, performance, and persistence patterns. Focusing on first year of college, the authors analyze the undergraduate experience, using institutional records from a Hispanic Serving Institution. Discussing one of the pools from which Latina/o doctoral students are selected, Mark Clark provides reflections on a dean-based approach to increasing recruitment and retention of Latina/o master's students.

Section Two—*Navegando el Camino* (Navigating the Path)

Challenges and supports both litter the educational highway for Latina/o doctoral students. Addressing the experiences, concerns, and considerations, Section Two provides conceptual, theoretical, and newly developed research regarding Latina/o doctoral students. Beginning this section, Frances Contreras and Patricia Gándara provide a historical and contemporary overview of Latina/o education. Their chapter addresses the need for continuity of students throughout the educational journey to develop a convoy of potential doctoral degree earners. Next, Tara Watford, Martha A. Rivas, Rebeca Burciaga, and Daniel Solorzano present the results of their doctorate records analyses for Latina doctoral students. Analyzing data from 1990 to 2000, the authors address micro and macro inequities experienced by Latinas, along with issues of marginality and resistance or coping. Continuing the conversation about coping and navigation of person and environment, Vasti Torres describes the Bicultural Orientation Model for Latina/o doctoral students. Bridging native and institutional values, this model provides a contextual framework from which to understand how Latina/os maintain, engage, and situate their ethnic identity within the educational context. Next, Aída Hurtado and Mrinal Sinha discuss gender socialization of Latina/o doctoral students and the effects this socialization has on their academic achievement. From qualitative interviews, the authors find gender differences that are contextualized within educational achievement and support for academic accomplishments. Finally, providing an integrative examination of the different dimensions of doctoral training, Alberta M. Gloria and Jeanett Castellanos provide a theoretical approach for understanding the experiences and providing effective interventions and programming suggestions for Latina/o doctoral students. In particular, the authors use vignettes to highlight various applications of the framework.

Section Three—*Aprendiendo de los Pasajeros* (Learning from the Passengers)

In accurately understanding the educational journey and experiences encountered along the highway, the most exact source of information is the travelers themselves. Eight Latina/o doctoral students from across the nation, who reflect different disciplines and have varied perspectives and experiences, share different yet interrelated dimensions of their stories. First, Mark Kamimura describes his enculturation process, as presented in phases, into the context and value-laden educational environment as a Latino. Similarly, Rocio Rosales discusses the social and cultural adjustments that she contends with in her educational persistence. In particular, Raul Ramirez addresses maintaining ethnic identity as one of the primary sources of support. Similarly, Theresa Segura-Herrera discusses the central importance of creating and maintaining family. In negotiating the doctoral process, Claudio Vera Sanchez and Marisa Garcia, in separate chapters, share how gender plays a salient role in understanding themselves as Latina/os in training. Both having recently completed their doctoral training, David Quijada discusses his experiences in being mentored into academia, while Petra Guerra describes the process of carrying out the final requirement of her doctoral degree—completing her dissertation.

With unique personal histories and stories, these Latina/o students represent the past, present, and future of the educational system—having survived and thrived along the educational highway and soon to graduate with doctoral degrees. ¡*Sí se puede*! (Yes we can!)

References

Aguirre, A., Jr., & Martinez, R. O. (1993). *Chicanos in higher education: Issues and dilemmas for the 21st century.* ASHE-ERIC Higher Education Report No. 3,

Washington, DC: The George Washington University, School of Education and Human Development.

Alvarez, R. R., Jr., (1986). The Lemon Grove Incident: The national first successful desegregation court case. *The Journal of San Diego History*, *32*(2), 116–135.

Castillo, E. M. (1998). Psychosociocultural predictors of academic persistence decisions for Latino adolescents. Unpublished dissertation. University of Wisconsin-Madison, Madison, WI.

Comas-Díaz, L. (2001). Hispanics, Latinos, or Americanos: The evolution of identity. *Cultural Diversity and Ethnic Minority Psychology*, *7*(2), 115–120.

Donato, R., Menchaca, M., & Valencia, R. R. (1991). Segregation, desegregation, and integration of Chicano students. In R. R. Valencia (Ed.), *Chicano school failure and success: Research and policy agendas for the 1990s* (pp. 26–63). London: Falmer Press.

Getz, L. M. (1997). *Schools of their own: The education of Hispanos in New Mexico, 1850–1940.* Albuquerque, NM: University of New Mexico Press.

Gloria, A. M. (2001). The cultural construction of Latinas: Practice implications of multiple realities and identities. In D. B. Pope-Davis and H. L. K. Coleman (Eds.), *The intersection between race, gender, and class: Implications for multicultural counseling* (pp. 3–24). Thousand Oaks, CA: Sage.

Gloria, A. M., Castellanos, J., Lopez, A., & Rosales, R. (2005). A psychosociocultural examination of academic persistence of Latina/o undergraduates. *Hispanic Journal of Behavioral Sciences*, *27*, 202–223.

Gloria, A. M., & Rodriguez, E. R. (2000). Counseling Latino university students: Psychosociocultural issues for consideration. *Journal of Counseling and Development*, *78*, 145–154.

Gloria, A. M., & Segura-Herrera, T. A. (2004). *Ambrocia* and *Omar* go to college: A psychosociocultural examination of Chicanos and Chicanas in higher education. In R. J. Velasquez, B. McNeill, & L. Arellano (Eds.), *Handbook of Chicana and Chicano psychology* (pp. 401–425). Mahwah, NJ: Lawrence Erlbaum.

González, G. G. (1990). *Chicano education in the era of segregation.* Philadelphia: Balch Institute Press.

Gonzales, P., & Rodriguez, R. (2004). Census pushes for Indian Removal. Universal Press Syndicate. Column of the Americas. Released week of December 17, 2004.

Guzmán, B. (2001). *The Hispanic population: Census Brief 2000.* Census Briefs, C2KBR/01-3. Washington, DC: U.S. Census Bureau.

Hendrick, I. (1977). *The education of non-whites in California, 1848–1970.* San Francisco: R&E Associates.

Martinez, J. L. (Ed.) (1977). *Chicano psychology.* Orlando, FL: Academic Press.

Meier, K. J., & Stewart, Jr., J (1991). *The politics of Hispanic education: Un paso pa'lante y dos pa'tras.* New York: State University of New York Press.

Mintz, S. (2003). Mexican American Voices. *Digital History*. Retrieved on December 16, 2004, from http://www.digitalhistory.uh.edu/mexican_voices/voices_display.cfm?id = 106.

Murillo, N. (1984) The works of George I. Sánchez: An appreciation. In J. L. Martinez & R. H. Mendoza (Eds.), *Chicano psychology*, 2nd ed. (pp. 23–33). Orlando, FL: Academic Press.

National Center for Educational Statistics (NCES). (1995). *The educational progress of Hispanic students.* NCES 95-767, U.S. Department of Education. Washington, DC: U.S. Government Printing Office.

National Center for Education Statistics (2000a). *Racial and ethnic distribution of elementary and secondary students.* NCES 2000-005. U.S. Department of Education. Washington, DC: U.S. Government Printing Office.

National Center for Education Statistics (2000b). *The condition of education 2000.* NCES 2000-062. U.S. Department of Education. Washington, DC: U.S. Government Printing Office.

National Center for Educational Statistics (2003). *Status and trends in the education of Hispanics.* NCES 2003-008. Washington D.C.: U.S. Department of Education, Institute of Education Sciences.

Padilla, A. M. (1984). Synopsis of the history of Chicano psychology. In J. L. Martinez & R. H. Mendoza (Eds.), *Chicano psychology*, 2nd ed. (pp. 1–19). Orlando, FL: Academic Press.

President's Advisory Commission on Educational Excellence for Hispanic Americans (1996). *Our nation on the fault line: Hispanic American education, September 1996. A report to the president of the U.S., the nation, and the secretary of education.* Washington, DC: U.S. Department of Education.

Ramirez, R. R., & de la Cruz, G. P. (2003). *The Hispanic population in the United States: March 2002: Population characteristics.* P20-545. Washington, DC: U.S. Bureau of the Census.

Rendón, A. B. (1971). *Chicano manifesto.* New York: Macmillan.

San Miguel, (1987). *"Let all of them take heed": Mexican Americans and the campaign for educational equity in Texas, 1910–1981.* Austin: University of Texas Press.

San Miguel, G., & Valencia, R. R. (1998). From the treaty of Guadalupe Hidalgo to Hopwood:The educational plight and struggle of Mexican Americans in the Southwest. *Harvard Educational Review, 68,* 353–412.

Secada, W. G., Chavez-Chavez, R., Garcia, E., Muñoz, C., Oakes, J., Santiago-Santiago, I., & Slavin, R. (1998). No more excuses: The final report of the Hispanic Dropout Project. Washington, DC.: U.S. Department of Education.

Suro, R., & Passel, J. S. (2003). *The rise of the second generation: Changing patterns in the Hispanic population growth.* Pew Hispanic Center: Author.

Valencia, R. R. and Black, M. S. (2002). "Mexican Americans don't value education!" On the basis of the myth, mythmaking, and debunking. *Journal of Latinos and Education, 1,* 81–103.

Vernez, G. & Mizell, L. (2001). *Goal: To double the rate of Hispanics earning a bachelor's degree.* Santa Monica, CA: Rand Education, Center for Research on Immigration Policy.

PART ONE

EL CAMINO RECORRIDO
(THE ROAD TRAVELED)

Patricia D. Quijada

Dr. Patricia D. Quijada is an assistant professor of counseling, educational psychology, and adult and higher education at the University of Texas at San Antonio. She has a Ph.D. in educational psychology with a designated emphasis in human development from the University of Wisconsin-Madison (2004); two master's degrees in counseling and human development from Harvard University; a multiple subject teaching credential from the University of San Diego; and two bachelor's degrees in political science and sociology from the University of California at Riverside. Dr. Quijada's research interests include indigenous Latina/o youth—adult relationships and identity formations, native epistemologies, and multicultural education in community and school contexts.

Leticia Alvarez

Dr. Leticia Alvarez is an American Educational Research Association/Institute of Education Sciences postdoctoral fellow at the University of Wyoming. She has a Ph.D. in educational psychology, with a designated emphasis in adolescent development, from the University of Wisconsin-Madison (2004). She received The School of Education-Spencer Doctoral Research Program Fellowship. Dr. Alvarez earned a master's degree in education from the Harvard Graduate School of Education (1995); a multiple subject bilingual teaching credential, social studies/language arts (1993); and a bachelor's degree in liberal studies, with a specialization in Spanish, from California State University, San Marcos (1992). Her research includes examining psychosocial processes that affect educational and healthy development for adolescents and focuses on how processes of acculturation affect educational and developmental outcomes for Latina/o youth. Dr. Alvarez's postdoctoral fellowship work involves a three-year, longitudinal project that deconstructs the relationship processes between adults and youth in schools for newcomer Mexican youth. Central to this research is identifying cultural influences and everyday experiences with classmates and teachers who assist in shaping the psychosocial factors that contribute to improving youth's engagement in schooling and optimize their chances of academic success. This work is being completed in collaboration with Dr. Alvarez's mentor, Professor Francisco Rios, at the University of Wyoming.

I

CULTIVANDO SEMILLAS EDUCACIONALES (CULTIVATING EDUCATIONAL SEEDS)

Understanding the Experiences of K–8 Latina/o Students

Patricia D. Quijada
Leticia Alvarez

Real education should consist of drawing the goodness and the best out of our own students. What better books can there be than the book of humanity? (Cesar E. Chavez, 1995)

Although Latina/o children spend the majority of their days in educational institutions that attempt to *foster* learning and creativity, recent policies and legislation advocate for censored learning. As a result, Latina/o children face institutional barriers embedded within an educational system that heightens their school challenges, hinders their opportunities for intellectual knowledge, and stunts children's imagination and ingenuity. Thus, the avenue leading to postsecondary education for Latinas/os is congested by institutionally based roadblocks. This congestion often causes policy makers and educators to dismiss the wealth of knowledge and experience Latina/o children and youth bring to classrooms. This chapter addresses K–8 Latina/o students' educational experiences and affirms the knowledge each student brings to school settings in supporting their pursuit of a postsecondary degree.

The purpose of this chapter is threefold. First, the status of U.S. Latina/o students enrolled in grades K–8 is overviewed. Second, demographic data is contextualized within the educational issues and challenges that Latina/o children engage. Finally, the chapter provides suggestions for educational institutions, educators, and policy makers to increase future representation of Latina/o children in institutions of higher education.

Latina/os are the fastest-growing and youngest minority population in the United States. Projections report that the overall U.S. Latina/o population will double in the next 50 years (U.S. Census Bureau, 2000a). In fact, it is projected that, by 2025, one-fourth of all U.S. public school students in grades K–8 will be Latina/o (U.S. Census Bureau, 2000b). Over the last 30 years (i.e., 1968 to 1998), a 245% increase in population was reported for Latina/os (Orfield, 2001). Today, Latina/os represent 12% of the total U.S. population and comprise the largest minority group with children under the age of 18 (34.4%) (U.S. Census Bureau, 2000a).

Residency Patterns

Residency patterns for Latina/os enrolled in public K–8 educational institutions in the United States are concentrated predominantly in five southwestern states: Arizona, California, Colorado, New Mexico, and Texas (see table 1.1). California had the highest percentage, with 6.3 million students enrolled in public elementary and secondary schools (California Department of Education, 2005). More specifically, 43.2% of the K–8 California public school students were Latina/os. Following California's enrollment numbers, Texas reported approximately 40.5% of its student population to be Latina/o. Similarly, New Mexico had a 49.3% enrollment of K–8 Latina/o students, even though it was smaller in population.

TABLE 1.1
**Latina/o K–8 School Enrollments by Percentage and Total Number
in Five Southwestern States**

State	*Percentage of Latina/o Students*	*Total number of Latina/o Students*
Arizona	31.6	268,098
California	43.2	2,613,480
Colorado	22.0	159,600
New Mexico	49.3	162,918
Texas	40.5	1,650,560

Source: Data from California Department of Education (2001); Texas Education Agency (2001); Arizona Department of Education (2000); Colorado Department of Education (2001); and New Mexico Public Education Department (2001).

Residency patterns for all Latina/os continue to be concentrated within the southwestern region of the United States. Noteworthy shifts in migration patterns, however, have resulted in dramatic increases of Latina/os in states that historically had limited representation. For example, Arkansas, Georgia, Nevada, North Carolina, and Tennessee reported a 200% or greater increase in Latina/o population during 1990–2000 (U.S. Census Bureau, 2003).

These residency patterns are important to contextualize within socioeconomic data. Almost one in five children in the United States under the age of 5 identifies as Latina/o, and one in three of these Latina/os lives below the poverty line. More specifically, 28% of Latina/o children under 18 years of age were living below poverty level, compared to 13.8% of their non-Latina/o counterparts in 2002 (U.S. Census Bureau, 2003).

K–8 Latina/o School Enrollment

In 2000, racial and ethnic minority students constituted 39% of public school K–8 enrollment; of these 44% were Latina/o, comprising 17% of the total enrollment (U.S. Census Bureau, 2000b). The Latina/o school-age community comprises the second largest U.S. racial and ethnic group (see table 1.2). A total of 37.1% of K–8 students are Latina/o, with 20.1% enrolled in kindergarten (U.S. Census Bureau, 2000d). Important to note is that most Latina/os students are enrolled in public K–8 schools in which minorities are numerically the student population majority. For example, 38% of Latina/o students attended schools in which the student enrollment was 90% or more minority. Also, 77% of Latina/os attended schools where total enrollment was 50% or more minority (NCES, 2003). As a result, Latina/o children are attending some of the most segregated schools in the United States despite the *Brown v. Board of Education* ruling (Orfield & Yun, 1999).

TABLE 1.2

K–8 U.S. Public School Enrollment by Race/Ethnicity, 2000 (in thousands)

	White	Latina/o	African American	Asian American	Total
Kindergarten	1,846	639	547	124	3,156
	58.2%	20.1%	17.2%	3.9%	
Elementary Grades	17,740	5,000	5,127	1,252	29,119
	60.5%	17.0%	17.5%	4.3%	

Source: Adapted from Bureau of the Census (2000b).

In these school contexts, where there is a high enrollment of culturally lin-guistic diverse students, less funding is allocated and fewer resources support student learning (Reyes & Rodriguez, 2004). For instance, fewer state and local dollars per student were allocated in 38 of 48 states in which school districts had high racial and ethnic minority student enrollment (The Educa-tion Trust, 2003).

Culturally Linguistic Latina/o Students

The number of English Language Learner (ELL) students in U.S. public schools is approximately three million, or 7% of the national public school population (NCES, 2004). In 1990, 14% (32 million) of the total U.S. popu-lation over the age of 5 spoke a language other than English in their homes (NCES, 2004). By 2000, that number had increased by 47% to nearly 47 million, encompassing nearly 18% of the total U.S. population (U.S. Census Bureau, 2000b).

Given immigration and population trends, Latina/os are culturally lin-guistically diverse. In particular, since 1998 Latina/os have comprised the largest percentage of culturally linguistic school-age children in the United States (Contreras, 2004). Their varying levels of Spanish fluency are influ-enced by generational status, ethnic background, and nationality (Flores & Yudice, 1993). Although 78% of Latina/o students age 5 and older enter school speaking Spanish, national policies continue to support English-only initiatives. These policies hinder students' ability to further refine their lin-guistic ability in Spanish. Paradoxically the majority of schools do not culti-vate language diversity for Latina/o students, as well as others, in elementary school, yet later in their educational training require a foreign language for university admission.

Resources and Teachers for K–8 Latina/os

Research suggests that schools populated by a majority of students who are economically disadvantaged and who are ELL have inadequate resources and opportunities for a quality education (Harris, 2004). For example, Harris found that California schools with large numbers of economically disadvan-taged and ELL students lacked qualified teachers and reported high teacher turnover rates, unacceptable working conditions, lack of textbooks and other instructional supplies, poor facilities, and ineffective parent programs. Spe-cifically, the study revealed that more than half (54%) of science teachers lacked equipment to conduct lab experiments (e.g., lab stations, lab tools, materials); 50% of social studies teachers lacked maps, atlases, and reference materials; and 32% of teachers reported not having enough texts for each child. Other salient findings included that teachers were more likely to be undercredentialed, and classroom conditions were poor (e.g., evidence of cockroaches, rats, or mice).

In addition to limited classroom resources, Latina/o students have teachers who are young (under 40 years of age), had a median of 15 years of classroom experience, and were likely to be White females (NCES, 2003; National Education Association, 2003). Also, evidence suggests that teacher salaries vary by racial and ethnic background. The base salary for Latina/o teachers was lower ($38,488) than the salaries for White ($40,022) and Black ($39,377) teachers (NCES, 2003). In addition, Latina/o teachers were more likely to teach in classrooms where 75% or more of the children were also Latina/o (Germino-Hausken, Waltson, & Rathbun, 2004).

These schools with high Latina/o concentrations are more likely to hire less-qualified teachers, many of whom cannot provide culturally relevant academic and support programs. For example, low-income and racially and ethnically diverse students are taught by twice as many inexperienced teachers as are White students (NCES, 2003). In California, approximately 16% of the teachers in schools with a majority of Latina/o students were not fully credentialed. Similarly, 40% of teachers were identified as teaching courses outside their field of expertise, twice that for White students (NCES, 2003). Further, 41% of math teachers lack certification to teach, often resulting in Latina/o students having less access to enroll in college preparatory courses (e.g., algebra II) (The Education Trust, 2004).

In a national report of school concerns, public elementary and secondary school teachers indicated five main concerns, including students' unpreparedness, lack of parental involvement, poverty, student disrespect for teachers, and student apathy (U.S. Department of Education, 2004). Each of these reasons is considered to be the fault of the students' families, thus perpetuating a deficit approach to student issues. Both elementary and secondary schoolteachers concern themselves minimally with student dropout, perceiving tardiness as of greater educational concern (U.S. Department of Education, 2004).

These conditions of schooling and discrepancies across school settings provide a contextualized understanding of and explanation for Latina/o students' limited academic achievement. Inadequate school conditions, less-qualified teachers, and inequitable funding equate to allocation discrepancies. What resiliency and stamina is required of Latina/o students who learn in such school conditions and achieve academically to pursue a postsecondary education? These school disparities and inequalities are not prevalent in wealthy and White neighborhoods, yet are salient in low socioeconomic and culturally diverse neighborhoods. These unequal distributions of resources are at the forefront of the issues that perpetuate low academic achievement among Latina/o students.

Achievement Gap and Dropout

Given the relationship of educational attainment and social mobility, within the context of an increasing Latina/o population (Chapa, 2002), it is critical to ease the educational journey for K–8 Latina/o students to the Ph.D., particularly as they transition into high school. Unfortunately, Latina/os lead the nation in dropout rates, with 43.0% earning less than a high school diploma, and 26% of these individuals dropping out before the ninth grade (NCES, 2003). Understanding why Latina/o students are not succeeding academically and are dropping out is a complex issue, yet it can be linked to school satisfaction, economics, language barriers, recent immigration status, and low academic achievement (Fashola & Slavin, 1997; Martinez, DeGarmo, & Eddy, 2004).

When examining dropout or stopout (a temporary leave from school with the intention of returning) rates, educational attainment varies by ethnic group. Specifically, Mexicans are least likely to have a high school education (51.0%), followed by Puerto Ricans and Central and South Americans (64.3% each). Cubans are most likely to have a high school degree (73.0%) (Therrien & Ramírez, 2001). By generational status, recent Latina/o immigrants have substantially higher dropout rates (44%) than Latina/os who arrived in the United States earlier (15%–16%) (NCES, 2002). The high school dropout rate for Latina/os (between 16 and 24 years of age) has been consistently higher than those of other races and ethnicities for almost 30 years.

Latina/o academic challenges have been attributed to lack of fundamental knowledge and skills (Farkas, 2000, 2003; PEW Hispanic Center, 2004; Snow, Burns, & Griffin, 1998). Research suggests that by the age of nine, Latina/o children are academically two years behind White children (PEW Hispanic Center, 2004), particularly in math and reading (NAEP, 1999). The academic gap widens further as Latinas/os continue on to middle and high school. In fact, by the time Latina/o students enter their senior year in high school, their math and reading levels are equivalent to those of White 13-year-olds (NAEP, 1999).

To date, much of this achievement gap has been attributed to fewer Latina/o children enrolling in pre-kindergarten educational programs. Specifically, only 35% of Latina/o children between the ages of 3 and 4 are enrolled in preschool and nursery schools, compared to 55% of White children the same age. Unfortunately, the achievement gap is also attributed to parents' limited foundational knowledge and support. However, scholars (Betsinger, Garcia, & Guerra, 2001; Garcia & Guerra, 2004; Valencia & Solorzano, 1997) have worked to debunk the familial deficit perspective for Latina/o student success by acknowledging sociocultural links.

Influences of *Familismo* for K–8 Students and Education

The influence of cultural values (e.g., *familismo*) and the need for different roles within in the family (e.g., language broker or cultural interpreter) are minimized within the educational system for Latina/o students. Although Latina/o groups are heterogeneous due to sociocultural variables, *familismo* is a common core value (Keefe, Padilla, & Carlos, 1978; Marín, 1993; Baca Zinn, 1998). In general, Latina/os have a strong connection to family, reinforced and affirmed by close relationships, interdependence, cohesiveness, cooperation, and parental authority. These extremely valuable culturally enriched resources and attributes that Latina/o students bring with them to school settings could and should be used as a platform to engage students in the learning process.

Being part of a cohesive family often translates into Latina/o elementary and secondary students of first- and sometimes second-generation families taking on leadership roles. Bilingual Latina/o students are taking on leadership roles that require a certain degree of maturity to ensure the well-being of their family. For instance, children and adolescents serve as primary translators for their parents or guardians with school administers and teachers, employers, and business settings. Balancing bank accounts and negotiating business and personal transactions are common responsibilities Latina/o youth assume for their parents/guardians. Although many Latina/o students assume familial responsibilities aligned with "adulthood," these valuable experiences and resources (e.g., negotiation and interaction skills) are not acknowledged or valued in everyday schooling experiences. If these culturally enriched experiences were legitimized, learning would become a dialogical process whereby Latina/o children and youth would feel validated and encouraged to engage in the learning process.

(De)constructing the Latina/o family-school links

K–8 Latina/o students' poor academic achievement is a serious concern (Chapa & de la Rosa, 2004; Garcia, 2001; Martinez, DeGarmo, & Eddy,

2004; Prelow & Loukas, 2003; Suárez-Orozco & Suárez-Orozco, 1995) in that academic functioning has been related to family detachment, delinquency, association with deviant peers, and substance abuse (Partida, 1996). For example, U.S.-born Latina/o children use alcohol and tobacco more than do immigrant Latina/o children (Secada et al., 1998; Vega & Gil, 1999).

Several theoretical models have attempted to explain the low academic performance of U.S. Latina/o students. Since the 1960s, the "cultural deprivation" model has been used to explain the underperformance of Latina/o school children. Perpetuated in the educational and psychological literature, this model ascribes minority school failure to "cultural" influences such as backgrounds that fail to instill children with the basic tools required for school achievement. In particular, parents are identified as the primary culprits behind their children's underperformance (Moreno & Valencia, 2002; Ramirez, 2003; Valencia & Black, 2002).

In contrast, Latina/o parents do not feel that schools are invested in their children's learning. Specific concerns of parents include schools not listening to parents, not providing translators, and communicating ineffectively regarding their children's grades, academic needs, and available services (Moll & Gonzalez, 1997; Ramirez, 2003). Contextual factors (e.g., parental adjustment, socioeconomic status, social support, immigrant status, and context of neighborhood) also contribute to children's educational adjustment indirectly through parenting practices (Martinez, DeGarmo, & Eddy, 2004; Quijada & Alvarez, 2003).

Quijada and Alvarez (2003) demonstrated the importance of talking about parenting processes by deconstructing parental daily roles within the family rather than focusing only on the behaviors of parenting. Parenting is contextualized through everyday life experiences, by incorporating traditions, practices, and native languages. In other words, parenting is more than a series of linear practices; it instead is a process that encompasses daily cultural interactions. In dimensionalizing parenting, the use of *consejos* could be implemented to create a deeper understanding of children's lives and educational experiences. For example, Delgado-Gaitan (1994) emphasizes the use of *consejos* as a powerful cultural narrative for nurturing advice. She argued that *consejos* is more than advice, it is problem solving. "*Consejos* implies a cultural domain of communication, imbued with emotional empathy, compassion, and familial expectations" (p. 314). Similarly, Quijada and Alvarez (2003) examined the opportunities that *consejos* created for parents to know more about their children's lives, unconsciously revealing their own identities and cultural beliefs. Latina/o parents implement their cultural traditions by integrating their personal identities with community affiliations and familial responsibilities through parental practices. Such integration of identities fused into the school environment would benefit Latina/o children similarly.

In this light, we advocate that policy makers and school officials legitimize Latina/o family-school relationships by recognizing that parenting is not a one-dimensional practice as often represented in the United States. Understanding parenting as a process embedded in cultural identity would contextualize how parenting occurs within Latina/o families. School officials must continue to foster a relationship with Latina/o parents by engaging parents in the daily lives of their children in school settings. For example, parental involvement should not be evaluated based on the frequency of parents' school visits. To this end, a continuous line of communication must be maintained with parents via multiple modes of communication (e.g., telephone calls) in parents' language of choice. Once a firm line of communication is established, students will trust that schools are sincere in building coalitions with their families.

Reteniendo los Estudiantes (Retaining Students): Implications for Latina/o Students, Families, and School Personnel

It is well-documented that Latina/o K–8 students have salient educational challenges and cultural adjustment concerns throughout their academic tenure. A plethora of literature relates Latina/o K–8 educational inequalities to the lack of interrelated roles among families, communities, and educational systems. Specific efforts (e.g., school and student assessments) have been advanced with limited success to address the educational disparities and shortcomings faced by the growing student population. As a result, the educational realities for Latina/o K–8 students require a closer examination, focusing on their daily life and school experiences as well as educational conditions and barriers.

In looking to the future, a series of fundamental questions merit consideration. First, how can adults and youth come together across differences to create learning relationships that inform, reform, and maintain cultural practices? Next, how can adults learn about and from cultural practices of youth as a means to engage in culturally relevant relationships and teaching practices? Third, how can educators establish reciprocal transformative learning relationships in school settings? These questions can prompt effective relationships between adults and adolescents in school and family communities—paving the way for Latina/o youth to advanced degree attainment.

If researchers, educators, and policy makers intend to increase postsecondary educational opportunities for Latina/o students in the United States, family resources and contexts need to be acknowledged and valued in school settings. Greater attention also needs to be paid to the learning contexts in which K–8 Latina/o students are being taught. In promoting academic success, Latina/o students must be offered curricula and opportunities equal to their Whites peers', while valuing cultural differences as assets (Darder, Torres & Gutierrez, 1997; Garcia & Guerra, 2004; Suárez-Orozco & Suárez-Orozco, 1998). The educational and psychological literatures (Garcia & Guerra, 2004) continue to use culturally deficit frameworks to examine and reform Latina/o achievement, blaming Latina/o cultures, languages, and parents and students themselves. Taking a cultural deficit approach has been an ongoing trend that is cited repeatedly, removing responsibility for the Latina/o achievement gap from school constituents (see Garcia & Guerra, 2004).

Taking a positive and strength-based approach to supporting Latina/o youth through elementary and secondary education, we provide the following recommendations for families, teachers, and administrators.

Para la Familia: *For the Family*

- Enroll your children in early outreach programs (e.g., Head Start) to provide a solid foundation for their educational careers.
- Establish partnerships with schools and teachers to be adequately informed about your child's educational rights and progress.
- Identify means of participation at your child's school, outside of teacher-parent school meetings. For example, volunteer as a teacher's assistant in your child's classroom.
- Integrate culture into the parenting of your child's daily activities, connecting core *familia* values and educational experiences.
- Initiate open and two-way communications through *consejos*, while maintaining *respeto*, to gain insight into and interconnection with your child.

Para los Maestros: *For the Teachers*

- Eliminate the application of a cultural-deficit approach when engaging with Latina/o students.
- Value the sociocultural resources (e.g., bilingualism) that students bring to the classroom by supporting and promoting ethnic and cultural pride. Doing so will shift from a "subtractive" mode of thinking (Valenzuela, 1999) to *valorizando* (valuing) students' assets.

- Incorporate transformative pedagogy that engages differential perspectives of the learning process. This teaching style reinforces multidirectional interactions, facilitating reciprocal transformation (Nakkula, 2003).
- Recognize and integrate the salient roles of family and community into students' curriculum and learning assignments. Serve as a facilitator in encouraging students to share their work with family and community, promoting a sense of collaboration through school-community and youth-adult relationships.
- Create venues for self-reflection and acquisition of accurate knowledge about Latina/o children, families, communities, and cultural values. For example, read biographies of racial and ethnic minorities, become involved in local community agencies and projects, and engage in difficult dialogues with other teachers to dispel personal biases and prejudices.

Para los administradores: *For the Administrators*

- Promote cultural appreciation and understanding on school campuses to ensure academic achievement at all educational levels and fuel culturally relevant discourse, including across school constituents.
- Scrutinize how institutional policies and systems hinder student achievement and implement and evaluate bilingual education, early outreach, and after-school programs.
- Hire teachers who are culturally integrative and knowledgeable about the diverse cultural practices of Latina/o students, families, and communities.
- Recruit and retain appropriately qualified teachers in all school districts without discrepancy in distribution of teachers to higher socioeconomic status communities.
- Acknowledge and remunerate teachers who are culturally engaged and trained to work effectively with Latina/o students, families, and communities.
- Find creative means to fund necessary school materials (e.g., books, laboratory materials) to ensure equity and a high-quality learning experience for Latina/o students.
- Take responsibility for teacher preparation and offer advanced curricula to provide Latina/os with equal access to learning opportunities and quality education. Doing so will allow students to have future doctoral pursuits as options.

References

Arizona Department of Education. (2000). Arizona enrollment figures, state of Arizona: October 1, 1998, enrollment, SY99. Phoeniz, AZ: Author.

Baca Zinn, M. (1998). Family, feminism, and race in America. In K. V. Hansen & A. I. Gary (Eds.), *Families in the U.S.: Kinship and domestic politics* (pp. 21–32). Philadelphia: Temple University Press.

Betsinger, A., Garcia, S. B., & Guerra, P. (2001). Addressing teachers' beliefs about diverse students through staff development. *Journal of Staff Development, 22*(2), 24–27.

California Department of Education. (2001). *Enrollment in California public schools by ethnic group, 2000–2001.* Sacramento, CA: Author.

California Department of Education. (2005). *Enrollment in California public schools by ethnic group, 2003–2004.* Sacramento, CA: Author.

Chapa, J. (2002). Affirmative action, X percent plans, and Latino access to higher education in the twenty-first century. In M. Suárez-Orozco & M. Páez (Eds.), *Latinos remaking America* (pp. 375–388). Berkeley: University of California Press.

Chapa, J., & de la Rosa, B. (2004). Latino population growth, socioeconomic and demographic characteristics, and implications for educational attainment. *Education and Urban Society, 36*(2), 130–149.

Chavez, C. E. (1995). Retrieved on March 15, 2005, from http://www.sfu.edu/~cecipp/cesar_chavez/cesarquotes.htm.

Colorado Department of Education. (2001). *Fall 2000 membership by county, district, and ethnic/racial group.* Denver, CO: Author.

Contreras, R. A. (2004). Epilogue: Latinos at the Portal for the 21st Century. *Education and Urban Society, 36,* 223–234.

Darder, A., Torres, R. D., & Gutiérrez, H. (1997). Introduction. In A. Darder, R. D. Torres, & H. Gutiérrez (Eds.), *Latinos and education: A critical reader* (pp. xi–xix). New York: Routledge.

Delgado-Gaitan, C. (1994). *Consejos:* The power of cultural narratives. *Anthropology and Education Quarterly, 25*(3): 298–316.

The Education Trust (2003). The funding gap report. Retrieved January 2005, from http://www2.edtrust.org/EdTrust/Product+Catalog.htm.

The Education Trust. (2004). *Thinking K–16. 8*(1), 1–44. Washington, DC: Author.

Farkas, G. (2000). Teaching low-income children to read at grade level. *Contemporary Sociology, 29,* 53–61.

Farkas, G. (2003). Racial disparities and discrimination in education: What do we know, how do we know it, and what do we need to know? *Teachers College Record, 105,* 1119–1146.

Fashola, O. S., & Slavin, R. S. (1997). Promising programs for elementary and middle schools: Evidence of effectiveness and replicability. *Journal of Education for Students Placed at Risk, 2,* 251–302.

Flores, J., & Yudice, G. (1993). *Divided borders: Essays in Puerto Rican identity.* Houston, TX: Arte Publico.

García, E. E. (2001). *Hispanic education in the United States: Raices y alas*. Boulder, CO: Rowen & Littlefield.

Garcia, S. B., & Guerra, P. L. (2004). Deconstructing deficit thinking: Working with educators to create more equitable learning environments. *Education & Urban Society, 36*, 150–168.

Germino-Hausken, E., Waltson, J., & Rathbun, A. H. (2004). *Kindergarten teachers: Public and private school teachers of the kindergarten class of 1998–1999*. Washington, DC: National Center for Education Statistics.

Harris, L. (2004). *Report on the status of public school education in California 2004*. The William and Flora Hewlett Foundation.

Keefe, S. E., Padilla, A. M., & Carlos, M. L. (1978). The Mexican American extended family as an emotional support system. In J. M. Casas & S. E. Keefe (Eds.), *Family and mental health in the Mexican American community* (pp. 49–67). Los Angeles: Spanish Speaking Mental Health Research Center.

Marín, G. (1993). Influence of acculturation on familialism and self-identification among Hispanics. In M. E. Bernal & G. P. Knight (Eds.), *Ethnic identity: Formation and transmission among Hispanics and other minorities* (pp. 181–196). New York: State University of New York Press.

Martinez Jr., C. R., DeGarmo, D. S., & Eddy, J. M. (2004). Promoting academic success among Latino youth. *Hispanic Journal of Behavioral Sciences, 26* (2), 128–151.

Moll, L. C., & Gonzalez, N. (1997). Teachers as social scientist: Learning about culture from household research. In P. M. Hall (Ed.), *Race, Ethnicity and Multiculturalism* (vol. 1). New York: Garland.

Moreno, R., & Valencia, R. (2002). Chicano families and schools: Myths, knowledge, and future directions for understanding. In R. R. Valencia (Ed.), *Chicano school failure and success: Past, present, and future* (pp. 227–500). Routledge Palmer: New York.

Nakkula, M. (2003). Identity and possibility: Adolescent development and the potential of schools. In M. Sadowski (Ed.), *Adolescents at school: Perspectives on youth, identity, and education* (pp. 7–18). Cambridge, MA: Harvard Education Press.

National Assessment of Educational Progress [NAEP]. (1999). Long term trends summary tables. Retrieved on October 9, 2004, from http://nces.ed.gov/nations reportcard/tables/Ltt1999/ltthelp.asp.

National Center for Education Statistics (NCES). (2000a). *Monitoring quality: An indicators report*. Washington: DC: U.S. Department of Education.

National Center for Education Statistics (2000b). *Dropout rates in the United States: 1999*. Washington: DC: U.S. Department of Education, Office of Educational Research and Improvement.

National Center for Education Statistics. (2003). *Digest of education statistics*. Washington, DC: Author.

National Center for Education Statistics (2003). *Status and trends in the education of Hispanics*. NCES 2003-008. Washington: DC: U.S. Department of Education.

National Center for Education Statistics (2004). *English language learner students in U.S. public schools 1994 and 2000.* Washington: DC: U.S. Department of Education Office of Educational Research and Improvement.

New Mexico Department of Education. (2001). *Percent of student enrollment ethnic category by district: School year 2000–2001.* Santa Fe, NM: Author.

Orfield, G., & Yun, J. T. (1999). *Resegregation in American Schools.* Cambridge, MA: Harvard University Press.

Orfield, G. (2001). *Schools more separate: Consequences of a decade of research.* Cambridge, MA: Harvard University.

Partida, J. (1996). The effects of immigration on children in the Mexican American community. *Child and Adolescent Social Work Journal, 13,* 241–254.

PEW Hispanic Center (2004). *Educational attainment: Better than meets the eye but large challenges remain.* Washington, DC: PEW Hispanic Center.

Prelow, H. M., & Loukas, A. (2003). The role of resource, protective, and risk factors on academic achievement-related outcomes of economically disadvantaged Latino youth. *Journal of Community Psychology, 31,* 513–529.

Quijada, P. D., & Alvarez, L. (2003, April 23). Indigenous parents (Re)claim self: Negotiating cultural and gender scripts within community and educational settings. In K. Watson-Gegeo and D. A. Quijada (chairs), *(Re)doing identity: Problematizing education and transformation in the margins.* Symposium conducted at the annual meeting of the American Educational Research Association, Chicago, IL.

Ramirez, A. Y. F. (2003). Dismay and disappointment: Parental involvement of Latino immigrant parents. *The Urban Review, 35*(2), 93–110.

Reyes, A. H., & Rodriguez, G. M. (2004). School finance: Raising questions for urban schools. *Education and Urban Society, 37,* 3–21.

Secada, W. G., Chávez-Chávez, R., García, E., Muñoz, C., Oakes, J., Santiago-Santiago, I., & Slavin, R. (1998). *No more excuses: The final report of the Hispanic dropout project.* Washington, DC: U.S., Department of Education.

Snow, C., Burns, M. S., & Griffin, P. (Eds.). (1998). *Preventing reading difficulties in young children.* Washington, DC: National Academy Press.

Suárez-Orozco, C. & Suárez-Orozco, M. (1995). *Transformations: Migration, family life, and achievement motivation among Latino adolescents.* Stanford, CA: Stanford University Press.

Texas Education Agency. (2001). *2000–2001 student enrollment: Statewide totals.* Austin, TX: Author.

Therrien, M., & Ramírez, R. R. (2001). The Hispanic population in the United States: Population characteristics (*Current Population Reports,* pp. 20–535). Washington, DC: U.S. Census Bureau.

U.S. Department of Commerce, Bureau of the Census (2000a). *Profile of general demographic characteristics for the United States: 2000.* Washington, DC: Author.

U.S. Department of Commerce, Bureau of the Census. (2000b). *Educational attainment of the population 15 years and over, by age, sex, race, and Hispanic origin: March 2000.* Washington, DC: Author.

U.S. Department of Commerce, Bureau of the Census (2000c). *Projections of the resident population by age, sex, race, and Hispanic origin: 1999 to 2100.* Washington, DC: Author.

U.S. Department of Commerce, Bureau of the Census. (2000d). *People in families by family structure, age, and sex iterated by income to poverty ratio and race.* Washington, DC: Author.

U.S. Department of Commerce, Bureau of the Census. (2003). Current population survey (March 2002). Washington, DC: U.S. Census Bureau, Population Division, Ethnic and Hispanic Statistics Branch.

U.S. Department of Education, National Center for Education Statistics. (2002). *Digest of education statistics.* Washington, DC: U.S. Government Printing Office.

U.S. Department of Education, National Center for Education Statistics. (2003). *Digest of education statistics.* Washington, DC: U.S. Government Printing Office.

U.S. Department of Education, National Center for Education Statistics. (2004). *The condition of education 2004* (NCES 2004-077). Washington, DC: U.S. Government Printing Office.

Valencia, R. (1997a). *The evolution of deficit thinking.* London: Falmer.

Valencia, R. R. (1997b). Genetic pathology model of deficit thinking. In R. R. Valencia (Ed.), *The evolution of deficit thinking: Educational thought and practice* (pp. 41– 112). The Stanford Series on Education and Public Policy. London: Falmer Press.

Valencia, R. R., & Black, M. S. (2002). "Mexican Americans don't value education!": On the basis of the myth, mythmaking, and debunking. *Journal of Latinos and Education, 1,* 81–103.

Valencia, R. R., & Solorzano, D. G. (1997). Contemporary deficit thinking. In R. R. Valencia (Ed.), *The evolution of deficit thinking: Educational thought and practice* (pp. 160–210). London: Falmer Press.

Valenzuela, A. (1999). *Subtractive Schooling: U.S. Mexican youth and the politics of caring.* Albany, NY: State University of New York Press.

Vega, W. A., & Gil, A. C. (1999). A model for explaining drug use behavior among Hispanic adolescents. *Drugs and Society, 14*(1–2), 57–74.

Milton A. Fuentes

Dr. Milton Fuentes is an assistant professor of psychology and co-director of the Latin American and Latino Studies program at Montclair State University; he is also a licensed psychologist. He is one of the founding members of the Latino Psychological Association of New Jersey and is the association's past president. Dr. Fuentes's interests are Latina/o mental health, child psychology, and family therapy. He serves as a consultant to several schools and community-based programs.

2

KEEPING OUR CHILDREN
IN HIGH SCHOOL
We Know What Works—Why Aren't We Doing It?[1]

Milton A. Fuentes

We stand at a crossroads. If we continue on our present course, one out of every three Hispanic students will be left without a basic high school education, no prospects for college and every likelihood of a life of poverty. If this populous group, growing at five and one half times the rate of non-Hispanic whites, does not take greater advantage of post secondary education, the effect on the United States economy will be gravely negative. If the gap in educational achievement is ignored for another generation, the result will be millions of Hispanics relegated to a minimum-wage and low-skilled existence that is likely to condemn their children to an upbringing of poverty and risk. (President's Advisory Commission on Educational Excellence for Hispanic Americans, 2002, p. 21)

Considering the substantial growth of the Latina/o population, their limited educational progress, and the opportunities that education can offer, it is imperative to understand the context in which Latina/o high school students are educated. This chapter discusses the status of Latina/o high school students in the United States. The first section briefly introduces my involvement in this area and provides some demographic data on Latina/o high

[1] This chapter was considerably influenced by the work of the Hispanic Adolescent Research Team (HART) at Montclair State University. I wish to acknowledge the following students for the countless hours they dedicated to HART: Marisol Aguila, William Clancy, Arturo Kiyana, Yanique Lockhart, Lyssett Martinez, Alex Renelt, Adriana Restrepo, William Reynolds, Elba Rosario, Denise Sulzer, and Maria Yapondjian. I also wish to acknowledge the Center of Pedagogy at Montclair State University for providing HART with financial and academic support.

school students. The second section, which discusses some of the concepts typically used when referring to Latina/os, defines my understanding of what it means to be Latina/o and briefly highlights the similarities and differences among Latina/o high school students. The next section, "Learning from Our Past," delineates the historical attempts made in the United States to understand and address Latina/o educational attainment issues. Since a preponderance of Latina/o high school students drop out of school, I give special attention to this phenomenon. One section is dedicated to defining the dropout rate, and another is devoted to factors associated with the dropout rate. The subsequent section discusses academic persistence and describes the elements in effective learning communities that promote persistence. The chapter concludes with some closing remarks and a list of recommendations for parents and professionals.

In the summer of 2001, a colleague e-mailed me an article that appeared in the *Home News Tribune*, titled "Hispanics Fall Behind" (Symons, 2000). The article addressed how the nation's education system was ill equipped to serve the fastest-growing group of school children—Latina/o children—appropriately. As an advocate of Latina/os, I was deeply concerned about these findings, and I reviewed the literature more closely. Upon careful investigation, I was disheartened by the continued trend of the Latina/o high school dropout rate. Although the majority of schools were failing our Latina/o children, a few select schools throughout the country were successfully educating and graduating them. The question that continually came to mind was: we know what works, why aren't we doing it?

The educational journey of Latina/o high school students is dreadfully challenging and often fraught with academic difficulties, discrimination, and disappointments. Given the growing numbers of Latina/o students in U.S. schools, it behooves educators, policy makers, politicians, and other relevant stakeholders to address issues related to high school dropout. To ensure that Latina/o student needs are adequately assessed and culturally and linguistically compatible academic programs are developed and accessible, the social and educational contexts warrant investigation.

Deconstructing Latina/o High School Student Experiences

Before discussing educational issues related to Latina/o high school students, it is essential to unpack the term *Latina/o* and other factors associated with it. Throughout this chapter the terms, Hispanic and Latina/o, are used interchangeably. Although there is a considerable debate regarding terminology, these arguments extend beyond the scope of this chapter. For purposes of this discussion, Hispanics and Latina/os are used synonymously and are defined as individuals who immigrated or whose ancestors immigrated to the U.S. from Mexico, Central America, South America, or the Caribbean (i.e., Cuba, Puerto Rico, or the Dominican Republic) and whose family and home background includes native speakers of Spanish.

With a variety of ethnicities, migration patterns, sociopolitical histories, and educational backgrounds, Latina/os are a highly heterogeneous group in the United States. The Latina/o high school population is no less diverse: 65% are native-born and 27% have migrated to the United States. Within the group of student immigrants, the number of years in U.S. schools varies, depending on age of arrival and previous schooling. For example, research indicates that Mexican and Central American students are less educated upon arrival in the United States than are students from the Caribbean and South America (Lowell & Suro, 2002). Nearly 40% of immigrant students of Mexican descent drop out of high school, compared to 13% of their South American counterparts (Fry, 2003).

The literature pays special attention to Mexican students, given that they are the largest Latina/o subpopulation in the United States (Fry, 2003; Lowell & Suro, 2002; President's Advisory Commission on Educational Excellence for Hispanic Americans, 2002). In particular, there is a persistently wide educational gap between foreign-born Mexican students and U.S.-born students of Mexican descent. However, when foreign-born students migrate to the United States before the age of 5, they graduate from high school at rates similar to their Hispanic counterparts. Similarly, a quarter of foreign-born Central American students drop out, whereas only 7% of their U.S.-born counterparts drop out (Fry, 2003). These initial data reveal the need for educators and policy makers to be aware of the ethnic diversity and trends that exist within Latina/o subpopulations when developing sound academic programs that adequately address the unique needs of the various student groups.

Learning from the past—*Si no sabes de donde vienes, no sabes a donde iras* (If you do not know where you are coming from, you do not know where you are going)

The United States has grappled with high school attrition for more than half a century. This section describes the history of Latina/o high school students in the U.S. school system, with special attention to reports and legislation that focus on or influence the status of Latina/o high school students.

In the 1950s, only 40% to 50% of the U.S. school population graduated from high school (Hispanic Dropout Project, 1998). However, between 1955 and 1972, the overall dropout rate for students between the ages of 16 and 24 dropped 30 points, to approximately 15%. By 1994, the dropout rate was estimated to be 13%. While the gap gradually narrowed for Whites and African Americans, it remained consistently wide for Latina/o high school students, ranging between 30% and 35% (Hispanic Dropout Project, 1998).

The 1973 Supreme Court decision on *Lau vs. Nichols* (1973) raised substantial awareness of the needs of limited-English learners. This significant ruling forced U.S. school districts to accommodate students who had limited proficiency in English, ensuring that they had equal access to educational opportunities. Although this ruling had the potential to influence the education of many Latina/o students substantially, little changed. Unfortunately, Latina/o students were considered intellectually inferior and were relegated to vocational programs or inappropriately classified and placed in special classrooms rather than enjoying an integrated educational context (Slavin & Calderon, 2000).

From 1976 to 1996, the proportion of Latina/o high school students doubled, from 6.4% to 12% (Garcia, 2001). The increase of Latina/os and the census projections of significant increases in the Latina/o population sparked considerable social and political interest in Latina/o academic achievement and failure. For instance, in 1990, the National Council of La Raza (NCLR) released *Hispanic Education: A Statistical Portrait*, a compelling document that examined the status of Hispanics in the U.S. school system. The report revealed discouraging statistics about Hispanic retention, academic achievement, dropout rates, and high school completion rates. It was evident that Latina/o high school students were struggling and that the U.S. school system was failing to address their needs.

In response to these troubling findings, Richard W. Riley, then U.S. Secretary of Education, invited a group of scholars to explore special issues contributing to the Hispanic student dropout rate. The group established the Hispanic Dropout Project, whose three primary goals were to raise awareness, develop a set of policy-related recommendations, and establish a group of interested stakeholders who could address the problems associated with the Hispanic dropout rate. The group generated a persuasive report, *No More Excuses*, in which they examined the roles of all the key players—Hispanic students, their parents and families, teachers, schools, policy makers, community members, and business leaders—and provided a set of recommendations to each, urging them to work together. Aptly stated, change for the better can begin with the actions of any adult player. But the actions of all players must work in concert to produce a move forward, to support change in other arenas, and to achieve longer lasting and more extensive improvements in Hispanic dropout rates than can be achieved through solitary action. (Hispanic Dropout Project, 1998, p. 11)

The committee asserted that Latina/o attrition has remained largely invisible to most, except for those who are directly affected. Rather than a general and non-race-specific examination of the dropout problem, the committee insisted special attention be given to the Hispanic student dropout problem. Its members recommended that Hispanic dropout and school completion be added to the national education agenda, and they urged researchers to study the mechanisms through which students of different backgrounds disengage from school, evaluate promising dropout prevention programs, and disseminate information about successful programs.

In 2001, President Bush signed an executive order establishing the President's Advisory Commission on Educational Excellence for Hispanic Americans. This federally based commission examined means and mechanisms to decrease the educational achievement gap for Hispanic Americans. It was expected that the commission would develop, monitor, and coordinate federal efforts to promote high-quality education for Hispanic Americans.

In September 2002, the President's Advisory Commission released its interim report, *The Road to a College Diploma: The Complex Reality of Raising Educational Achievement for Hispanics in the United States*. After reviewing extensive census data and countless studies and reports, the committee identified the following five strategic imperatives that would guide its work for the subsequent year: "Coordinating a national campaign for action; putting college on the radar screen; establishing measurable strategies and goals; abandoning one-size-fits-all-thinking; and asking what works and for whom" (p. 3). Mindful of the role of parents and families in academic achievement, the committee also established a working subcommittee dedicated exclusively to the family's influences on academic aspirations and attainment. The committee's ultimate goal was to develop a road map that would integrate sound public policy and effective classroom practice, successfully guiding all of the relevant stakeholders in a coordinated effort to improve the educational attainment of Latina/os.

On March 31, 2003, the commission released its final report, *From Risk to Opportunity: Fulfilling the Educational Needs of Hispanic Americans in the 21st Century*. The commission found that Latina/o students were indeed at risk, and the current education system was ill-equipped to handle one of the nation's largest and fastest-growing minorities. Commission members established that Latina/o families often lacked the knowledge and resources needed to achieve the high academic goals set for their children. They found that too many educators set low expectations for their Latina/o students, and they recognized that the federal government was not effectively measuring, monitoring, or managing the programs considered necessary for Latina/o students and their families. To help address these deficiencies and problems, the commission offered the following six recommendations:

> set new and high expectations across America for Hispanic American children . . . full implementation and full enforcement of the *No Child Left Behind* Act . . . reinforce a high quality teaching profession . . . initiate a new coherent and comprehensive research agenda . . . ensure full access for Hispanic American students to enter college and demand greater accountability in higher education for Hispanic graduation rates . . . and increase the accountability and coordination of programs within the federal government to better serve Hispanic American children and their families. (p. viii)

Overall, these reports and commissions on Latina/o student education came to similar conclusions. Although significant efforts have been put forth nationally, Latina/o students continue to have limited access to and lower-quality educational preparation. These challenges make for a nation that has not served the needs of all its society's members adequately.

Defining the Dropout Rate

As each of the national reports and commissions addresses the ever-increasing Latina/o high school dropout rate, it is imperative to define the term *dropout* accurately and understand the factors that both moderate and mediate dropout decisions for Latina/os. According to Fry (2003), the most common measure is "the status dropout rate which represents the fraction of the population in a given age bracket that has not completed high school and is not enrolled in school" (p. 2). When examining the dropout rate from this approach, as the National Center for Educational Statistics (2001) and others (President's Advisory Commission) commonly do, Latina/os are four times more likely than White students and three times more likely than African American students to drop out of school. This "status dropout rate," however, inaccurately portrays the problem by distorting the numbers and failing to capture important nuances. Fry (2003) contends that, within the high school age group, particular students present with different backgrounds, intentions, and aspirations. Specifically, his analyses revealed that there are "three sub-groups of the Latina/o youth population that need to be examined separately: the native born, foreign born who attend U.S. schools and the foreign born who emigrate primarily for employment purposes and do not enroll in U.S. schools" (p. 2). When categorized in this manner, the dropout rates vary considerably. For example, using the Census 2000 Supplementary Survey (U.S. Bureau of the Census, 2001), the dropout rate for U.S.-born Latina/o students was 14%, compared to 18% for U.S.-educated immigrants and 90% for Latina/os educated abroad (Fry, 2003). Fry also noted that nearly all of the Latina/o students educated exclusively abroad are dropouts because they immigrate to the United States primarily to secure employment.

Similarly, the age range selected when calculating dropout significantly influences dropout estimates. For example, when varying age brackets are selected (16–19, 18–24, 16–24), the dropout rates range from 21% to 28% to 33%, respectively (Fry, 2003). Regardless of the calculations used, the dropout rates remain discouraging and disconcerting since they are still twice as high for Latina/os as they are for non-Latina/os.

Factors Associated with the High School Dropout

The National Council of La Raza (NCLR, 1990) aggregated and re-analyzed data from several prominent reports and studies conducted in the 1980s on Latina/o education. Findings revealed common risk factors for school failure for Latina/o students as "single-parent family, low parent education, limited English proficiency, low family income, sibling drop out, and home alone more than three hours on weekdays" (p. 41). Although these analyses were conducted more than 20 years ago, the recent President's Advisory Commission on Educational Excellence for Hispanic Americans' 2003 report regrettably corroborated the council's findings, revealing that these factors remain today.

More recently, the NCLR released its annual report, *State of Hispanic America 2004*, similarly enumerating the educational challenges that Latina/o high school students encounter. Specific contextual factors that influence Latina/o educational experiences include inadequate funding, poor teacher quality, and unchallenging coursework. It is not surprising that the factors associated with high school dropout and academic failure are a complicated phenomenon caused by a complex interplay of factors (Garcia, 2000; Reyes, Scribner, & Scribner, 1999). Garcia conceptualized three categories of academic failure risks for Latina/o children. The first, youth- and child-focused factors include personal features and characteristics that are unique to the student (e.g., migration history, learning disability, language ability). These factors "begin to define a child's readiness to learn" (p. 312). The second category of factors is environmentally based. These factors essentially surround the student and/or are embedded within his or her environment (e.g., parents with low levels of education, disorganized neighborhood, single-parent or guardian household). Finally, the conditions conducive to learning, the third category, uniquely define those aspects of the school environment that contribute to the learning process. It is this category of factors that ultimately places schools at risk of failing Latina/o children. High turnover of key teaching and administrative staff, unqualified and noncredentialed teachers, and inappropriate or inept curriculum aptly focus the responsibility for Latina/o school failure on the schools.

Both Fry (2003) and Garcia (2000) emphasize that limited English proficiency plays a critical role in academic success. Garcia observed that a number of Latina/o students speak primarily Spanish at home, contributing to "low levels of skills in the four English Language Arts domains (listening, speaking, reading and writing)" (p. 309). This dilemma places students at a considerable disadvantage and compromises their academic skills and abilities, preventing them from succeeding in school. Fry's analyses revealed that Latina/o students who have poor English-language skills have a significantly higher dropout rate than those students who are English-proficient. Findings indicate that the non-English-proficient student dropout rate is 60%, compared to English-proficient Latina/os, 15% of whom drop out.

Family income is another risk factor associated with the Latina/o dropout rate. Limited family income creates additional challenges and responsibilities for Latina/o students (Garcia, 2000). In particular, the literature indicates that inadequate resources compel Latina/o high school students to work. For example, more than 50% of Latina/o high school dropouts held jobs while attending school (Fry, 2003; Reyes, Scribner, & Scribner, 1999). Although they earned higher wages than their White and African American counterparts, as a function of working longer hours (Fry 2003), their time for studies and educational activities was compromised.

Finally, when examining Latina/o high school experiences, gender disparities are evident. Specifically, males drop out at significantly higher rates than their female peers (NCLR, 1990; Fry, 2003). Males tend to drop out to secure employment, whereas females do so for personal reasons (e.g., familial responsibilities). Females also are more likely to drop out slightly earlier in their educational path than males. In contrast, males are more prone to repeat a grade (NCLR, 1990).

Dropping Out or Being Pushed Out?

In the Latina/o dropout literature, researchers often adopt a deficit model in which Latina/o students are portrayed as lacking the personal resources or academic ability needed to succeed in school. The term *dropout* presumes a willful, deliberate decision to leave or withdraw from school. A closer examination of the literature, however, reveals that Latina/os drop out of school due to faulty administrative policies, inept academic practices, questionable teacher expectations, and/or fiscal inequities (Fuentes, Kiyana, & Rosario, 2003; Secada et al., 1998). As a result, scholars have questioned whether Latina/o students drop out or, in essence, are pushed out (Fuentes, Kiyana, & Rosario, 2003; Secada et al., 1998).

To answer the question of Latina/o student pushout, Jordan, Lara, and McPartland (1994) analyzed data from the National Education Longitudinal Study of 1988 (i.e., NELS 88) consisting of 25,000 eighth graders in 1,000 schools across the nation. Reasons for dropout and educational patterns across adolescent subgroups by race/ethnicity and gender were investigated. Study findings revealed that the most frequent dropout influences were disliking school; poor school performance; poor student-teacher relations; inability to keep up with academic work; and feeling that they did not belonged in school. In examining the list of influences, school and contextual factors were cited most frequently, rather than personal factors, as reasons for dropping out.

Related to this point, Marín (1995) interviewed 10 Puerto Rican high school dropouts about personal, school, family, and community factors in relation to their educational experiences. The sample consisted primarily of students who came from large families and whose parent(s) had limited education. Overall findings suggested that the participants shared common high school experiences. For example, characteristics included being retained in the same grade multiple times, poor academic performance records, feelings of alienation, poor teacher-student relationships, and increased suspensions.

Finally, Aviles et al. (1999) also investigated perceptions of 72 Chicana/o/Latina/o dropout students from a Midwestern high school. Student responses consistently revealed specific challenges of attendance, school participation, teacher and staff expectations, racism and prejudice, and personal situations (e.g., family concerns). These students consistently and distinctly reported factors that contributed to what the authors termed being "facilitated" out. That is, they frequently described a process by which administrators and teachers engaged in practices that made dropping out of high school a viable and appealing option.

Sí, Se Puede (Yes, We Can), but It Takes a *Barrio*

Successful navigation through adolescence depends on student characteristics as well as families, neighborhoods, schools, health care systems, and other related institutions (National Research Council, 1993; Reyes, Scribner, & Scribner, 1999). Clearly, schools play the most salient role in the academic achievement and success of Latina/o students; however, research is primarily conducted on Latina/o students who have already dropped out of school. Fewer studies have examined Latina/os who stay in school and graduate, a phenomenon commonly referred to as persistence: the ability to remain in school until completion or graduation (Miller, 1989). To promote academic persistence among Latina/o students, it is essential to examine the associated positive elements.

Lucas, Henze, and Donato (1997) found that school context plays a substantial and vital role in the academic success of Latina/o high school students throughout the United States. Schools that are staffed by high-quality personnel, set high expectations, allocate appropriate resources, and honor diversity are bound to promote academic persistence and excellence among their students. For example, Reyes, Scribner and Scribner (1999) examined the school cultures and related academic practices of eight schools that were effectively educating and successfully graduating their students. These eight schools, primarily Latina/o-populated, were selected based on their consistently successful state standardized test scores. Four contextual dimensions were identified as critical elements of their successes: collaborative governance and leadership, community and family involvement, culturally responsive pedagogy, and advocacy-oriented assessment. Using these dimensions, the following section defines and integrates various studies that demonstrate their relevance and value.

Collaborative governance is perhaps of greatest importance as it underlies each of the dimensions. Guided by the principle that all students can and will learn, effective schools have a common mission and/or vision directing their work. Furthermore, a culture of ownership and accountability permeates these schools. When relevant and possible, decisions are made collaboratively, and there is recognition that all school personnel play a critical role in creating and maintaining a learning community. Principals often serve as facilitators who acknowledge teachers as experts and provide the necessary resources and support to perform their responsibilities successfully. It is through this dimension that proactive and effective learning communities are created and maintained.

Lucas, Henze, and Donato's (1997) study corroborates the importance of collaborative governance for schools. Examining instructional practices and related academic cultures of six secondary schools in California and Arizona, the authors determined eight key features that were responsible for school successes. These variables included placing value in the students' languages and cultures; making the high expectations of language-minority students concrete; ensuring that the education of language-minority students is a priority; creating staff development programs that are explicitly designed to help teachers and other staff serve language-minority students more effectively; offering a variety of courses and programs for language-minority students; implementing a counseling program that gives special attention to language-minority students; encouraging parents to become involved in their children's education; and promoting a strong, shared commitment throughout the schools that empowered language-minority students through education. As noted earlier, effective learning prevails when schools are deliberately designed to address the unique needs of students. School authorities cannot expect academic success and persistence to occur naturally; they must be cognizant of the variables that ensure effective integration for all students.

The role of effective learning communities, the second dimension of success, is facilitated by community and family involvement. Parents and families serve a critical role in Latina/o student success (NCLR, 2004; Hispanic Dropout Project, 1998). Despite the recognition of the family's importance, some schools have not capitalized on this valuable support resource (Curiel, 1991; Sanchez, 1997). Rather than viewing families and communities as tolerated and avoided obstacles, successful schools recognize families and community members as partners who easily complement the school missions and enhance the cultures of schools with rich perspectives and useful resources.

Curiel (1991) maintained that school officials hold negative stereotypes about Latina/o parents based on language barriers, cultural differences, different educational expectations, and false assumptions regarding parents' interests in their children's education. As a result of discrimination and marginalization, Latina/o parents have reported feeling powerless and resentful that they are unable to make a difference in their children's education. Sanchez (1997) found a similar sentiment among Latina/o parents, that they were consistently excluded from active, policy-making roles within their children's education. It is important to note, however, that there are legitimate barriers—language differences, work schedules, transportation problems, and child care needs—that were often misperceived as parental disinterest in their child's education and a lack of educational or intellectual ability. Many studies have found that Latina/o parents, despite their limited education, play an instrumental role through successful partnerships with teachers and by fostering academic resiliency (Duran, 2000; Lucas, Henze, & Donato, 1997; Ruiz, 2002).

Fuentes, Kiyana, and Rosario's (2003) exploratory study illustrated parents' critical role. In this study, the majority of the participants (87%) reported never considering dropping out of school and credited their parents and teachers as the most influential factors in their decision to finish school. A number of the students described parents who had an authoritative parenting style; that is, their parents collaborated with them in major decisions and maintained an open and understanding relationship with them, while maintaining definitive authority in the household. Moreover, parents clearly communicated expectations of high school graduation to their children—dropping out was not an option. In establishing parental influence, families had high academic expectations demonstrated by attending to their children's progress, being available, and providing necessary school resources (e.g., school supplies).

Within family and community involvement, a common theme of wanting a "better life" and more opportunities for their children also emerged (Fuentes, Kiyana, & Rosario, 2003). Latina/o parents either directly or indirectly communicated to their children that education was the primary vehicle for social, economic, and political mobility. Just as important, the schools also acknowledged that there were other critical players who transcended the traditional community boundaries but who held considerable power and influence. Maintaining a broad sense of community by including state, regional, and federal players helped these schools recognize the critical roles these political forces play in creating and maintaining sound learning communities.

The third dimension, culturally responsive pedagogy, is guided by the premise that all children can learn. In effective schools, differences in culture and language are perceived as commodities rather than obstacles. The primary languages of students are honored, and coursework is taught in their native languages while incorporating their experiences and backgrounds. Moreover, students are encouraged to play active roles in the teaching and learning process and are perceived as educational collaborators, rather than as passive recipients of information. In addition, teachers challenge students to consider the practical aspects of knowledge for application in their lives. Culturally responsive pedagogy is developed and implemented by teachers committed to student learning, thus fulfilling a critical role in academic persistence (Lucas, Henze, & Donato, 1997; Reyes, Scribner, & Scribner, 1999). For example, Fuentes, Kiyana, and Rosario (2003) found that high school students appreciated teachers who had high expectations and were academically demanding, yet were supportive and approachable.

Assessment, the fourth dimension, can have both positive and negative consequences for Latina/o high school students. When implemented successfully, assessment processes can provide useful information regarding students' progress and teachers' ability and efforts. However, when implemented incorrectly, assessment inaccurately identifies and exaggerates student limitations while minimizing or disguising teacher ineffectiveness and difficult school climates. Effective learning communities use advocacy-oriented assessment (Reyes, Scribner, & Scribner, 1999), perceiving assessment processes as a means to learn about the students, instructors, and schools. A student's lack of skills is not interpreted as a lack of ability, but rather as a possible lack of opportunity to learn or lack of access to effective instruction. In other words, if a student is failing, it may mean that the teaching process is not a good fit for the student. Teachers within these effective learning communities are not guided by elements of the Bell Curve theory; instead, students serve as their own comparisons because each student has his or her own unique potential. Advocacy-oriented assessment promotes the crafting of innovative assessment procedures (e.g., portfolio assessment, informal inquiries, and qualitative procedures).

A careful review of Latina/o educational experiences underscores the connection between teaching and learning and the considerable overlap among the four dimensions—governance and leadership, community and family involvement, culturally responsive pedagogy, and advocacy-oriented assessment. In fact, the interconnection among the dimensions emphasizes their relationships and highlights their influences on each other. For example, creative learning can only be initiated in an environment with supportive instructors who have the necessary resources in the classroom to facilitate learning. Without funding and administrative support, classroom enhancement and school environment are negatively affected, hindering student learning and persistence. Similarly, testing and sound assessment can only be implemented in a school environment where a culturally responsive pedagogy is valued. Hence, without a culturally sensitive orientation, proper assessment cannot be conducted, and without such assessment, culturally sensitive services cannot be provided.

Conclusion

The United States has grappled unsuccessfully with Latina/o dropout for numerous decades. Despite the growing number of successful academic programs throughout the United States, a large number of schools still push out our children by engaging in poor and maladaptive academic practices. One theme that has emerged repeatedly in this chapter is the relevance and importance of context for Latina/o high school educational persistence. Historically, the system has blamed Latina/o students and their families for lack of academic persistence. Yet, as education aims to maintain learning communities for all children, particularly Latina/os, it is critical to determine the contextual factors (psychological, social, and cultural) that enhance or compromise educational growth and progress. Moreover, it is essential to acknowledge the education systems' shortcomings and their societal implications.

To seriously address Latina/o educational issues related to a quality experience and, ultimately, persistence, one question must be reexamined—we know what works, why aren't we doing it? If this question is considered openly and honestly, we may be seriously disturbed by what we discover (e.g., negligence, resistance, and apathy). Despite such sentiments and limited historical progress, it is only through intentional and consistent advocacy efforts that change will occur. Hence, whenever I become disheartened, I turn to the wise words of Antonio Machado (1875–1939), who said, "*Caminanta, no hay camino, se hace el camino al andar*" (Traveler, there is no path, you make it as you walk). Machado underscores the importance of making our own paths to influence the current educational conditions.

Specific directives to consider as parents, teachers, and administrators, who also walk to make their paths, include:

Parents:

- Have high expectations of your children and play an active role in their learning.
- Consistently communicate that dropping out or failing out of school is not an option.
- Be actively involved in your children's education and develop and maintain a collaborative partnership with teachers and administrators.

Teachers and Administrators:

- Know and understand the influence of background variables and contextual factors on academic persistence.

- Implement a culturally integrative pedagogy that facilitates learning and incorporates the students' background, including their history, values, beliefs, and practices.
- Move away from a "one size fits all" mindset when considering issues and concerns for Latina/o students. Each Latina/o subpopulation has its own unique characteristics, and educators must be mindful of them when developing and implementing academic program and interventions.
- Collaborate with families and surrounding communities to foster and maintain an effective learning environment for Latina/o high school students.

References

Aviles, R. M., Guerrero, M. P., Howarth, H. B., & Thomas, G. (1999). Perceptions of Chicano/Latina/o students who have dropped out of school. *Journal of Counseling and Development, 77,* 465–473.

Curiel, H. (1991). Strengthening family and school bonds in promoting Hispanic children's school performance. In M. Sotomayor (Ed.), *Empowering Hispanic families: A critical issue for the '90s* (pp. 75–95). Milwaukee, WI: Family Service America.

Duran, D. (2000). *A retrospective study of academic resilience in successful Latina/o students from a rural California community.* Unpublished doctoral dissertation. Stanford University.

Fry, R. (2003). *Hispanic youth dropping out of U.S. schools: Measuring the challenge.* Washington, DC: Pew Hispanic Center.

Fuentes, M., Kiyana, A., & Rosario, E. (2003, August). *Keeping Latina/os in high school: The role of context.* Paper presented as part of a symposium, Academic Persistence of Latina/o Students: Personal, Social, & Contextual Factors, 111th Annual Meeting of the American Psychological Association, Toronto, Canada.

Garcia, E. E. (2001). *Hispanic education in the United States.* New York: Rowman and Littlefield Publishers.

Garcia, G. N. (2000). The factors that place Latina/o children and youth at risk of educational failure. In R. E. Slavin & M. Calderon (Eds.), *Effective programs for Latina/o students* (pp. 307–329). Mahwah, NJ: Lawrence Erlbaum Associates.

Hispanic Dropout Project (1998). *No more excuses: The final report.* Washington, DC: U.S. Department of Education.

Jordan, W. J., Lara, J., & McPartland, J. M. (1994). *Exploring the complexity of early drop out causal structures.* (Rep. No. 48, pp. 4–38). Baltimore: Center for Research on Effective Schooling for Disadvantaged Students, John Hopkins University.

Lau v. Nichols, 414 U.S. 563, 566 (1973).

Lowell, B.L., & Suro, R. (2002). *The improving educational profile of Latino immigrants.* Washington, DC: Pew Hispanic Center.

Lucas, T., Henze, R., & Donato, R. (1997). Promoting the success of Latino language-minority students: An exploratory study of six high schools. *Harvard Educational Review, 60,* 315–340.

Marín, P. (1995). Using open ended interviews to determine why Puerto Rican students drop out of school. *Journal of Multicultural Counseling and Development, 23,* 158–170.

Miller, A. P. (1989). Student characteristics and the persistence/dropout behavior of Hispanic students. In J. M. Lakebrink (Ed.), *Children at risk* (pp. 119–139). Springfield, IL: Charles C. Thomas.

National Center for Education Statistics (1990). NEL: 88. *Base, year, sample, design, report.* Washington, DC: U.S. Department of Education.

National Center for Education Statistics (2001) *Dropout rates in the United States: 2000.* Washington, DC: U.S. Department of Education.

National Council of la Raza (NCLR) (1990). *Hispanic education: A statistical portrait.* Washington, DC: Author.

National Council of la Raza (2004). *State of Hispanic America 2004.* Washington, DC: Author.

National Research Council (1993). Losing generations: Adolescents in high-risk settings*: Panel on high-risk youth, National Research Council.* Washington, DC: National Academy Press.

President's Advisory Commission on Educational Excellence for Hispanic Americans (2002). *The road to a college diploma: The complex reality of raising educational achievement for Hispanics in the United States.* Washington, DC: U.S. Department of Education.

President's Advisory Commission on Educational Excellence for Hispanic Americans (2003). *From risk to opportunity: Fulfilling the educational needs of Hispanic Americans in the 21st century.* Washington, DC: U.S. Department of Education.

Reyes, P., Scribner, J. D., & Scribner, A. P. (1999). *Lessons from high performing Hispanic schools.* New York: Teachers College Press.

Ruiz, Y. (2002). *Predictors of academic resiliency in Latina/o middle school students.* Unpublished doctoral dissertation. Boston College.

Sanchez, W. (1997). Special education and Latino clients: Empowerment and becoming a good consumer. *Special Services in the Schools, 12,* 23–29.

Secada, W. G., Chavez-Chavez, R., Garcia, E., Muñoz, C., Oakes, J., Santiago-Santiago, I., & Slavin, R. (1998). *No more excuses: The final report of the Hispanic Dropout Project.* Washington, DC: U.S. Department of Education.

Slavin, R. E., & Calderon, M. (2000). *Effective programs for Latina/o students.* Mahwah, NJ: Lawrence Erlbaum Associates.

Symons, M. (2000, March 16). Hispanic students fall behind: Report calls for dual language school. *Home News Tribune,* pp. A1, A2.

U.S. Bureau of Census (2001). *The Hispanic population.* Retrieved May 31, 2004, from http://www.census.gov/prod/2001pubs/c2kbr01-3.pdf.

Alfredo G. de los Santos Jr.

Alfredo G. de los Santos Jr. is a research professor at Arizona State University Main, Tempe, Arizona. He has an academic assignment in the Division of Educational Leadership and Policy Studies in the College of Education and research and development responsibilities at the Hispanic Research Center in the College of Liberal Arts and Sciences. He is also a Senior League Fellow of The League for Innovation in the Community College.

From 1978 through October 1, 1999, Dr. de los Santos served as vice chancellor for student and educational development at the Maricopa Community Colleges. He has received a number of awards and recognitions, including the National Leadership Award from the American Association of Community Colleges in April 2004; the Reginald Wilson Award, American Council on Education, October 2001; the 1998 Harold W. McGraw Jr. Prize in Education, from the McGraw-Hill Companies, September 1998; the Special Recognition Award for Scholarly Research in Bilingual Education from the National Association for Bilingual Education, 1994; and the Education Achievement Award from the National Science Foundation in 1993.

Gerardo E. de los Santos

Gerardo E. de los Santos is interim president and chief executive officer of the League for Innovation in the Community College, an international organization dedicated to catalyzing the community college movement. The League hosts conferences and institutes, develops Web resources, conducts research, produces publications, provides services, and leads projects and initiatives with more than 750 member institutions, 100 corporate partners, and a host of other governmental and nonprofit agencies in its continuing effort to make a positive difference for students and communities.

Dr. de los Santos manages the organizational, fiscal, and cultural operations of the League. He also directs the League's annual Innovations Conference, which is dedicated to improving student and organizational learning through innovation, experimentation, and institutional transformation.

Dr. de los Santos began his own education at Mesa Community College in Arizona, where he earned an A.A. degree, and subsequently transferred to the University of California at Berkeley, where he earned a B.A. in rhetoric. He earned his master's in English from Arizona State University, where he was honored as a Graduate Regents Fellow. He received his Ph.D. in educational administration from the University of Texas at Austin, where he was named Distinguished Graduate.

3

LATINA/OS AND COMMUNITY COLLEGES[1]

A Pathway to Graduate Studies?

Alfredo G. de los Santos Jr.
Gerardo E. de los Santos

Dramatic changes are occurring in the demographic makeup of the United States at a time when the importance of a high-quality education for all of the country's citizens is necessary if the nation is to be competitive in the global marketplace. Carnavale and Desrochers (2003) note that "meeting high educational standards has become a prerequisite for economic growth and social inclusion in the 21st century. Knowledge has become the engine of growth among nations, and individuals need a solid academic foundation in order to meet the increasing skills demands on the job" (p. 2). Given the inequities of the educational system, which has not provided equal opportunities for all students, it is clear that the negative implications are far-reaching. For example, these educational inequities have led to an increasingly underprepared workforce, which has resulted in an unequal distribution of

[1] The authors wish to thank a number of people for their generosity in sharing information and helping the authors access data. Dennis Jones, president of the National Center for Higher Education Management in Boulder, Colorado, provided information from National Center for Higher Education Management Systems databases specifically on Latina/os. Melinda Gebel, assistant director of the Office of Institutional Analysis and Data Administration at Arizona State University (ASU), prepared a special report of recent ASU baccalaureate graduates by racial/ethnic group who attended the Maricopa Community Colleges and shared it with the authors. Kent Phillippe, senior research associate at the American Association of Community Colleges in Washington, D.C., provided recent trend data and helped the authors access other data. John Tsapogas, senior analyst in the Division of Science Resources Studies at the National Science Foundation, provided information specific to Latina/os from the study he wrote earlier this year. Richard Fry, senior research associate at the Pew Hispanic Center in Washington, D.C., not only shared his earlier reports, but helped the authors access more recent data as well.

the country's wealth. Carnavale and Desrochers write that, among the "world's advanced economics, America's increasing divide between 'college haves' and 'college have-nots' has resulted in the United States surpassing Great Britain as the nation with the widest income differences" (p. 7).

Latina/os, now the nation's largest minority, will play an increasingly important role in the economic and social life of the country in this century if they have access to an education system that provides them with the opportunity to be more "college haves" than "college have-nots." To Latina/os, community colleges are an important gateway to America's educational opportunities.

This chapter addresses one overarching question regarding Latina/os in community colleges: What do more recent data indicate about Latina/os' success in transferring from community colleges to four-year colleges and universities and their persistence in earning degrees? This main question will be answered by addressing three different, but related questions: (1) How do Latina/os compare with White students along the educational pipeline? (2) How many Latina/os who earn degrees at four-year colleges and universities began their studies in community colleges? (3) How many Latina/os who earned degrees at four-year colleges and universities attended community colleges?

The American Community College

The community college, an American invention, dates back to the late 19th century and the beginning of the 20th and is now an important part of the nation's system of higher education. Although these institutions initially were called *junior colleges*, several terms have been used over the years to refer to them, including *county college*, the *people's college*, *two-year colleges*, *democracy's college*, *technical institutes*, *contrary college*, *learning college*, and so forth. The term most commonly used now is *community college* (Cohen & Brawer, 2003).

Cohen and Brawer (2003) define the community college as "any institution regionally accredited to award the associate in arts or the associate in science as its highest degree" (p. 5). The Carnegie Foundation for the Advancement of Teaching defines community colleges as *associate's colleges*: "These institutions offer associate's degree and certificates programs but, with few exceptions, award no baccalaureate degrees. This group includes community, junior, and technical colleges" (Carnegie Foundation for the Advancement of Teaching, 2001, p. 2).

The community colleges provide comprehensive curricular offerings that include academic transfer preparation, vocational-technical education, continuing education, developmental education, and community services (Cohen & Brawer, 2003, p. 20). As well, community colleges supplement the instructional process with a wide variety of student personnel services (Cohen & Brawer, 2003, p. 197). In addition, by the early 1990s, community colleges had become an important part of the economic and workforce development efforts in the United States (Zeiss & Associates, 1997).

According to the American Association of Community Colleges (AACC), there are 1,173 community colleges in the United States. Of these, 997, or almost 85%, are public institutions. A total of 145 are private community colleges, and 31 are tribal colleges (AACC, 2004).

In 2003, 11.3 million students were enrolled in America's community colleges, 6.3 million in credit courses and 5 million in noncredit offerings. The students enrolled in community colleges represented 44% of all undergraduates and 45% of all first-time freshmen (AACC, 2004).

Latina/o Population—Largest Minority Group

The Latina/o population in the United States grew from 22,354,059 in 1990 to 35,305,818 in 2000—a 57.93% increase—making them the country's largest minority group. In the same period, the total population increased from 248.7 million in 1990 to 281.4 million in 2000, a 13.15% increase (see Table 3.1). In 2000, the Latina/o population represented 12.5% of the total U.S. population (U.S. Bureau of the Census, 2000); one of every eight persons in the country is Latina/o.

As shown in Table 3.1, the number of Latina/o individuals of Mexican

TABLE 3.1
U.S. Latina/o Population Increase, 1990 and 2000

	1990	*2000*	*% Increase*
Grand Total, U.S. Population	248,709,873	281,421,906	13.15%
Total Latina/o Population	22,354,059	35,305,818	57.93%
Mexican	13,495,938	20,640,711	52.94%
Puerto Rican	2,727,754	3,406,711	24.87%
Cuban	1,043,435	1,241,685	18.94%
Other*	5,086,435	10,017,244	96.96%

* This category represents Latina/os from Central America, South America, and other parts of the world.

Source: U.S. Bureau of the Census, 2000.

descent increased from 13,495,938 in 1990 to 20,640,711 in 2000, an increase of 57.93%. The number of Puerto Ricans increased by 24.87%, from 2,727,754 in 1990 to 3,406,711 in 2000, and the number of Cubans, from 1,043,435 in 1990 to 1,241,685, an 18.94% increase. It is interesting to note that the "other" Latina/o population almost doubled, from 5,086,435 in 1990 to 10,017,244 in 2000; these include Latina/os from Central and South America and other parts of the world.

Given the increase in the Latina/o population in the United States, the projected increase in Latina/os who will graduate from high school and enroll in college should not come as a surprise.

Projections: Latina/o High School Graduation and College Enrollment

The number of Latina/o students who will graduate from high school is projected to increase in the next decade, from 326,198 in 2002–2003 to 634,280 by 2017–18. By 2017, Latina/o students will represent 22.1% of all high school graduates, compared to the 13.2% that African Americans will represent that year (WICHE, ACT, & College Board, 2003, p. 89) (see Table 3.2).

In some states, such as Arizona and New Mexico, the number of Latina/o high school graduates will exceed non-Latina/o White graduates by 2012. In

TABLE 3.2
Projected High School Graduates in the United States, 2002–03 through 2017–8, by Racial/Ethnic Group

	Growth by Race/Ethnicity				
Total	American Indian	Asian Pac Is	African American	Latina/o	White Non-Latina/o
2002–2003					
	27,048	132,618	349,869	326,198	1,817,190
% total	1.01%	4.99%	13.19%	12.29%	68.49%
2017–18					
2,872,141	34,035	227,298	379,827	634,280	1,596,701
% total	1.19%	7.91%	3.22%	22.08%	5.59%
% increase 8.26%	25.83%	71.14%	8.56%	94.44%	decrease

Source: WICHE, ACT, & College Board, 2003.

Arizona, for example, in 2017–2018, 32,772 Latina/os (45.1% of the total) are projected to graduate from high school, compared to 31,122 White, non-Latina/os (42.8% of the total) (WICHE, ACT, & College Board, 2003).

In 2017–18, a total of 9,045 Latina/o students are projected to graduate from New Mexico high schools, 54.7% of the total, compared to 4,509 White, non-Latina/o graduates, or 27.3% of the total (WICHE, ACT, & College Board).

The number of Latina/o students enrolling in college will increase from 1.4 million in 1995 to 2.5 million in 2015. The additional 1.1 million Latina/o students represent a 73% increase over a 20-year period—1995–2015. By 2006, Latina/o students are expected to outnumber African American students enrolled in college (Carnavale & Fry, 1999).

Latina/o Educational Pipeline, College Enrollment, and Degree Achievement

As shown in Table 3.3, of 100 Latina/os who begin their studies in the ninth grade, 53 graduate from high school, compared to 75 White students. While 41 of the White students who do graduate from high school enroll in college, only 27 Latina/o students do.

Only 10 of the 100 Latina/o ninth graders earn a two- or four-year degree within 150% time; that is, within three years for two-year college degrees or six years for four-year degrees. In contrast, more than twice the number of White students, 23, graduate with a two- or four-year degree in the same time frame (Jones, 2004).

TABLE 3.3
Latina/o Pipeline—Ninth Grade through Earned Degree

Race/Ethnicity	For every 100 ninth graders	Graduate from high school	Enter College	Graduate within 150% time*
Total	100	67	41	19
White	100	75	48	23
African American	100	49	27	9
Hispanic	100	53	27	10

*Graduation rates are weighted based on the percentage of full-time, first-time freshmen enrolled in two-year and four-year colleges.

Source: Jones, 2004.

Latina/o High School Graduates

While Latina/os have made some progress in educational achievement, they continue to trail behind non-Hispanic Whites. For example, in 2000–01, the gap in the high school graduation rate between White and Latina/o students for persons 18 to 24 years old was 27.9 percentage points: 59.5% for Latina/o students, compared to 87.6% for White students (Harvey, 2003, pp. 49–50).

Rate of Latina/os Enrolled in College

In 2000–01, the enrolled-in-college rate for 18- to 24-year-old Whites was 38.7%, compared to 21.7% for Latina/o students, a gap of 17 percentage points. Thus, a smaller percentage of those Latina/o students who did graduate from high school pursued further education. However, in the period between 1990–01 and 2000–01, the number of Latina/o students enrolled in all institutions of higher education increased by almost 87%, from 782,000 in 1990–01 to 1,462,000 in 2000–01 (Harvey, 2003, pp. 49–50).

Latina/os in Community Colleges

Of the total number of Latina/o students enrolled in institutions of higher education in 2000–01, 844,000, or more than half (57.7%), were enrolled in community colleges (Harvey, 2003, p. 57). The AACC also reports that more than half (55%) of all Latina/o undergraduates are enrolled in community colleges (2002, p. 4). It is clear that community colleges have been Latina/os' primary point of entry to higher education (Cohen & Brawer, 2003).

Of all the students enrolled in community colleges, Latina/os represented 11.8% of the total enrollment in 1997, compared to 9.3% of the total that Latina/os represented in 1992 (retrieved May 26, 2004, from www.aacc .nche.edu/pdf/aboutCC_Racial/pdf.). By 2000–01, the 844,000 Latina/os enrolled in two-year colleges represented 14.19% of the total enrolled in community colleges: 5,948,000 (Harvey, 2003, p.57). The AACC reported in 2004 that Latina/os represented 13.6% of all community college students (AACC, 2004). To summarize, Latina/os represent an increasing percentage of the enrollment in community colleges, ranging from 13.6% to 14.19% of the total.

Degrees Earned by Latina/os

Latina/o students represented 9.6% of all the students enrolled in institutions of higher education in 2000–01 (Harvey, 2003, p. 57), and they earned 9.9% of the associate degrees granted (Harvey, 2003, p. 63). The number of

Latina/os who earned associate degrees increased by more than 135% between 1990–01 and 2000–01. In 1990–01, Latina/os earned 24,251 associate degrees; 10 years later, in 2000–01, Latina/os earned 57,288 associate degrees (Harvey, 2003, p. 62).

Historically, more Latinas have earned associate degrees than Latinos for more than a decade. In 1990–01, of the 24,251 associate degrees awarded to Latina/os, Latinas earned 14,041 associate degrees, compared to 10,210 associate degrees earned by Latino males. That year, Latinas earned 57.9% of all associate degrees earned by Latina/os. In 2000–01, Latinas earned 33,938 of the 57,288 associate degrees earned by Latina/os, or 59.4% (Harvey, 2003, p. 62). Thus, almost 6 of every 10 associate degrees earned by Latinos were earned by females.

As noted above, while Latina/o students represented 9.6% of all the students enrolled in institutions of higher education in 2000–01, Latina/os earned only 5.9% of the bachelor's degrees (Harvey, 2003, p. 57); 4.3% of the master's degrees (Harvey, 2003, p. 64), and 4.8% of the first-professional degrees awarded that year (Harvey, 2003, p. 65). Latina/o individuals earned 1,119 of the 40,744 doctoral degrees awarded in 2000–01, or 2.7% of all doctoral degrees (Harvey, 2003, p. 66).

Characteristics of Community College Students

Of the 11.3 million students enrolled in America's community colleges, a majority of the students (57%) were females; 43% were males. The average student age was 29 (AACC, 2004). Almost two-thirds (62%) of the students were enrolled part time, and 37% were full-time students (AACC, 2002).

A higher percentage of students from the lowest and the middle quartiles of SAT scores were enrolled in community colleges in 1995–96 (Coley, 2000). Of the students who scored in the lowest quartile on the SAT, 43% were enrolled in community colleges, compared to 17% in public four-year colleges and 12% in private four-year colleges. That same year, 47% of students in the middle quartiles were enrolled in community colleges. Only 10% of students in the highest quartile were enrolled in community colleges (Coley, 2000, p. 4).

Perhaps the most current description of community college students was written by Thomas R. Bailey:

> Our findings show that, when compared to students at four-year institutions, community college students are more likely to come from households with lower incomes, to be from a minority population, to be first

generation students, to be older than the average college students, to have children, to delay enrollment after high school, and to have lower achievement in high school.

Thus, when compared to their counterpart student population, community college students—in general . . . are more likely to enter postsecondary education with weaker academic and economic backgrounds, and to have other major life responsibilities like jobs and families. They often face a complex situation of juggling academic, family, and work commitments that make it difficult for them to succeed in school. (2004, p. 1)

Coley (2000) reported that community college students represent a much higher percentage experiencing "risk factors" than do students in private or public four-year colleges. Of those community college students beginning their education in 1995–96, almost half (48%) delayed entry into college after graduating from high school, and 46% enrolled part time. More than a third (35%) worked full time, and the same percentage was financially independent. As well, one in five (21%) had dependents; one in ten (11%) were single parents, and a similar number had no high school diploma (Coley, 2000, p. 15).

Research has shown that community college students come from the lower socioeconomic levels of society and that finances are an important issue (Cohen & Brawer, 2003). In 2000, community college students reported that the top five problems associated with taking classes included personal financial problems (63%), cost of books/materials (62%), job-related responsibilities (59%), cost of computer (50%), and cost of child care (50%) (Phillippe & Valiga, 2000). In effect, four of the top five problems faced by students are directly related to financial issues. Only job responsibilities are not related to financial issues; however, there may be an indirect relationship.

Latina/o students enrolled in community colleges have the same characteristics of community college students in general. That is, they have weak academic preparation, come from lower socioeconomic backgrounds, work either full- or part-time, have family responsibilities, enroll late, have financial constraints, and so forth (Rendón & Garza, 1996). Other authors add at least two more characteristics: many Latina/os are the first in their family to enroll in an institution of higher education and many have parents with low academic preparation (Fry, 2002; Villareal, 2004).

Latina/os, Community Colleges, Transfer, and Earned Degrees

Over the years, some authors have been critical of community colleges and the role they have played in helping students, particularly minority students, transfer successfully to four-year colleges and universities (Zwerling, 1986; Karabel, 1972; Brint & Karabel, 1989; Dougherty, 2001). These critics have argued that community colleges have focused on vocational education and have not helped minority students to transfer. Others have argued "that community colleges are no more able to overturn the inequities of the nation than the lower schools have been, that all schools are relatively low-influence environments when compared with other social institutions" (Cohen & Brawer, 2003, p. 388).

Other authors have arrived at qualified opinions about the success of community colleges in assisting minority students to transfer to four-year colleges and universities (Olivas, 1979; Jalomo, 2003). In one of the first in-depth studies of minorities in two-year colleges, Olivas (1979) concluded that

> The dilemma is clear: do two-year institutions provide opportunities for minorities or do they perpetuate inequities? The data examined in this book suggest that the answer to both questions is a qualified "yes." To the extent that easily-available institutions do increase access, opportunities are provided to all who would enroll. However to the extent that full time access for minorities occurs predominantly in the public two year section, it cannot be said that this system represents an equitable distribution. (p. 170)

More recent studies continue to show that a very large proportion of Latina/os enroll in institutions of higher education, but too few earn degrees and pursue graduate studies (Fry, 2002). More than 20 years after Olivas noted the dilemma of access, Fry reported in 2002 that "Latinos are far more likely to be enrolled in two-year colleges than any other group. About 40% of Latino 18- to 24-year-old college students attend two-year institutions compared to about 25 percent of white and black students in that age group" (p. vi). Fry further reported that, "Latinos very clearly lag behind in the pursuit of graduate and professional degrees. Among 25- to 34-year-old high school graduates, nearly 3.8 percent of whites are enrolled in graduate school. Only 1.9 percent of similarly aged Latino high school graduates are pursuing post-baccalaureate studies" (2002, p. vi). Thus, the "equitable distribution" that Olivas wrote about in 1979 is not yet a reality in American higher education almost 25 years later.

So what do more recent data indicate about Latina/os' success in transferring from community colleges to four-year colleges and universities and earning degrees? This issue can be approached by asking different questions, the first of which focuses on the educational pipeline. Another approach is to ask a different question: Of the Latina/os who earn degrees at four-year colleges and universities, how many *began their studies* in community colleges? One can ask yet a third question: Of the Latina/os who earned degrees at four-year colleges and universities, how many *attended* community colleges?

The question related to the issue of the educational pipeline might be answered by the data in Table 3.4. Of 100 White students who began in the ninth grade four years earlier, 74.6% graduated from high school in 2001, or more than 7 of 10. That same year, a little more than half (52.6%) of Latina/os who were ninth graders four years earlier graduated (Jones, 2004).

In the fall 2001 semester, 64.2% of White high school graduates enrolled directly in college, compared to 51.7% of Latina/o students. More than 6 of 10 White students enrolled directly in college, while only one of two Latina/os enrolled. In the fall 2002 semester, one-third of White, full-time, first-time freshmen enrolled in two-year colleges, while almost half (49.2%) of full-time, first-time Latina/o freshmen enrolled in two-year colleges.

In 2002, the three-year graduation rate of White students in two-year colleges was 30.4%, compared to 26.6% for Latina/os. That same year, the six-year graduation rate at four-year colleges for Latina/os was 44.7%, compared to 57.1% for White students.

The second question, that is, the number of Latina/os who earned baccalaureate degrees and began their postsecondary education in community colleges might be answered by a recent study (see Table 3.5). The 2000–01 Baccalaureate and Beyond Survey (NCES, 2002) shows that 19.5% of all 1999–2000 bachelor's degree recipients started their postsecondary education at community colleges, and almost one in four (23.6%) of Latina/os who earned baccalaureate degrees that year began their education in community colleges (Bradburn et al., 2002; Fry, 2004). One of five non-Hispanic White (19.7%) baccalaureate graduates in 1999–2000 attended a community college.

The third approach to determining the role of community colleges as a pathway for graduate education of Latina/os, as noted above, is to ask this question: Of the Latina/os who earned degrees at four-year colleges and universities, how many attended community colleges? Recent reports indicate that a large percentage of baccalaureate, master's, and doctoral degree graduates attended a community college (see Table 3.6). Almost 6 of 10 Latina/os (58.6%) who earned baccalaureate degrees in 1999–2000 attended one or more community colleges (NCES, 2004; Fry, 2004).

More than half (50.8) of non-Hispanic White baccalaureate graduates in 1999–2000 attended one or more community colleges, while 52.3% of *all*

TABLE 3.4
Educational Attainment of Full-time, First-time Freshmen, by Racial/Ethnic Group (Percentage)

Race/Ethnicity	2001 High school graduates as a percent of 9th graders 4 years earlier (public high schools) (NCES common core data)*	Percent going directly to college, fall 2001 (NCES Digest of Education Statistics, Table 183)	Percent of full-time, first-time freshmen enrolled in 2-year colleges (IPEDS 2002 Fall Enrollment Survey)	Percent of full-time, first-time freshmen enrolled in 4-year colleges (IPEDS 2002 Fall Enrollment Survey)	Three-year graduation rates at 2-year colleges (IPEDS 2002 Graduation Rate Survey, Early Release Data)	Six-year graduation rates at 4-year colleges (IPEDS 2002 Graduation Rate Survey, Early Release Data)
Total	67.3	61.7	35.4	64.6	29.1	54.3
White	74.6	64.2	33.0	67.0	30.7	57.1
African American	49.4	54.6	42.9	57.1	23.0	38.1
Hispanic	52.6	51.7	49.2	50.8	26.6	44.7

*High school graduation percentages by race/ethnicity are based on data from 41 states.

Note: Race/ethnicity data for 1997 ninth graders and 2000–01 high school graduates are not available for AZ, ID, KS, NC, NH, NJ, SC, TN, VT.

Source: Jones, 2004.

TABLE 3.5
1999–2000 Baccalaureate Graduates Who Began at a Community College, by Racial/Ethnic Group

Race/ethnicity (historical) 1999–2000	Percent
White, non-Hispanic	19.7
Black, non-Hispanic	16.3
Hispanic or Latina/o	23.6
Asian	20.9
American Indian/Alaska Native	35.2
Native Hawaiian/other Pacific Islander	32.4
Other	24.1
Total	19.5

Sources: NCES, 2004; Fry, 2004.

graduates who earned the baccalaureate that year attended community college.

At Arizona State University, of the 8,324 baccalaureate recipients in fall 2002, spring 2003, and summer 2003, a total of 5,551 (66.66%) had attended one or more of the Maricopa Community Colleges. That same year, Latina/os earned 926 degrees, or 11.12% of the total, and 672 of all Latina/os—72.57%—had attended one or more of the Maricopa Community Colleges (Gebel, 2004). Seven of 10 Latina/os who earned baccalaureate degrees in 2002–2003 had attended a community college.

Another recent report on the role of community colleges in the educa-

TABLE 3.6
1999–2000 Baccalaureate Graduates Who Attended a Community College, by Racial/Ethnic Group

Race-ethnicity (historical) 1999–2000	Percent
White, non-Hispanic	51.2
Black, non-Hispanic	50.8
Hispanic or Latina/o	58.6
Asian	55.6
American Indian/Alaska Native	69.7
Native Hawaiian/other Pacific Islander	76.5
Other	52.6
Total	52.3

Sources: NCES, 2004; Fry, 2004.

tion of recent science and engineering (S&E) graduates indicates that in 1999–2000, 44% of S&E baccalaureate graduates, about one-third of graduates with master's degree, and more than 8% of doctorate recipients attended community colleges (Tsapogas, 2004).

The report further shows that "Hispanic S&E graduates are more likely to have attended a community college than any other racial/ethnic group" (Tsapogas, 2004, p. 2). More than half (51%) of all "Hispanic S&E graduates reported attending community college before receiving their bachelor's or master's degree" (Tsapogas, 2004, p. 2).

In 1999–2000, of the 86,896 S&E doctorate recipients who are U.S. citizens or permanent residents, 3,143 or 3.62% were Hispanic. Of these, 346, or 11%, attended community colleges. Of the Hispanic subgroups, 18% (156 of 864) of Mexican Americans attended community colleges (Tsapogas, 2004, p. 2). Almost one of five of all Mexican American S&E doctoral graduates attended community colleges.

To summarize, the answers to the questions posed at the beginning of the chapter are provided below.

1. How do Latina/os compare with White students along the educational pipeline?

   As shown above, a little more than half (52.6%) of Latina/os who began in the ninth grade graduate from high school four years later, compared to 74.6% of White students. After graduation from high school, only one of two Latina/os enrolled directly in college, compared to 6 of 10 White students. Almost half (49.2%) of Latina/o full-time, first-time freshmen enrolled in community colleges, compared to one-third of White students. The three-year graduation rate at two-year colleges for Latina/os is 26.6%, compared to 30.4% for Whites. The six-year graduation rate for Latina/os at four-year colleges is 44.7%, while White students had a 57.1% six-year graduation rate.

2. Of the Latina/os who earn degrees at four-year colleges and universities, how many began their studies in community colleges?

   Almost one of four (23.6%) Latina/os who earned baccalaureate degrees in 1999–2000 began their postsecondary education in a community college, compared to 19.7% of Whites who earned baccalaureate degrees that year.

3. Of the Latina/os who earned degrees at four-year colleges and universities, how many attended community colleges?

   Almost 6 of 10 (58.6%) of Latina/o 1999–2000 baccalaureate recipients attended a community college. At Arizona State University, 7 of 10 (72.57%) Latina/os who earned baccalaureate degrees in 2002–2003 attended one or more of the Maricopa Community Colleges. More than half (51%) of Latina/os who earned either a bachelor's or master's degree in science and engineering in 1999–2000 attended a community college. Finally, of the all Latina/o doctorate recipients in 1999–2000, 11% attended a community college. Almost one in five (18%) of all Mexican American doctorate recipients attended a community college.

Summary, Findings, and Conclusions

Latina/os are now the largest minority group in the United States. By 2017, one-fifth (22.1%) of all high school graduates are projected to be Latina/o. In some states (Arizona and New Mexico) Latina/o high school graduates will exceed all other groups in this decade. In addition, Latina/o enrollment is projected to increase by 1.1 million to 2.5 million by 2015. Of 100 Latina/os who begin the ninth grade, only 10 will earn a degree within 150% time. More than half of all Latina/o undergraduates (55%–58%) enrolled in institutions of higher education are enrolled in community colleges. Almost one in four (23.6%) of all Latina/o baccalaureate recipients began their postsecondary education in a community college. One in two Latina/os who earned either baccalaureate or master's degrees in sciences and engineering attended a community college, and one of 10 Latina/os who earned the doctorate in sciences or engineering attended a community college.

The community college has been Latina/os' primary point of entry into higher education. In the view of the authors, if it were not for the community college, it is highly probable that fewer Latina/os would earn baccalaureate, master's, or doctorate degrees. Given the projected increase in the number of Latina/os in higher education, the community college will continue to play a very important part in their education.

Recommendations for Research and Practice

Because community colleges have emerged as essential engines of educational, economic, and social development, they are currently experiencing a rising prominence on the national scene (Milliron & de los Santos, 2004). This relatively new prominence and recognition are indications that policy makers, as well as community and business leaders, are beginning to embrace community colleges as linchpin institutions. Consequently, community colleges are being called on more frequently to strengthen partnerships among local public schools, neighboring four-year colleges and universities, and local businesses to help ease student transitions from one sector to another. Furthermore, K–12 and senior institutions are increasingly recognizing the value of partnering with their local community colleges.

As community colleges continue to gear up to meet the economic, educational, and social challenges our society faces during these dynamic times, the following questions about research and practice are intended to help frame further opportunities for exploration:

1. What model partnerships between community colleges and four-year colleges and universities have resulted in increased Hispanic student transition? Retention? Increased degree attainment, particularly at the graduate level?
2. What model partnerships between K–12 systems and community colleges have resulted in increased Hispanic student transition? Retention? Increased degree attainment, particularly at the graduate level?
3. What state policies encourage and empower partnerships among community colleges, K–12 systems, and four-year colleges and universities?
4. What model partnerships exist between local businesses and community colleges that have resulted in increased Hispanic student transition to graduate school? Workplace?
5. To what extend are community colleges perceived as nexus educational institutions in the pre-K–16 continuum?

References

American Association of Community Colleges (AACC) (2002). *Facts: Community college facts at a glance.* Washington, DC: AACC.

American Association of Community Colleges (AACC) (2004). *Facts Sheet 2004: Community college fast fact.* Washington, DC: AACC. Retrieved May 26, 2004, from www.aacc.nche.edu/pdf/aboutcc_Racial/pdf.

Bailey, T. R. (2004). Community college students: Characteristics, outcomes, and recommendations for success. *CCRC Currents.* New York: Community College Research Center, Teachers College, Columbia University.

Bradburn, E. M., Berger, R., Xiaojie, L., & Rooney, K. (2002). *A descriptive summary of 1999–2000 bachelor's degrees recipients 1 year later: With an analysis of time to degree.* Retrieved May 27, 2004, from http//nces.ed.gov/programs/quarterly/vol_5/5_3/4_3.asp.

Brint, S., & Karabel, J. (1989). *The diverted dream: Community colleges and the promise of educational opportunity in America, 1900–1985.* New York: Oxford University Press.

Carnavale, A. P., & Desrochers, D. M. (2003). *Standards for what? The economic roots of K–16 reform.* Princeton, N.J.: Educational Testing Service.

Carnavale, A. P., & Fry, R. A. (1999). *Crossing the great divide: Can we achieve equity when generation Y goes to college?* Princeton NJ: Educational Testing Service.

Carnegie Foundation for the Advancement of Teaching (2001). *The Carnegie Classification of institutions of higher education.* Menlo Park, CA: Author.

Cohen, A. M., & Brawer, F. B. (2003). *The American community college* (4th ed.). San Francisco: Jossey-Bass.

Coley, R. J. (2000). *The American community college turns 100: A look at its students, programs, and prospects.* Princeton, N.J.: Educational Testing Service.

Dougherty, K. J. (2001). *The contradictory college: The conflicting origins, impacts and futures of the community college.* Albany: State University of New York Press.

Fry, R. (2002). *Latina/os in higher education: Many enroll, too few graduate.* Washington, DC: Pew Hispanic Center.

Fry, R. (May 4, 2004). Personal correspondence.

Gebel, M. (May 19, 2004). Personal correspondence.

Harvey, W. B. (2003). *Minorities in higher education, 2001–2002: Twentieth anniversary annual status report.* Washington, DC: American Council on Education.

Jalomo, R., Jr. (2003). Being there for us: Latina/o students and their first-year experience in urban community colleges. In D. J. Leon (Ed.), *Latina/os in higher education* (pp. 85–105). San Francisco: JAI.

Jones, E. (April 16, 2004). Personal correspondence.

Karabel, J. (1972). Community college and social stratification. *Harvard Educational Review, 41,* 521–562.

Milliron, M. D., & de los Santos, G. E. (2004). Making the most of community colleges on the road ahead. *Community College Journal of Research and Practice,* February 28, 105–122.

National Center for Educational Statistics (NCES), U.S. Department of Education (2002). *A descriptive summary of 1999–2000 bachelor's degrees recipients 1 year later: With an analysis of time to degree.* Retrieved May 27, 2004, from http//nces.ed .gov/programs/quarterly/vol_5/5_3/4_3.asp.

Olivas, M. A. (1979). *The dilemma of access: Minorities in two year colleges.* Washington, DC: Howard University Press.

Phillippe, K. A. & Valiga, M. J. (April 2000). *Faces of the future: A portrait of America's community college students.* Washington, DC: American Association of Community Colleges.

Rendón, L. I., & Garza, H. (1996). Closing the gap between two- and four-year institutions. In L. I. Rendón, R. O. Hope, & Associates. *Educating a new majority: Transferring America's educational system for diversity* (pp. 289–308). San Francisco: Jossey-Bass.

Tsapogas, J. (April 2004). The role of community colleges in the education of recent science and engineering graduates. *InfoBrief: Science Resources Statistics. NSD 04-315.* Arlington, VA: National Science Foundation. Also available at http://www.nsf.gov/sbe/srs/infbrief/nsf04315/start.html. Retrieved May 13, 2004.

U.S. Bureau of the Census (2000). *Profile of general demographic characteristics for the United States, 1990 and 2000.* Retrieved April 20, 2004, from http://www.census.gov/;prod.www.abs/decennial.html.

Villareal, H. (April 2004). *Personal, institutional, and environmental influences on Hispanic community college transfer students who completed the baccalaureate degree.* Unpublished dissertation. Arizona State University.

Western Interstate Commission for Higher Education (WICHE), American College Testing [ACT], & College Board (2003). *Knocking at the college door: Projections of high school graduates by state and race/ethnicity, 1998 to 2018.* Denver, CO: WICHE.

Zeiss, T., & Associates (1997). *Developing the world's best workforce: An agenda for America's community colleges.* Washington, DC: Community College Press.

Zwerling, L. S. (Ed.) (1986). *The community college and its critics.* New Directions for Community Colleges, 54. San Francisco: Jossey Bass.

Amaury Nora

Dr. Amaury Nora is professor and associate dean for research in the College of Education at the University of Houston, Texas. His research focuses on student academic achievement, precollege and collegiate psychosocial factors affecting adjustment to college and student persistence, the role of college in diverse student populations across different types of institutions, academic and social experiences influencing cognitive as well as noncognitive student outcomes, and theory building and testing. His inquiries have contributed to the development of theoretical perspectives related to traditional lines of research on college persistence and have helped to focus on research related to minorities in both two- and four-year institutions. Dr. Nora has served as consultant to the American Council of Education, the Ford Foundation, Hispanic Association of Colleges and Universities, and U.S. Department of Education and as a reviewer for the National Research Council.

Dr. Nora has served on the editorial boards of *Research in Higher Education*, *The Review of Higher Education*, *The Journal of Higher Education*, *Journal of Hispanic Higher Education*, and *The Journal of College Student Retention: Research and Theory*. He assumed the position of editor for *The Review of Higher Education* in January 2004.

Libby Barlow

Dr. Libby Barlow is executive director of institutional research and institutional effectiveness at the University of Houston, Texas. Her primary research interest focuses on the persistence of nontraditional students, and she is currently overseeing a longitudinal study of the factors influencing degree completion among undergraduates at a public, urban, diverse, nonresidential, four-year campus. As chief officer of institutional research, Dr. Barlow has integrated multiple databases that capture a variety of theoretical frameworks on the retention of college students. Her efforts provide a means of testing different perspectives holistically within a single model as well as informing the institutional practices and policies affecting undergraduates. Currently Dr. Barlow serves as an associate editor of *The Review of Higher Education*, the journal of the Association for the Study of Higher Education.

Gloria Crisp

Gloria Crisp is a doctoral student in educational leadership with a focus on higher education in the department of educational leadership and cultural studies, College of Education at the University of Houston, Texas. Her research interests include college student access and persistence, mentoring, and institutional effectiveness. Ms. Crisp is currently managing editor of *The Review of Higher Education* and adjunct psychology professor at San Jacinto College.

4

AN ASSESSMENT OF HISPANIC STUDENTS IN FOUR-YEAR INSTITUTIONS OF HIGHER EDUCATION

Amaury Nora
Libby Barlow
Gloria Crisp

Hispanic student persistence, a longitudinal and multifaceted process, remains an area of investigation that has received attention in the literature only recently. While some Latina/o students may return to college for a second or even third year, dropping out is still a major consideration for this group of students. Much has been written on student persistence during the past three decades that focuses on the impact of such variables as the academic and social integration of students on campus (e.g., Bean, 1980; Pascarella & Terenzini, 1979; Terenzini & Pascarella, 1980), different sources and forms of support systems (e.g., Nora, 2004; Nora & Cabrera, 1996), student finances (e.g., Cabrera, Nora, & Castaneda, 1992; Olivas, 1986; St. John, Cabrera, Nora, & Asker, 2001), and even discriminatory behaviors and gestures (e.g., Cabrera & Nora, 1994; Nora & Cabrera, 1996) on student engagement, academic performance, first-to-second-year persistence, and, ultimately, degree attainment. In spite of these efforts, little is known in the persistence literature on Hispanic student retention at the end of that critical first year in college and in subsequent years.

The intent of the current chapter is to provide an overview of findings on Latina/o student persistence in four-year institutions, focusing mainly on the first year in college. Because even less has been studied following

Latina/o students' first year in college, this chapter also attempts to provide a preliminary profile of Hispanic student characteristics, academic perform- ance, and attrition rates over a six-year period using institutional records from a highly diverse Hispanic-serving research institution. For purposes of comparing those factors that play a role in Hispanic student withdrawal deci- sions with those found in the literature on all student populations, the con- ceptual framework for this chapter is directed by current theoretical perspectives used in studying the persistence of first-time-in-college (FTIC) students.

Much of what has been found related to student persistence (e.g., Brax- ton & Lien, 2000; Nora, 2004; Nora & Cabrera, 1996; Nora et al., 1996) has relied on different yet often overlapping frameworks. The early work in this area was based mainly on Tinto's (1975) model of student integration. Those studies that followed modified Tinto's original hypotheses and led to the infusion of such models as Bean's (1985) student model, Pascarella and Ter- enzini's (1980) interpretation of Tinto's (1975) theoretical framework, and even Astin's (1984) student involvement perspective.

During the last three decades, quantitative and qualitative studies have contributed to the literature base on student persistence. Investigations such as those conducted by Braxton and Brier (1989), Rendón (1994), Hurtado and Carter (1997), Pascarella and Terenzini (1990), and others have explored and identified an assortment of factors that bear on the decisions of minority and nonminority students to remain enrolled in college or to withdraw tem- porarily or permanently from higher education. Among those efforts is re- search by Nora and associates (e.g., Nora & Cabrera, 1996; Cabrera & Nora, 1994; Cabrera, Nora, & Castaneda, 1992; Nora & Garcia, n.d.; Nora & Lang, n.d.; Nora, 2002, 2004). The culmination of those efforts has led to the conceptualization of the student engagement model (Nora, 2004). Figure 4.1 displays the theoretical framework used in examining an array of factors affecting withdrawal/persistence decisions of undergraduates once they are enrolled in college.

Hispanic (and Other Minority) Students at Four-Year Institutions: An Overview

Most studies that touch on the issue of student persistence among minority students do not specifically study Hispanic students in isolation. For exam- ple, Bowen and Bok (2000) mention as an aside the exclusion of Hispanics

FIGURE 4.1
Student/Institution Engagement Model Theoretical Framework

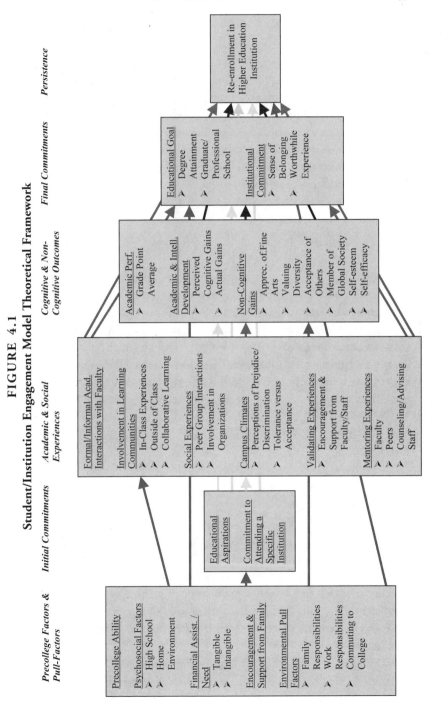

from their book simply because an appropriate sample size was not available to make comparisons with Whites and African Americans. Consequently, data on Latina/o students in higher education has been derived from studies that collect and analyze information on both minority and nonminority student populations. Collectively, those studies on which data on Latina/os are available and meaningful have identified eight major constructs of interest: minority students' educational aspirations, finances and financial aid, academic and social campus experiences, institutional commitment, academic ability, precollege psychosocial factors, undergraduate academic performance, and student persistence.

Educational Aspirations

Nora and associates (e.g., Cabrera & Nora, 1994; Cabrera, Nora, & Castaneda, 1992; Nora 2002, 2004; Nora & Cabrera, 1996; Nora & Lang, 2001) have identified five factors that influence the educational aspirations of Hispanic college students. Findings from several studies revealed that three such environmental factors pull students away from engaging fully in their on-campus experiences: family responsibilities, working off-campus, and long-distance commutes. All three were found to negatively influence the commitments to attaining an undergraduate degree that Hispanics brought with them on entering college. The reality of having to leave campus immediately after class to work or attend to a family member, plus the time it took to travel between their campuses and home (or work), served to diminish their hopes of earning a college degree and, ultimately, led to the decision to drop out of college.

In three separate studies (Cabrera & Nora, 1994; Cabrera, Nora, & Castaneda, 1993; Nora & Cabrera, 1996), another environmental characteristic was found to negatively affect both the educational aspirations and withdrawal behavior of Hispanics. Perceptions of prejudice and discrimination on campus, in as well as outside the classroom, were extremely harmful to the goal of attaining an undergraduate degree. Of specific importance was the finding that it was not only the direct exposure to discriminatory words and gestures that led to the negative impact on the hopes and expectations of Hispanic students but also the perception that an environment of intolerance and discrimination existed on their campus and, more specifically, in the classroom.

Yet another factor that was found to impel Hispanic students to give up on their higher education goals and withdraw from college was their academic performance (Hu & St. John, 2001; Nora & Cabrera, 1996; Nora et

al., 1996). While this finding is not surprising, what was of significant importance was the fact that the studies from which this finding was extracted
consisted only of students who voluntarily withdrew from college and not
those who were asked to leave for academic reasons. What the studies revealed was that, for Hispanics, earning less than "good" grades made these
students question their ability to attain a college degree. The result was a
sense of giving up and a decision to drop out.

Still another unexpected result was the finding that parental support and
encouragement had the greatest impact on Latina/o educational goal commitments (Nora & Cabrera, 1996). The surprise was not so much that access
to a support system would result in increased desire to earn a college degree,
but that a strong family support system that provided words of encouragement and different sources and forms of support (Nora, 2002) not only
would positively affect this group of students' educational goals, it also
would serve to negate the harmful effects of those discriminatory and preju-
dicial words and gestures experienced by Latina/os, thereby convincing these
students to remain in college.

Finally, it comes as no surprise that positive academic experiences during
the first year of college were found to inspire Latina/o students' degree commitment and their determination to stay in college. Positive and validating
classroom experiences, as well as positive experiences in labs, study groups,
and discussions, encouraged Latina/os to stick to their goals and return to
college the following academic year (Rendón, 1994).

Financial Aid

A second area where some data can be found on Hispanic students is student
finances and financial assistance. Hu and St. John (2001) examined the effects of financial aid on the within-year persistence of Hispanic, African
American, and White students. Data from a state higher education system
were analyzed for three cohorts of full-time undergraduate resident students
enrolled in a four-year university at three different points (1990–91, 1993–94,
and 1996–97). Their findings revealed an overall disparity in the persistence
among ethnic groups—White students persisted at higher rates than did
Hispanic and African American students.

Hu and St. John (2001) confirmed that receiving financial assistance
serves an important role in equalizing the playing field and opportunities for
Hispanic and African American students. In comparing the odds of persisting between those who had received financial aid compared to those students
of each ethnic/racial group who did not receive aid, Hispanic and African

American students who received financial aid were more likely to persist than were their counterparts who did not receive financial aid. The link between financial aid and student persistence has long been established (Cabrera, Nora, & Castaneda, 1993; Stampen & Cabrera, 1986; St. John, Cabrera, Nora, & Asker, 2001). What have been missing are much more insightful investigations on Latina/os' finances and financial aid patterns as they relate to their adjustment to college, their performance in the classroom, and their decisions to remain committed to their educational goals.

Social Interactions

Very early in the investigation of those factors that contributed to student dropout behavior, Pascarella and Terenzini (1980) established the importance of the student's social integration on campus. While many earlier studies substantiated the influence of social integration on persistence (e.g., Bean, 1980; Braxton & Brier, 1989; Terenzini & Pascarella, 1980), its conceptualization and importance were questioned as appropriate for minority students (Rendón, Jalomo, & Nora, 2001; Tierney, 1992). Nonetheless, several studies on minority and nonminority students in two- and four-year institutions indicate some overall conclusions regarding the social interactions of Hispanics and their relationship to student persistence. In Nora and Cabrera's (1996) study on the role of perceptions of prejudice and discrimination within a theoretically based model of college persistence, their results indicated that the encouragement and support provided by parents had a significant and positive effect on Hispanic students' social experiences. However, the expectation that those social interactions with peers and faculty were positively influencing student persistence decisions was not substantiated. In contrast to what had been established previously among White student populations, it was found that such experiences had only a minimal, indirect effect on the persistence of minority students. In a second study conducted by Nora et al., (1996), researchers found that student interactions were not significantly related to the persistence of minority students.

Institutional Commitment/Fit

Padilla, Trevino, Gonzalez, and Trevino (1997) have examined the different forms of informal knowledge that minority students required to be able to handle their academic and social environments while enrolled in college and to be able to succeed, operationally defined as graduating from college. Their findings indicated that sophomore, junior, and senior minority students who had successfully involved themselves in their college campuses took specific actions to overcome four major categories of barriers: discontinuity, lack of nurturing, lack of presence, and resources. To overcome any discontinuity barriers, successful minority students took actions such as joining an organization, making their own decisions, and researching the profitability of their own majors. They dealt with a lack of nurturing by addressing issues of self-worth, dealing with their specific needs, or pursuing nurturing from others such as joining support groups or accessing mentoring resources on campus.

The lack of presence on a university campus involved the institutional culture and practices that devalued and ignored ethnic minority students. For those students who met such challenges successfully, overcoming this barrier meant having to seek out the ethnic presence on campus, participating fully in ethnic student organizations, and making themselves known on campus one way or another. Finally, successful minority students had to overcome barriers brought on by a lack of resources by preparing and applying early for financial aid, talking to people familiar with the financial aid process, and developing time management skills.

Precollege Factors

Few studies have focused on the educational experiences of Hispanics prior to their enrollment in college, as those specific experiences influence subsequent academic performance in college and withdrawal decisions. Nora and Cabrera (1996) relied on structural modeling to examine student persistence among African American and White students. Their results addressed a long-held belief that traditional precollege academic ability, as measured by Scholastic Aptitude Test (SAT) verbal and quantitative scores, was highly predictive of first-semester grade point average (GPA). However, and most important, the findings established empirical evidence that high school academic achievement/performance in the form of GPA and standardized test scores was not significantly related to retention of undergraduate student groups. These initial results indicated that the persistence of both minority and nonminority groups could be attributed better to noncognitive variables such as a realistic self-appraisal, positive self-concept, preferring long-range goals, and having leadership experience.

In a later study, Nora and Lang (2001) not only confirmed earlier findings by Nora and Cabrera (1996) but further identified a set of precollege psychosocial factors experienced in high school that were much more predictive of withdrawal decisions. Thirteen precollege domains were part of a logistic regression analysis examining student persistence: (1) academic anticipation of going to college, (2) anticipation of being enrolled in a more diverse student population, (3) resiliency in the face of adversity in high school, (4) perceived academic self-efficacy as established through high school academic experiences, (5) perceived social self-efficacy as established through high school social experiences, (6) a sense of pride in academic endeavors while in high school, (7) degree of shyness as reported by the student, (8) nature and degree of involvement in leadership activities in high school, (9) perception of the existence of a friendship support group while in high school, (10) degree of encouragement and support received by that support group while in high school, (11) degree of encouragement and support provided by parents, (12) parental expectations of students before enrolling in college, and (13) patterns of internal or self-directed explanations when the student experienced a setback or unstable causes while in high school, causes that were likely to change quickly and not have long-term consequences. Nora and Lang's (2000) findings, while based on a student population limited by a small number of minority students, substantiated the argument that precollege factors other than a student's academic performance are influential in affecting subsequent withdrawal decisions at the end of the student's first year in college.

Recent findings from a longitudinal study found that Hispanic students consistently had higher attrition rates than White students, regardless of academic preparation (Fry, 2004). DesJardins, Ahlbrug, and McCall (2002) found that not only were Latina/o students less likely to graduate, but those who were retained took longer to graduate than did White students. One of their major conclusions was that the quality of the school from which Hispanic students were enrolled made a difference in whether they persisted. Another major finding was that the socioeconomic status with which minority students entered college negatively affected their retention. However, earlier studies by Nora and associates (Cabrera, Nora, & Castaneda, 1992; Cabrera, Nora, & Castaneda, 1993; Nora, 1987) had indicated that socioeconomic status as measured by the educational attainment of the student's parents or through the total family income earned were associated only minimally with a student's integration into his or her social environment and were not related to a student's decision to re-enroll in college.

Studies on Hispanic Student Persistence

A review of current literature reveals that very little has been studied with regard to Hispanic students at four-year institutions. Three studies, described below, examined factors related to the different intermediate and long-term college outcomes of Hispanic students at four-year universities. In the first study, Hurtado, Carter, and Spuler (1996) attempted to better understand those features that affect Latina/os' adjustment and attachment to college. Latina/o students who were semifinalists for a national scholarship award were selected on the basis on being freshman students at a four-year university in fall 1991. Participants completed the National Survey of Hispanic Students (NSHS) and the Student Adaptation to College Questionnaire. The adjustment to college by Latina/o students was operationally defined as comprising four areas: social, academic, personal-emotional, and attachment to the institution.

Results indicated that the size of the college enrollment and type of college attended had a significant effect on Latina/o students' social adjustment and attachment to their campuses. Hispanic students who attended private four-year colleges scored significantly higher on measures of social adjustment and attachment to the institution they were attending. Those factors that were found to be related positively to the academic adjustment of Latina/o students were the size of the Latina/o population at the university and the students' perceptions of their interactions with faculty. A large concentration of Hispanic students enrolled and positive interactions between students and faculty were identified as two major factors contributing to the retention of Hispanic students.

The academic adjustments of Hispanic students during the second year, as well as the students' personal-emotional adjustment, were affected positively by the students' ability to manage resources such as time, money, and schedules. Perceiving the amount of college-related work as quite manageable was also found to be associated with the academic and personal-emotional adjustment of Latina/o students during the first two years in college. Those highly influential transitional experiences that affected the adjustment of Hispanics during their second year in college included knowing that there was a support system provided by the student's family and time spent time socializing with friends on campus. For those reasons, resident advisors, academic counselors, and upper-class students were believed to have a positive affect on the adjustment of Latina/o students to their respective institutions. However, for those students who indicated that they received help from other freshman like them, it was found that they were less well-adjusted academically in their second year. The authors concluded that Latina/o students may need guidance and support from more mature individuals, such as faculty and upper-class students, if they are to adjust well to college following their first two years of enrollment.

In an earlier study, Hurtado and Carter (1997) attempted to apply Tinto's theoretical model of student departure to a population of Latina/o students. A major focus of the study was to clarify the structure of a conceptual model that specified those factors that led to a sense of belonging on the part of the student. The authors examined the extent to which Latina/o students' background characteristics (i.e., gender and academic self-concept) and academic and social experiences in the first and second years of college contributed to a sense of belonging in the third year. Data on Latina/o students who entered college in 1990 and completed the NSHS and the Student Descriptive Questionnaire (SDQ) were analyzed.

The authors' findings confirmed that the first-year academic and social experiences of Latina/o students at four-year institutions led to a strong sense of belonging at their respective institutions in their third year of college. Hurtado and Carter (1997) also established that: (1) a strong relationship was found between Hispanic students' sense of belonging on campus and the frequency with which they engaged in discussions with other students outside of class; (2) membership in religious and social-community organizations was strongly associated with a student's sense of belonging; and (3) Latina/o students' perceptions of a hostile racial climate on their campuses had direct negative effects on those students' sense of belonging in the third year. In other words, in an environment that encourages tolerance and acceptance and engages students and faculty in academic and social discourse, Latina/o students' sense that they belong in college and are accepted at that institution is established and nourished.

A recent study of Latina/o student retention conducted by Longerbeam, Sedlacek, and Alatorre (2004) reported on the results of an online questionnaire, the University New Student Census (UNSC), developed by the study institution to examine Latina/o and non-Latina/o students' reasons for dropping out of college. Based on a series of multivariate analyses, significant differences were found between the two groups of students studied. The analysis revealed differences between Latina/o and non-Latina/o students in their perceptions that most likely led to attrition. Among those factors identified among Latina/o students were financial reasons, a perceived lack of academic capital needed to be successful in college, or a desire to enter military service. As anticipated, Latina/os, more so than White students, were significantly more likely to work off-campus, a condition previously found to have a negative impact on student persistence (Nora et al., 1996). Financial reasons included the expectation of sending money home to help with family finances. Another factor identified in the retention study was diversity on the college campus as it related to student persistence. The results indicated that those Latina/o students who perceived the campus as being diverse were more likely to remain enrolled.

Undergraduate Hispanic Trends: FTIC Demographics, Second- to Third-year Student Performance and Subsequent Sixth-year Graduation Rates

National Databases: The Need for In-depth Longitudinal Data

Data on Hispanic students are minimal, at best, and are almost nonexistent past their first year in college. This situation is largely based on the shortcomings associated with large national databases. Although those data sets may incorporate longitudinal information, the depth of that information on individual students is limited. The next section focuses on attrition rates, academic performance, specific course grades, and performance on core curriculum, data that are only available at the institutional level. The profile that follows is based on first-time-in-college Latina/o students at a large, research, Hispanic-serving university. The institution is the most highly diverse among research and comprehensive four-year institutions with regard to racial and ethnic student representation. It is believed that such a diverse student population can be used to begin to examine retention, academic performance, and graduation patterns past the first academic year, particularly since more and more students seeking a higher education today reflect this diversity.

Demographic Profile

The population selected for examining the persistence rates of Hispanic students consisted of 659 first-time-in-college (FTIC) Latina/o students entering in the fall 1997 semester at a major public, commuter, doctoral-granting institution. Hispanic FTICs comprised 22.7% of all first-time entering students. Students were considered to be FTIC's based on a record of no prior attendance at any other university or community college. Demographically, 43.4% of the Hispanic students were male, and 56.6% were female (see Table 4.1). The large majority of students were classified as full time. Only 11.2% of those students were classified as part-time students, defined as students enrolled in fewer than 12 student credit hours for the semester. The profile that follows is specific to the 23% of students who are Hispanic.

As Hispanic students entered college for the first time and were asked to declare a major, 39.3% of those students—the great majority of whom are

TABLE 4.1
Demographic Profile of FTIC Hispanic Students, Fall 1997*

	Hispanic Cohort	*Retained to 2nd year*	*Retained to 3rd year*	*Graduated within 6 years*
	(*n* = 659)	(*n* = 470)	(*n* = 366)	(*n* = 223)
Gender				
Male	286	196	145	83
Female	373	274	221	140
Tuition Status				
In-state tuition	643	458	358	215
Nonresident tuition	5	3	3	3
Tuition exempt	11	9	5	5
High School Quartile				
Top 10%	125	100	84	54
10–24%	214	150	122	80
25–49%	134	91	67	32
50–74%	67	47	27	14
Bottom 25%	12	9	5	4
High School GPA				
Mean	3.17	3.22	3.28	3.36
Percentiles 25	2.78	2.82	2.93	3.03
50	3.22	3.28	3.33	3.40
75	3.59	3.62	3.67	3.74
Total *N*	628	451	350	212
SAT Scores				
Mean Total Score	1,001	1,008	1,013	1,027
St. Dev. Total	136	138	136	133
Total *N*	621	449	350	214

*Data collected from institutional records, University of Houston, Texas.

undeclared—were classified under university studies.[1] Among those declaring a major, their fields of choice included biology (11.2%), prebusiness administration (7.7%), psychology (5.0%), communications (3.8%), architecture (3.0%), and interdisciplinary studies (3.0%). A comparison with findings from the National Center for Education Statistics (Llagas, 2003) on

[1] Includes students that require advisement for preprofessional studies in premedical, predental, and prelaw and all undeclared students.

the highest percentage of bachelor's degrees earned by Hispanic students provides an indication of those areas where Hispanics have declared an interest, where they have been successful, and where they have not. For instance, while only 5% of FTIC Hispanic students declared psychology as a major, nationally, 8.5% of degrees earned by Hispanics are in that field. In contrast, while 11.2% might desire a degree in biology, nationally, not even 1% of undergraduate degrees in biology are awarded to Hispanics. Another discrepancy can be seen in business, which includes finance, marketing, and management. Only 7.7% of Latina/o students indicated interest in earning a business degree, and yet nationally, 17.8% of degrees awarded annually to Hispanics are in a business-related field. While some gains have been made in other areas, the majority of Hispanic students remain clustered in business and the social sciences.

Nearly a third (29.1%) of the entering Hispanic cohort was classified as developmental students, defined as students who enrolled in at least one developmental course[2] in their first year. Hispanic students enrolled in developmental courses performed slightly below the entire cohort academically. For instance, the cumulative grade point average (GPA) of developmental students at the end of their first year in college was 2.04, compared to 2.35 for nondevelopmental Hispanic students. It is not surprising that Hispanics classified as developmental students were less likely to graduate from college. The six-year graduation rate for Hispanic developmental students was 28.6%, compared to 36.1% for nondevelopmental Latina/o students. Although not supported by existing research, these findings suggest that developmental courses may be another significant barrier to Hispanic and other minority student success.

Profile of Academic Performance

Precollege Academic Performance

Prior academic ability has been found to be an influential factor on the academic achievement of minority students (Nora & Cabrera, 1996). In the current investigation, the mean high school GPA for the Hispanic cohort was 3.17 (see Table 4.1). As anticipated, Latina/o students who returned for a second year[3] had entered college in their first year with higher grade point averages than did those who dropped out, 3.22 and 3.04, respectively. As could also be projected, Latina/o students who graduated within a six-year period had entered college with a high GPA from their high schools ($\bar{x} = 3.36$).

---

[2] Includes developmental courses in mathematics, reading, and English.
[3] Students enrolled in the fall semester of 1998.

Similarly, Hispanics scoring in the top quartile of their high schools were more likely than were Hispanics scoring in the second, third, or fourth quartiles to graduate within six years. Of those Hispanics who remained enrolled in college until graduation, 39.5% had scored in the top quartile of their high school graduating class, compared to 23.5% of Latina/os who had scored in the second, third, or fourth quartiles.

Another indicator of precollege academic performance is standardized test scores as measured by the SAT. The mean score on the test for FTIC Hispanic students was 1001 (SD = 136). Of those Hispanic students who were retained to the second year, their scores were only slightly higher ($\bar{x}$ = 1008) than those of students who were not retained ($\bar{x}$ = 983). Similarly, the average SAT score for Hispanic students who graduated within six years ($\bar{x}$ = 1,027) was only slightly higher than the average score for Hispanics who did not graduate ($\bar{x}$ = 987). Furthermore, the average SAT score for Latina/o students who enrolled for at least one developmental course during their first academic year and returned for a second year was 908.

Much controversy has always surrounded the use of standardized test scores for admissions purposes. The reason provided for their use is that they are a good indicator of future success in college, but the findings from this investigation would indicate otherwise. Differences in SAT scores between Latina/os who were retained compared to those who dropped out at different points were small. One would expect that those students who withdrew would have done so because of the academic disadvantages they possessed as measured by the SAT. However, any major differences between Hispanic persisters and nonpersisters could hardly be attributed to their performance on standardized tests. Based on these findings, an implication can be made that the use of SAT scores as a predictor of future college success (degree completion) may not be valid.

Semester Hours Completed

Latina/o students entering college in fall 1997 successfully completed 91% of the classes they enrolled in at the beginning of their first academic semester in college. Hispanic students persisting from their second year to their third year completed a larger proportion of their classes during the fall 1998 semester (88%) than did those Hispanics who dropped out (74%). Likewise, Hispanics persisting from the third year to the fourth completed 87% of their classes during the fall 1999 semester, compared to those who dropped out, who completed 67% of those classes, a pattern that was maintained throughout the six-year period. This evidence suggests that the ratio of student credit hours completed[4] may be associated with student retention.

Academic Performance in College

The academic performance of students during their first semester in college has been observed to have an influence not only on subsequent academic performance but also on student persistence, specifically for Hispanic students (Nora & Cabrera, 1996). The cumulative GPA at the end of the first semester in college (fall 1997) for Latina/o students retained to the second year was 2.48, compared to 1.39 for Latina/os not retained. Of those Hispanics persisting to the third year, an examination of their academic performance during their first semester in college revealed a GPA of 2.62, compared to those Hispanics who did not return for a third year, whose average GPA was 2.00. As anticipated, Hispanic students who graduated within six years had a cumulative GPA of 2.83 at the end of their first semester in college, compared to an average GPA of 1.83 for nongraduates. The evidence reveals that how Hispanic students perform academically during their initial semester in college may influence their subsequent withdrawal decisions, a finding consistent with research on minority students (Nora & Cabrera, 1996; Cabrera & Nora, 1994).

The impact of how well Latina/os perform academically extends well past their first semester in college. The cumulative GPA for Latina/o students persisting to the second year was found to be 2.53. For those Latina/o students who were not retained, their academic performance was substantially different (GPA of 1.53). The cumulative GPA for Hispanics returning to the third year was 2.72, compared to a cumulative GPA of 1.86 for students not re-enrolling after the first two years following their initial enrollment in fall 1997. Cumulative GPA has been found to affect the likelihood that students will graduate within six years (DesJardins, Ahlbrug, & McCall, 2002). In the present investigation, the cumulative GPA for Hispanics who graduated within six years was substantially higher than for students who did not graduate, 3.02 compared to 1.86, respectively. Nora and Cabrera (1996) found that, in comparing the impact of academic performance (GPA) of minorities and nonminorities, how minorities perceive their academic performance (discounting academic withdrawal) plays a much greater role in their decision to remain in college than it does for Whites. While both minorities and nonminorities may have a pedestrian academic performance during their first

---

[4] Calculated by dividing the number of student credit hours attempted by the number of hours earned.

two years in college, minorities may question whether they belong in college and may ultimately decide to withdraw.

Profile of Attrition Rates

Within the group of Hispanics who enrolled in the study's four-year university right out of high school, nearly three-quarters (71.3%) persisted from the first year to the second. Of the original FTIC Hispanic cohort, 55.5% persisted to the third year. In other words, approximately 29% of the entering Hispanic cohort withdrew from college at the end of their first year, and an additional 16.3% of Hispanics were lost between the second and third year. Although the purpose of this chapter is not to compare Hispanics and other groups, one finding was quite startling. Contrary to recent findings (Fry, 2004), the attrition rates for White students at this four-year institution were higher than for Hispanic students. Only 66.4% of FTIC White students entering college in fall of 1997 were retained to the second year, and 49.6% were retained to the third year.

Educational Costs

Tuition and other college-related expenses have been found to affect both the academic performance of students and the retention decisions of minority students (Nora & Cabrera, 1996; Nora et al., 1996; Nora & Lang, 2001; St. John et al., 2001). It should be noted that the rise in university and college tuition costs around the country has placed a sizeable burden on students and their families, regardless of socioeconomic status. This line of reasoning may help to explain why tuition costs may negatively impact minority student achievement when socioeconomic status has a minimal effect.

In the current investigation, Hispanic students who paid in-state tuition[5] were much more likely to re-enroll the following year than were students paying out-of-state or nonresident tuition. Tuition costs at the four-year institution studied in this investigation rank among the lowest at both the state and national levels. As expected, 71.2% of students paying in-state tuition returned to college for the second year. A comparison with those Hispanic students paying out-of-state tuition was not very meaningful, as only a handful of such students were enrolled in the entering cohort. However, the evidence indicates that those Hispanic students classified as nonresidents and paying out-of-state tuition were less likely to return for a second year. More important, the retention rate for Hispanic students who were exempt

[5] Students who have been Texas residents for at least 12 months.

from tuition[6] was higher than for students paying tuition, a finding that is in line with previous research on persistence and financial assistance (e.g., Cabrera, Nora, & Castaneda, 1993; Nora & Cabrera, 1996; Nora, 2004).

Enrollment Status

Part-time Latina/o students or those enrolled for fewer than 12 credit hours were less likely than were Hispanics attending college full time to be retained for the second and third years; 40.7% of Latina/os not returning for a second year and 26.9% of Latina/os not re-enrolling for a third year were classified as part-time students. Among those students who re-enrolled for a second and third year, only 8.7% and 12.6%, respectively, attended college part time. Moreover, students from the original Hispanic cohort who persisted to the second and third years were likely to try to take more student credit hours in both years ($\bar{x} = 12.8$, fall 1998; $\bar{x} = 13.1$, fall 1999) than were students who dropped out of college ($\bar{x} = 12.0$).

Profile of Six-year Graduation Rates

Of the 659 Hispanic students who enrolled in college as first-time-in-college students, only 33.8% graduated within six years (fall 1997–spring 2003). Several findings worthy of note were associated with the population of graduating students. First, female Hispanic graduation rates were 8.5 percentage points higher than those of Hispanic males. A total of 62.8% of the graduates were female, despite the fact that only 56.6% of the Hispanic cohort was female. A second finding of interest indicated that although a smaller percentage of White students were retained to the second and third years, the six-year graduation rates for Whites (35.6%) was higher than that for Hispanics (33.8%). Further, a sizeable percentage of Hispanic students (18.4%) were retained to the sixth year but had not yet graduated. Finally, and consistent with current theory, nearly half (45.5%) of the Hispanic students exempt from tuition graduated within six years.

Course-Taking Patterns

Developmental Courses

Of the 192 developmental students who were enrolled in the fall 1997 Hispanic cohort, 58.8% enrolled in a developmental English course (ENGL

---

[6] Tuition-exempt students include students who are blind, deaf, rank in the highest percentage of graduating high schools in Texas, children of firefighters and peace officers with disabilities, children of prisoners of war or persons missing in action, veterans, and children of members of the armed forces who were killed in action.

1300) and 20.3% enrolled in a developmental math course (MATH 1300) during their first year. Although only 30.9% of Latina/o students who successfully completed the English course during the first year were found to graduate within a six-year time span, nearly half (43.4%) of those who completed the developmental math course graduated within that same period. These figures compare to the overall Hispanic cohort graduation rate of 33.8%.

Core Courses

As in all four-year institutions, students are required to enroll and complete a set of core requirements (or courses) successfully. The large majority of the Hispanic students (87.3%) enrolled in a core English course (ENGL 1303) during their first year, of whom 69.0% earned a grade of A, B, or C for the course, while only 6.4% failed or withdrew. A total of 36.8% of the students who graduated within six years took this course in the first year.

Grades lower than a C have been found to have a significant negative relationship to student success (Hu & St. John, 2001). The current investigation found that students who withdrew or failed ENGL 1303 were less likely to graduate than were students who took the course and earned a C or better. While 41.3% of Hispanic students who took the course and earned a grade of C or better graduated, none of the students who failed or withdrew from the course in the first year graduated within the six-year time period.

Similarly, 53.4% of Latina/o students enrolled in a second core English course (ENGL 1304) during their first year. Of those students, 65.1% earned an A, B, or C for the course; only 1.1% failed; and 9.9% withdrew from the course. Almost half (44.3%) of those students who enrolled in the course during their first year in college graduated within six years. Furthermore, 52.8% who earned a grade of C or higher, none of the four students who failed, and 20% of the 35 students who withdrew from the course graduated within six years.

Regarding a core math course (MATH 1310) in the curriculum, 72.8% of the Hispanic cohort was enrolled in that course in their first year. Although nearly half (48.8%) of the students earned a grade of C or higher, 20.6% of those taking the course either failed or withdrew. Slightly over a third (34.2%) of the students who enrolled in the course during their first year graduated within six years. Of the students who earned a grade of C or better, 44% graduated within six years. In contrast, students who failed or withdrew from the course in the first year (requiring them to retake the course), were less likely to graduate within six years. Among that latter group of Hispanic students, only 14.5% took the course and failed, and 8.1% of those students who withdrew from the class graduated within six years.

Three-quarters (75.1%) of the Hispanic cohort enrolled in the first of two core history courses (HIST 1377) during their first year. Over half (53.5%) of the students who enrolled in the course earned a grade of C or better, while 20.2% of the students either failed or withdrew from the course. Once more, the link between completion of core courses during a student's first year in college and subsequent graduation were indicated in the data: 45.6% of students who took the course and earned a grade of C or better graduated within six years, while a mere 4.8% of Latina/o students who took the course and failed and 8.1% who withdrew from the course graduated within six years. Similar results were found with the second core history course (HIST 1378).

Summary

These findings suggest that several factors may have a negative impact on the academic success of first-time-in-college Hispanic students. Students enrolled in developmental courses are more likely to be unable to stay on course with the required curriculum and are more than likely to become discouraged from continuing their pursuit of a degree. Hispanic students who complete fewer credit hours during an academic semester are also quite likely to withdraw from college. Poor academic performance during the first semester of college, as well as a poor academic record overall, increases the likelihood of Hispanics dropping out of college.

While it may be difficult for all Hispanic students to attend college full time, attending college part time only serves to increase their chances of dropping out and not earning a degree. Related to this issue is students having to enroll in college part time because they must pay out-of-state or non-resident tuition. Many Hispanic students are forced to work so they can pay for their college-related expenses, while others must pay higher tuition rates because they have not established state residency requirements, imposing an added burden that ultimately may prevent Hispanic students from attaining a college degree. For Hispanics specifically, failing or withdrawing from core courses during the first year assures that they will not be around for a second year. While this situation does not affect White students adversely, Hispanic students are more likely to become extremely discouraged and convinced that they don't belong in college.

In contrast, those Hispanic students who arrive on a college campus with a record of academic success in high school (i.e., graduating in the top quartile) increase their odds of remaining enrolled until graduation. Hispanic students who perform well academically during their first semester of college are also more likely to stay in college. As discussed earlier, tuition rates have a negative impact on Hispanic persistence, but receiving a tuition exemption (eliminating the need to work off-campus) positively influences their chances of staying in college. Related to this factor is the link between not having to work and being able to take a larger course load, which increases the chances of succeeding and earning a college degree in a timely manner. For those students who must pay for room and board, taking a part-time rather than a full-time course load makes no difference in how much they must pay to eat and sleep while they are attending college. And, finally, as the chances of successfully completing core courses during the first year in college increase for Hispanics, so will their chances of persisting and earning a degree.

A Closing Note: The Need for Perceptual, Behavioral, and Attitudinal Data

Traditionally, this is the point where research and practical implications are introduced. Because the emphasis of this chapter is more focused on identifying a research agenda (as not much is known of Hispanic students at four-year institutions), and because the empirical findings are based on a trend analysis and are only suggestive of future research efforts, no practical implications are included in this final section.

If one is to derive an extensive profile of those factors that affect the persistence of Hispanic college students, many more data and different sources of information need to be collected and analyzed. The data that were examined from the current institution must be combined with perceptual, behavioral, and attitudinal data that capture the academic and social experiences of Hispanic students, not only at the end of their first year in college but also into their second year and beyond. Although there are student survey instruments such as the National Survey of Student Experiences that allow institutions to establish points of reference for their students' experiences in these areas, institutions also must develop their own tools that fully capture the unique connections between Hispanic students and institutions, from the interaction of students with different peer groups and faculty, to attitudes related to financing a college education, to student engagement with campus support systems. Because universities are so diverse with regard to academic policies, emphasis on research opportunities, faculty types, class sizes, and student demographics, they also generate classroom settings, academic and organizational cultures, and faculty practices that will differ from those at other higher education institutions. These institution-specific experiences have been established as playing an increasingly larger role in student persistence as time passes. For this reason, a more productive investigation of the interplay among factors that affect the re-enrollment of Hispanics in higher education, both cognitive and attitudinal, cannot be reached without a good understanding of those academic and social experiences. More important, how colleges and universities may influence such experiences for Hispanics must be based not on data sets that combine data from many types of institutions, but from single- and like-institution studies that are designed to capture the persistence process over time within the unique context of an institution.

References

Astin, A. (1984). Student involvement: A developmental theory for higher education. *Journal of College Student Personnel, 25*, 297–308.

Bean, J. (1980). Dropouts and turnover: The synthesis and test of a causal model of student attrition. *Research in Higher Education, 12*, 155–187.

Bean, J., & Metzner, B. (1985). A conceptual model of nontraditional undergraduate student attrition. *Review of Educational Research, 55*, 485–540.

Bowen, W. G., & Bok, D. (2000). *The shape of the river: Long-term consequences of considering race in college and university admissions.* Princeton, NJ: Princeton University Press.

Braxton, J., & Brier, E. (1989). Melding organizational and interactional theories of student attrition: A path analytic study. *Review of Higher Education, 13*, 47–61.

Braxton, J. M., & Lien, L. A. (2000). The viability of academic integration as a central construct in Tinto's interactionalist theory of college student departure. In J. Braxton (Ed.), *Reworking the student departure puzzle* (pp. 11–28). Nashville, TN: Vanderbilt University Press.

Cabrera, A. F., & Nora, A. (1994). College students' perceptions of prejudice and discrimination and their feelings of alienation: A construct validation approach. *The Review of Education/Pedagogy/Cultural Studies, 16*(3–4), pp. 387–409.

Cabrera, A. F., Nora, A., & Castaneda, M. B. (1992). The role of finances in the student persistence process: A structural model. *Research in Higher Education, 33*(5), 571–594.

Cabrera, A. F., Nora, A., & Castaneda, M. B. (1993). College persistence: The testing of an integrated model. *Journal of Higher Education, 64*(2), 123–139.

DesJardins, S. L., Ahlbrug, D. A., & McCall, B. P. (2002). A temporal investigation of factors related to timely degree completion. *Journal of Higher Education, 73* (5), 555–582.

Fry, R. (2004). Latino youth finishing college: The role of selective pathways. *Pew Hispanic Center*. Retrieved on June 24, 2004, from www.pewhispanic.org.

Hu, S., & St. John, E. P. (2001). Student persistence in a public higher education system: Understanding racial and ethnic differences. *Journal of Higher Education, 72* (3), 265–286.

Hurtado, S., & Carter, D. F. (1997). Effects of college transition and perceptions of the campus racial climate on Latino college students' sense of belonging. *Sociology of Education, 70,* 324–435.

Hurtado, S., Carter, D. F., & Spuler, A. (1996). Latino student transition to college: Assessing difficulties and factors in successful college adjustment. *Research in Higher Education, 37* (2), 135–154.

Llagas, C. (2003). Status and trends in the education of Hispanics. National Center for Education Statistics (Publication No. NCES 2003008). Retrieved on June 22, 2004, from http://nces.ed.gov/pubs2003/2003008.pdf.

Longerbeam, S. D., Sedlacek, W. E., & Alatorre, H. M. (2004). In their own voices: Latino student retention. *NASPA Journal, 41* (3), 538–550.

Nora, A. (1987). Determinants of retention among Chicano college students: A structural model. *Research in Higher Education, 26*(1), 31–59.

Nora, A. (2001). The depiction of significant others in Tinto's "Rites of Passage": A reconceptualization of the influence of family and community in the persistence process. *Journal of College Student Retention, 3* (1), 41–56.

Nora, A. (2002). A theoretical and practical view of student adjustment and academic achievement. In W. Tierney and L. Hagedorn (Eds.), *Increasing access to college: Extending possibilities for all students* (pp. 41–56). Albany: State University of New York Press.

Nora, A. (2004). The role of habitus and cultural capital in choosing a college, transitioning from high school to higher education, and persisting in college among minority and non-minority students. *Journal of Hispanic Higher Education, 3*(2), 180–208.

Nora, A. & Cabrera, A. F. (1996). The role of perceptions of prejudice and discrimination on the adjustment of minority students to college. *Journal of Higher Education, 67* (2), 120–148.

Nora, A., Cabrera, A. F., Hagedorn, L. S., & Pascarella, E. T. (1996). Differential impacts of academic and social experiences on college-related behavioral outcomes across different ethnic and gender groups at four-year institutions. *Research in Higher Education, 37* (4), 427–451.

Nora, A., & Garcia, V. (n.d.). The role of perceptions of remediation on the persistence of developmental students in higher education. Unpublished manuscript, University of Houston, Houston, TX.

Nora, A., & Lang, D. (June 2001). Precollege psychosocial factors related to persistence. Paper presented at the annual meeting of the Association for Institutional Research.

Nora, A., & Lang, D. (n.d.). Precollege psychosocial factors related to persistence. Unpublished manuscript, University of Houston, Houston, TX.

Olivas, M. A. (1986). *Latino college students*. New York: Teachers College Press.

Padilla, R., Trevino, J., Gonzalez, K., & Trevino, J. (1997). Developing local models of minority student success in college. *Journal of College Student Development, 38*, 125–135.

Pascarella, E. T., Pierson, C. T., Wolniak, G. C., & Terenzini, P. T. (2004). First generation college students. *Journal of Higher Education, 75*(3), 249–284.

Pascarella, E. T., & Terenzini, P. T. (1979). Student-faculty informal contact and college persistence: A further investigation. *Journal of Educational Research, 72*, 214–218.

Pascarella, E. T., & Terenzini, P. T. (1980). Predicting freshman persistence and voluntary dropout decisions from a theoretical model. *Journal of Higher Education, 51*, 60–75.

Pascarella, E. T., & Terenzini, P. T. (1990). *How college affects students: Findings and insights from twenty years of research*. San Francisco: Jossey-Bass Publishers.

Rendón, L. I. (1994). Validating culturally diverse students: Toward a new model of learning and student development. *Innovative Higher Education, 19* (1), 23–32.

Rendón, L.I., Jalomo, R., & Nora, A. (2001). Minority student persistence. In J. Braxton (Ed.), *Rethinking the departure puzzle: New theory and research on college student retention* (pp. 126–156). Nashville, TN: Vanderbilt University Press.

St. John, E. P., Cabrera, A. F., Nora, A., & Asker, E. H. (2001). Economic perspectives on student persistence. In J. Braxton (Ed.), *Rethinking the student departure puzzle* (pp. 29–47). Nashville, TN: Vanderbilt University Press.

Stampen, J. O., & Cabrera, A. F. (1986). Exploring the effects of student aid on attrition. *Journal of Student Financial Aid, 16*, 28–37.

Terenzini, P. T., & Pascarella, E. T. (1980). Student/faculty relationships and freshman year educational outcomes: A further investigation. *Journal of College Student Personnel, 21*, 521–528.

Tierney, W. (1992). An anthropological analysis of student participation in college. *Journal of Higher Education, 63*, 603–618.

Tinto, V. (1975). Dropout from higher education: A theoretical synthesis of recent research. *Review of Educational Research, 45*, 89–125.

Torres, V. (2003). Influences on ethnic identity development of Latino college students in the first two years of college. *Journal of College Student Development, 44*(4), 532–547.

Mark W. Clark

Dr. Mark Clark is currently a professor of education in the Foundations of Education Department at the University of Wisconsin-Eau Claire. Before his return to full-time teaching in September 2004, he spent the previous 18 years in a dean's office (graduate or academic). He has worked extensively in education, sport, and career mobility and is currently working on a book on the African American experience in baseball.

5

DEAN-BASED LEADERSHIP

Reflective Comments on Latina/o
Master's Degree Participation

Mark W. Clark

Setting the Stage . . . a Time for Reflection

Emerging voices representing a diverse college population are calling for change in higher education, but are institutions of higher education and their leadership listening? Considering the growing number of Latina/os in the United States, and the relationship between higher education and professional advancement, it is essential to increase current Latina/o master's-level enrollment and graduation rates. Moreover, taking into account the influence the Latina/o population will have on national development, Latina/os' educational training and professional advancement should be of serious concern to all. It is the responsibility of higher education officials to recognize the call to assist American educational institutions to recruit and retain the Latina/o student population.

Gary Orfield (2002) describes why U.S. educational institutions must consider race-conscious policies:

> [t]he 2000 census marks a watershed in American history, showing that we are clearly on a path to becoming a predominantly non-European country in which historically excluded groups will be a much larger presence and often a majority of the population of states, regions, and communities. In this era, the question of civil rights remedies arises with special urgency and in a multiracial rather than a black-white context. In fact, the census shows that the largest "minority" group is now Latinos, a group that is not a distinct racial group since many of its members are from multiracial back-

grounds, not a nationality, only partly defined by language, and extremely diverse. Latinos are the most segregated group in American schools and extremely disadvantaged in terms of high school completion and college access. (p. x)

This quotation speaks to current circumstances that have been emerging for many years. Rendón (2003) addresses similar issues specific to Latina/o students in higher education. Simply put, people of color in particular will soon comprise the majority of Americans, and the same situation will occur in the educational system. The social, political, and economic position of the United States is at stake, and the nation will require a populace educated beyond the bachelor's degree.

For many years, leaders of higher education institutions have discussed the need to recruit and retain students of color at all levels of education. Within this context, is the number of college students of color (and in particular, master's-level Latina/o students) increasing in a proportional manner? And what do graduation outcomes indicate?

In answering these questions, I reflect on a book chapter I wrote 10 years ago as a graduate dean; it examined the unique role the graduate dean played in the potential improvement of minority participation in higher education. The premise was

the graduate dean and graduate education holds a unique position relative to improving the current situation of minorities in higher education. The graduate dean straddles both the student service and academic components of the university. Graduate education straddles educational preparation and entry into the professional workplace. It also holds the "key" to upward professional mobility. (Clark & Garza, 1994, p. 298)

Since that writing, I have served as academic dean at two different institutions overseeing programs in education, nursing, and professional health care. During this past year, I assumed additional duties as a university-wide graduate dean and reconstituted a centralized graduate school office. Re-assuming responsibilities I had not held in almost 10 years, I re-acquainted myself with the various aspects of a graduate deanship. To my surprise, it seemed as if little had changed in relative circumstance, administrative attitude, and cultural climate in the 10-year period. For instance, Latina/o graduate enrollments nationally and locally (i.e., my current campus) were unchanged, and few campus leaders seemed disturbed about this circumstance. As a result, I can only conclude that deans and institutions have not made a "true" commitment to Latina/o graduate student enrollment. Campus leadership and deans should take responsibility for providing an education for students that fosters a sense of possibility for their educational attainment (Moses, 2002).

The remainder of this chapter sets forth an agenda of how personal involvement of dean-based leadership can make a real difference in Latina/o participation in master's-level programs. This chapter is intended to be more reflective than analytic; it comments on data trends rather than analyzing data. First, national data are limited and have a variety of shortcomings. For example, a few of the data set problems include self-reported ethnicity, cross-sectional rather than longitudinal designs, nonstandard operationalization of constructs (e.g., master's, graduate), and a range of respondents across years. Accurately understanding educational data for Latina/os is complicated further by the within-group heterogeneity and differential uses of self-reference (i.e., Latina/o and Hispanic). The use of singular terms to define a diverse population is an inaccurate and unrealistic approach to understanding this group fully, a problem that is well documented among scholars (Comas-Díaz, 2001; Ibarra, 1996). Adding to the complexity of definitions for Latina/os is whether they are U.S.- or foreign-born (Pew Hispanic Center/Kaiser Family Foundation, 2004). The influence of geographic location for Latina/os may also provide some insight into the cultural identification (Thierren & Ramírez, 2001). Despite each of the challenges in interpreting the data sets, the statistical trends remain relatively constant over time, validating an educational circumstance unchanged since the 1980s.

The Council of Graduate Schools (Syverson, 2003) has reported positive increases in graduate/master's-level enrollments for students of color generally and Latina/o students specifically. Table 5.1 highlights these increases from 1986 to 2001. The same data over time also indicate that the relative proportion of degree attainment decreases as Latina/o students move higher in the educational hierarchy. The inverse relationship of Latina/os and their higher education degree attainment is particularly troubling given their substantial growth and presence in the United States (WICHE, 2003). Because Latina/os account for a smaller portion of baccalaureate degrees earned, the prospective pool of master's degree applicants simultaneously decreases (The Tomas Rivera Policy Institute/Sallie Mae Fund, 2004).

The pool of prospective master's-level Latina/o students is further affected by low grades at the undergraduate level, less satisfactory Graduate Record Examination (GRE) performance scores, and lack of educational funding. For example, these students are less knowledgeable about navigating admissions and the financial aid processes (The Tomas Rivera Policy Institute/Sallie Mae Fund, 2004). In particular, many Latina/o students are

TABLE 5.1
Graduate Enrollment by Ethnic Group and Field, 1986 to 2001
(U.S. citizens and permanent residents only)

	African American			American Indian			Asian		
	2001	% Change 2000 to 2001	Average Annual % Change 1986 to 2001	2001	% Change 2000 to 2001	Average Annual % Change 1986 to 2001	2001	% Change 2000 to 2001	Average Annual % Change 1986 to 2001
Total	**98,307**	4		**6,514**	6	4	**56,513**	7	6
Biological Sciences*	1,840	-4	5	289	7	7	3,361	-3	6
Business	15,889	4	4	723	-7	3	11,887	9	7
Education	26,305	6	6	1,770	-2	3	6,150	2	7
Engineering	2,164	-1	4	200	10	5	6,590	6	2
Health Sciences	5,973	3	5	473	-2	6	5,599	4	9
Humanities and Arts	3,475	4	7	512	8	5	2,964	4	4
Physical Sciences	3,306	4	3	303	2	5	7,094	8	3
Public Admin. & Serv.	6,683	6	4	478	15	7	1,271	3	8
Social Sciences	7,266	4	5	726	6	6	3,517	3	6
Other Fields**	9,116	17	5	505	6	5	3,674	-3	5

	Hispanic/Latino			White		
	2001	% Change 2000 to 2001	Average Annual % Change 1986 to 2001	2001	% Change 2000 to 2001	Average Annual % Change 1986 to 2001
Total	**69,066**	6	6	**741,235**	1	0
Biological Sciences*	2,072	-2	4	34,829	0	0
Business	10,365	6	6	108,794	1	-1
Education	18,855	3	6	187,143	-1	0
Engineering	2,251	1	4	31,341	-2	-2
Health Sciences	3,511	9	9	58,345	-4	2
Humanities and Arts	4,899	4	3	58,694	0	-2
Physical Sciences	2,706	9	3	39,422	0	-2
Public Admin. & Serv.	3,521	8	6	26,711	-1	1
Social Sciences	6,060	5	6	56,127	0	0
Other Fields**	6,419	-2	5	61,112	3	0

NOTE: Because not all institutions responded to all items, detail variables may not sum to total. Percentages are based on total of known field.

*"Biological Sciences" includes agriculture.

**The category "Other Fields" includes architecture, communications, home economics, library science, and religion.

Source: CGS/GRE Survey of Graduate Enrollment

unaware of institutional graduate assistantships (e.g., teaching and research) that, combined with other institutional, federal, and private funding, can approximate entry-level salaries earned with a bachelor's-degree-type job. Many assistantships provide tuition remission, health benefits, access to graduate student housing, and a modest living stipend. In addition to limited knowledge of finances, Latina/o students have less interaction with faculty regarding the "processes" of entering into graduate studies at the master's level (Herrera, 2003; Ibarra, 1996). For example, Latina/o students do not have any formalized training on seeking out appropriate recommenders, writing comprehensive and persuasive personal statements, and following protocol to track their graduate application materials.

Increasing the number of Latina/o bachelor's degrees conferred is the first step toward ensuring a pool of students who can enter into master's-level graduate training programs. Although the number of bachelor's degrees conferred to Latina/os has increased, college and university administrators should not become complacent. In particular, we cannot rest on our laurels; master's degrees are the next, critical step to doctorate degrees in many fields.

Further affecting the representation of Latina/o graduate students is their educational path to degree attainment. In particular, for many first-generation college students, the bachelor's degree represents a milestone that temporarily satisfies Latina/o students' educational needs. Consequently, Latina/o students often work for several years before entering a master's-level program. A consistent theme supported by literature (Ibarra, 1996) describes this later-life entry to graduate school to gain higher job satisfaction, a better salary, and career advancement.

Although entering graduate school after having spent time in the work-force, many Latina/os persist at the master's level. Literature supports the adjustment and retention of Latina/o master's-level students once admitted. For example, Herrera (2003) describes his journey of working multiple years and entering the military before pursuing graduate training. Ibarra (1996) similarly reports students' persistence once enrolling in graduate school.

Considering the limited entry access and persistence trends, university professionals and deans must understand student characteristics and cultural misconceptions to improve Latina/os' participation rates in master's-degree-level education. Student-centered and culturally effective recruitment is the primary means of developing a potential pool of master's candidates. Equally important to recruitment are retention efforts, which warrant consideration of the complexities of background characteristics and cultural nuances (Nettles, 1990).

Dean-based Leadership—What Is It?

My experience in graduate-level program administration, and many years of networking with academic and graduate deans throughout the country, has exposed me to a wide range of discussions on providing dean-based leadership on issues related to recruitment and retention of students of color. These discussions have led me to formulate various questions for deans and directions for productive educational outcomes. Proactive dean-based leadership that intentionally seeks diversity and opportunities for students of color in graduate education distinguishes ethnically inclusive institutions from those with few students of color at graduate levels. The increased national attention to Latina/o educational issues is placing increasing demands on both academic and graduate deans. Such deans have academic power and should serve as committed leaders, particularly regarding access and degree attainment for Latina/o students.

What must deans do to demonstrate leadership in this area? Regardless of the level of their institutions, deans first must recognize and advocate the importance of their roles in student-focused recruitment. In particular, deans have a role of symbolic leadership and are challenged to be role models. Although others (including assistant/associate deans and support staff) are critical to the success of recruiting Latina/o students for graduate studies, deans, being the most visible symbol of institutional commitment, must demonstrate exemplary leadership. Hence, consistent professional and personal commitment to diversity initiatives and graduate education is paramount.

Today, with the various demands on deans and the significant amount of time and energy required, many responsibilities related to Latina/o recruitment and retention are frequently delegated to lower levels in the administrative structure. In particular, a person of color is often designated to address diversity issues. Many argue that university professionals of color are better prepared to manage minority agendas and policies; however, these positions are often seen as nonfunctional in terms of "real" decision-making power. While active involvement of administrators of color in master's-level education is key to Latina/o student success, these administrators' contributions should be complementary to (not separate from) the work of all other university professionals, including the full academic and graduate dean. This intentional dean-based leadership, founded on a commitment to increasing diversity, leads to positive outcomes—decreased regressive enrollment and increased numbers of students of color and Latina/o students in graduate studies (Geisinger, 2004; Syverson, 2003).

Institutional Roles and Responsibilities

On college and university campuses, minority representation is typically discussed relative to undergraduate student population and faculty/staff. The under-representation of master's education of Latina/o students receives attention only in discussions about minority faculty recruitment. College and university administrators must recognize that the crisis of minority faculty under-representation stems from and is perpetuated by low levels of minority graduate student enrollment and completion rates. This concept is fairly simple to understand, and the benefits of rectifying the problem are clear. Many institutions, however, continue to de-emphasize the issue, particularly as it relates to master's-level Latina/o degree attainment.

Some institutions attempt to address complex cultural diversity issues by providing faculty development programs and seminars focusing on the academic experience of students of color, pedagogical approaches, and different student learning styles. Although these seminars are useful, they fall short of presenting and promoting opportunities for open and candid discussions of university core values, beliefs, and assumptions that marginalize and isolate people of color in graduate education. Thus, limited change is typically gained from these professional development programs.

Nettles (1988) suggested that, when discussing students of color, institutional administrators should concentrate on quantitative rather than qualitative factors in higher education. That is, student experiences are secondary to increases in the number of students. Considering the numbers and experiences of students of color, the quality of their lives is a more important indicator of success (Castellanos & Jones, 2003; Ibarra, 1996; Nettles, 1988). Reflecting on my own experience and evaluation of higher education institutions, administrators and deans today continue to focus on the quantitative rather than the qualitative aspect of student experiences.

Another area in which deans have substantial influence is with the faculty. Faculty members assume key decision-making and gate-keeping roles in graduate education, and the academic and social integration of graduate students is, in large part, under their control. For example, faculty determine who is admitted into their graduate programs, what financial and research opportunities are made available to students, who serves as presenters at national conferences, and who is offered opportunities to co-author manuscripts and scholarly works. Given their significant role, academic and graduate deans must reach faculty to increase the recruitment and retention of Latina/o students in graduate programs. Yet, the literature continues to point out that Latina/os graduate students enter the system through their own persistence and determination, rather than as a result of faculty intervention and assistance (Herrera, 2003; Ibarra, 1996).

Although some progress has been made in reaching out to Latina/o student populations, these efforts tend to be special initiatives that are often dependent on time-limited grant funding. Unfortunately, when the grant ends or the invested individual leaves, the initiative also terminates. Few institutions have implemented formal and ongoing early identification and graduate-level preparation programs for Latina/o undergraduates. For the most part, ethnic-specific outreach programming has not been internalized as institutional practice. As a result of limited outreach, Latina/o students operate with limited and inaccurate information about master's-level study.

Over the course of my experiences as a dean, and after having read much of the literature, I pose several challenges for academic and graduate deans. I have personally committed to a dean-based leadership that is culturally relevant for Latina/o students, and I implore other deans to do the same.

Action Plan for Academic/Graduate Deans

Deans must

- Be proactive, community-minded leaders.
- Take responsibility for Latina/o master's degree attainment.
- Personally seek the financial resources and commitments to recruit and retain Latina/o graduate students.
- Initiate institutional priorities and policies to encourage outreach to Latina/os and persistence programming.
- Become personally involved in and learn about Latina/o cultures.
- Learn about what Latina/o groups are in their respective local communities and use this knowledge to encourage/enhance Latina/o participation at this level of degree attainment.
- Address Latina/o groups, both on- and off-campus, regarding the costs and benefits of master's-level degree attainment.
- Work directly with faculty and staff to identify, recruit, and nurture specific Latina/o students into master's-level programming.
- Personally mentor Latina/o students before and after their admission to graduate school.
- Help develop policy that addresses recruitment, retention, and degree attainment for Latina/os and other students of color.
- Move policy development beyond the numbers of students to include their educational experiences.

- Be active and visible in departments related to Latina/o student recruitment/retention.
- Reward successful programs! Deans can (and should) take a role of moral persuasion or "moral-suasion" when working with individual departments.
- Be directly involved in financial aid distribution and decision making.
- Develop and implement active multicultural professional development programs and ethnic-specific training for all faculty and staff at their institutions.
- Provide support for faculty and staff on issues related to Latina/o-based scholarship.

American higher education institutions are at a crossroads for change (Ibarra, 1996) and must genuinely invest in recruiting Latina/o students to and retaining them in graduate-level programs. In the 1980s and 1990s, Latina/o recruitment and enrollment in graduate programs was a *potential*; currently, it is a requirement for tomorrow's future.

References

Castellanos, J., & Jones, L. (2003). An infrastructure that facilitates the retention of Latina/os in higher education. In J. Castellanos & L. Jones (Eds.), *The majority in the minority: Expanding the representation of Latina/o faculty, administrators and students in higher education* (pp. 285–291). Sterling, VA: Stylus Publishing.

Clark, M., & Garza, H. (1994). Minorities in graduate education: A need to regain lost momentum. In M. J. Justiz, R. Wilson, & L. G. Björk (Eds.), *Minorities in higher education* (pp. 297–313). Phoenix, AZ: Oryx Press.

Comas-Díaz, L. (2001). Hispanics, Latinos or Americanos: The evolution of identity. *Cultural Diversity and Ethnic Minority Psychology, 7*, 115–120.

Geisinger, K. (2004). Improving the graduate admissions process: How deans can influence program decision making. *Council of Graduate Schools (CGS) Communicator, 37*(6), 1–2, 5–7.

Herrera, R. (2003). Notes from a Latino graduate student at a predominantly white university. In J. Castellanos & L. Jones (Eds.), *The majority in the minority: Expanding the representation of Latina/o faculty, administrators and students in higher education* (pp. 111–125). Sterling, VA: Stylus Publishing.

Ibarra, R. (1996). *Latino experiences in graduate education: Implications for change.* Washington, DC: Council of Graduate Schools.

Moses, M. S. (2002). *Embracing race: Why we need race-conscious education policy.* New York: Teachers College Press.

Nettles, M. (1988). *Toward Black undergraduate student equality in American higher education.* New York: Greenwood Press.

Nettles, M. (1990). *Black, Hispanic, and White doctoral students: Before, during and after enrolling in graduate school.* Princeton, NJ: Educational Testing Service.

Orfield, G. (2002). Foreword. In M. S. Moses, *Embracing race: Why we need race-conscious education policy* (pp. ix–xii). New York: Teachers College Press.

Pew Hispanic Center/Kaiser Family Foundation. (2004). *National survey of Latinos: Education.* Washington, DC: Pew Hispanic Center.

Rendón, L. I. (2003). Foreword. In J. Castellanos & L. Jones (Eds.), *The majority in the minority: Expanding the representation of Latina/o faculty, administrators and students in higher education* (pp. ix–xii). Sterling, VA: Stylus Publishing.

Syverson, P. D. (2003). *Graduate enrollment and degrees: 1986–2001.* Washington, DC: Council of Graduate Schools.

Therrien, M., & Ramírez, R.R. (2001). The Hispanic population in the United States: Population characteristics (*Current Population Reports,* pp. 20–535). Washington, DC: U.S. Bureau of the Census.

Tomas Rivera Policy Institute/Sallie Mae Fund. (2004). *Caught in the financial aid information divide: A national survey of Latino perspectives on financial aid.* Claremont, CA: The Tomas Rivera Center.

Western Interstate Commission for Higher Education (WICHE) (2003). *Knocking at the college door—2003.* Boulder, CO: WICHE.

PART TWO

NAVEGANDO EL CAMINO (NAVIGATING THE PATH)

Frances E. Contreras

Dr. Frances Contreras is an assistant professor of higher education in the College of Education at the University of Washington. She is also a research associate with the Diversity Scorecard Project at the University of Southern California and was a UC ACCORD Postdoctoral Fellow at the University of California, Davis from 2002 to 2004. Dr. Contreras received her Ph.D. in education from Stanford University, with a concentration in administration and policy analysis. She earned a bachelor's degree in history and mass communications from the University of California, Berkeley, and a master's degree in administration, planning, and social policy from the School of Education at Harvard University. Dr. Contreras has taught in the School of Education at UC-Davis and the Department of Ethnic Studies at UC-Berkeley. She has also served as a research associate for the Stanford Institute for Higher Education Research and as director of institutional planning and evaluation for the National Hispanic University in San Jose. Dr. Contreras has worked for the Vanguard Public Foundation and the Latino Issues Forum in San Francisco and has managed her own nonprofit consulting business. She currently researches equity and access for under-represented students in higher education.

Patricia Gándara

Professor Gándara leads the education policy studies emphasis at the University of California, Davis, and her research focuses on access to higher education for low-income and minority students and the education of English learners. She has been a social scientist with RAND Corporation (1980–85), directed education research in the California legislature (1985–87), and served as a commissioner for postsecondary education in California (1981–86). Currently she is director of the Institute for Education Policy, Law, and Government, co-director of Policy Analysis for California Education (PACE—a research consortium of UC-Davis, UC-Berkeley, and Stanford University) and associate director of the UC Linguistic Minority Research Institute. Professor Gándara also chairs the Committee on Scholars of Color for the American Educational Research Association. Her recent publications include *The Crisis in Access to Higher Education* (editor, with C. Horn and G. Orfield), a special issue of *Educational Policy*, May 2005.

6

THE LATINA/O PH.D. PIPELINE

A Case of Historical and Contemporary Under-representation

Frances E. Contreras
Patricia Gándara

Education is the great engine of personal development. It is through education that the daughter of a peasant can become a doctor, that a son of a mine worker can become the head of the mine, that a child of farm workers can become the president of a great nation.—Nelson Mandela

There is little debate that education is the primary vehicle of social and economic mobility in the developed world. Unless an individual is born into wealth and privilege, that person's life chances will be determined to a very large extent by the amount and type of education that he or she is able to receive. Moreover, the economic strength of society as a whole depends to a large extent on the educational attainment of its population (Cohn, 1979). Thus, education and economic well-being are inextricably linked for both groups and individuals. Table 6.1 shows the relationship between education and earnings for four major ethnic groups in the United States in 2002.

TABLE 6.1
Mean Earnings by Race and Education Level 18 Years or Older, 2002

Race	Not High School Graduate	High School Grad/GED	Bachelor's Degree	Advanced Degree
Latina/o	$18,981	$24,163	$40,949	$67,679
Black	16,516	22,823	42,286	59,944
Asian	16,746	24,900	46,628	72,852
White	19,423	28,756	53,185	74,122

Source: U.S. Census Bureau, 2003.

While Latina/os[1] never reach the same earnings as Whites with the same education level, they nonetheless improve their own situation significantly with each additional level of education. Education pays—for Latina/os as well as others. However, Latina/o youth are far less likely than Blacks, Whites, or Asians to graduate from high school, go on to college, and earn a degree. For this reason, the pool of young Latina/os who apply, and are admitted, to doctoral programs in the United States is extraordinarily small—smaller than for any other ethnic group.

The undereducation of Latina/o youth begins early. By the time they enter kindergarten, Latina/os are already significantly behind their non-Hispanic peers in reading and math readiness. For about half of Latina/o youth in the United States, English represents a chronic barrier to achievement in K–12 schools (Olsen, 1997); for many others, poverty, inadequate schooling, and lack of models of academic success also play a significant role in underachievement. By 12th grade, an estimated half of all Latina/o students have dropped out of high school (Orfield, 2003), and only about half of those who graduate from high school will go on to college. However, the great majority of these students will go to two-year colleges from which they are unlikely to transfer or receive a college degree (see Watford, Rivas, Burciaga, & Solorzano, chapter 7). On the basis of U.S. Census data, it is estimated that only 7% of Chicano students who begin school in the United States actually complete a college degree, thereby becoming eligible to be part of the graduate school pool; only 2% will receive some graduate degree, and less than 1% will complete the Ph.D. (Watford et al., 2005). Of all Latina/o subgroups, Chicanos—or individuals of Mexican origin—are the most at risk educationally. This is highly problematic, as they are also the most numerous of the Latina/o subgroups, comprising about 56% of all Latina/os nationally and up to 80% of the Latina/os in the Southwest (Guzman, 2001).

The myriad reasons for the early and chronic underachievement of Latina/o students have been well documented elsewhere (see, for example, Gándara, 2005) as well as in other chapters of this book. We will not belabor those issues here; we have charged ourselves in this chapter simply to lay out

---

[1] Throughout this document the terms, "Hispanic" and "Latina/o," are used interchangeably, as "Hispanic" is the preferred term for national data collection efforts, but Latina/o is often preferred in the literature and by members of the group. In some cases, data are presented separately for Mexican Americans, the largest subset of the Latina/o groups, and nationally the group most at risk. The reason for the focus on a particular group, for example, Mexican Americans or Puerto Ricans, is to reduce variation where possible with respect to the educational experiences of the group in question. For example, some Latina/o groups, notably Cuban Americans and foreign nationals, enter the United States to attend college and are not particularly at risk academically, while Mexican Americans or Puerto Rican students consistently fare very poorly in U.S. schools and colleges.

the educational situation as it exists and focus on policy levers within higher education that might contribute to stimulating the pool of eligible students who go on to pursue the Ph.D. and add to the ranks of university faculty and administrators.

In an effort to understand the pool of potential doctoral students, Table 6.2 illustrates the production of B.A.s and higher degrees for Latina/os compared to Blacks and Whites.

The most notable characteristic of these data is the relatively flat rate of growth in B.A. and other degrees over the last two decades for Latina/os. While both Blacks and Whites are increasing their overall educational levels, Latina/os have made very little progress. With such a small pool of students eligible for doctoral study, it is not surprising that the pipeline slows to a trickle at the level of the Ph.D. Table 6.3 shows the proportion of Ph.D.s conferred for four major ethnic groups for the 10-year period, 1992–2002.

The distribution of Ph.D. degrees across disciplines is also especially uneven for Latina/os. They earn nearly twice as many degrees in social sciences, humanities, and education as in other areas, as Table 6.4 illustrates, and most Latina/os who go on to graduate school actually go to professional schools rather than pursuing the Ph.D. In 2001, 4.8% of students who earned a graduate/professional degree in the United States were Latina/o, and the great majority of these degrees were awarded in law, medicine, and pharmacy (NCES, 2002a, 2002b). Of these professional degrees, more than half (55.9%) were in law (NCES, 2002a, 2002b).

Charting Educational Progress: The Impact of Generational Status and Gender

A consistent finding in the literature on Latina/o educational attainment is that Latina/os tend to "stall out" after the second generation. Reviewing

TABLE 6.2
Percent of 25- to 29-year-olds Completing a Bachelor's Degree or Higher, Selected Years, 1975–2000

Race/Ethnicity	1975	1980	1985	1990	1995	2000
Latina/o	9	8	11	8	9	10
Black	11	12	12	13	15	18
White	24	25	24	26	29	34

Source: U.S. Department of Education, National Center for Education Statistics, Digest of Education Statistics, 2001 based on the U.S. Department of Commerce, Bureau of the Census, March Current Population Survey.

TABLE 6.3
Percent of Doctorate Recipients by Race/Ethnicity, 1992–2002

	1992	1993	1994	1995	1996	1997	1998	1999	2000	2001	2002
Asian	21.3	21.8	22.8	23.3	23.2	21.2	20.1	19.5	19.6	19.9	19.7
Black/African American	3.7	4.1	4.1	4.4	4.3	4.2	4.5	5.0	5.1	4.9	5.0
Latina/o	3.6	3.6	3.7	3.7	3.8	4.0	4.4	4.6	4.7	4.7	5.1
White	66.7	66.5	66.1	65.0	64.1	61.7	62.9	64.4	63.6	62.4	60.7
Total (N)	38,890	39,800	41,034	41,742	42,413	42,545	42,634	41,060	41,368	40,790	39,955

Note 1: Includes all students, including U.S. citizens, permanent visas, temporary visas, and unknown citizenship.

Note 2: Data from 1990–2000 are from Survey of Earned Doctorates, 2000. Data for the 2001 and 2002 years are from Survey of Earned Doctorates, 2002.

Note 3: American Indian students are not included because the percentage point is well below 1%.

TABLE 6.4
Ph.D.s Conferred as Share of Total, by Field and Ethnicity, 1980, 1990, and 2000 (percent)

Field	Black			Latina/o			Asian[1]			White		
	1980	1990	2000	1980	1990	2000	1980	1990	2000	1980	1990	2000
Physical Sciences	1.0	1.0	2.6	1.0	2.0	3.5	2.4	3.3	6.1	88.4	90.9	84.9
Engineering	1.0	1.4	3.4	1.4	2.0	3.1	5.8	8.0	11.2	85.1	70.8	79.5
Life Sciences	1.5	1.6	3.5	1.0	2.3	3.8	2.3	3.3	7.3	89.7	91.2	82.8
Social Sciences	3.6	3.9	6.4	1.9	3.7	4.8	1.6	1.8	4.0	88.2	88.6	81.7
Humanities	2.8	2.3	3.6	2.4	3.6	4.2	1.2	1.1	3.2	89.0	91.2	86.2
Education	8.8	8.1	12.3	2.1	3.2	4.9	1.0	1.2	2.3	83.7	85.9	77.9
Other/Professional	4.7	4.0	7.5	1.2	2.0	3.3	1.8	2.0	4.7	87.6	90.2	82.7

[1] Includes Pacific Islander and Alaskan Native.

Note: The data are derived from U.S. citizen doctorate recipients. American Indian student percentages are not shown.

Source: Survey of Earned Doctorates, 2000.

1980 U.S. Census data, McCarthy and Burciaga (1985) reported that Hispanics were failing to increase their share of college-goers after the second generation, and Rumbaut (1995) noted a similar finding in his study of Latina/os on both U.S. coasts, conducted in the early 1990s. A more recent study by Grogger and Trejo (2002), looking at Mexican Americans in California, reports the same conclusion. Mexican Americans (the single largest portion of the Latina/o population, and the most at risk for school failure) appear to make significant gains in educational attainment from the first to the second generation; however, educational progress slows considerably after this point, with few gains made after the second generation. The reason for this is that while high school graduation improves substantially between the first and second generation, there is relatively little growth in college-going or college degree completion after the second generation. This finding illustrates how the longer a student's family is in the country, the greater the impact of institutional and contextual barriers, such as poverty, in inhibiting successful progression through high school and into postsecondary education (Grogger & Trejo, 2002). Mexican-origin students appear to hit a glass ceiling with respect to college-going and do not improve their situation over time. This is contrary to patterns established by other immigrant groups where succeeding generations tend to convert increasing family economic well-being into higher educational attainment across generations (Perlmann, 1987).

Gender is also a critically important factor in the educational progress of Latina/o students. When data were first collected on Latina/o educational progress in the early 1970s, women lagged considerably behind men in high school graduation and college-going. However, since the mid-1970s males have made relatively little progress, while females are responsible for almost all of the educational advances of the group. Table 6.5 shows the changing percentages of B.A. recipients between male Latinos and female Latinas for the 20-year period, 1980–2001. The dramatic increase in female degree pro-

TABLE 6.5
Percentage of Latina/os (25 to 29 years old) with a Bachelor's Degree or Higher, by Gender, 1980–2000

Ethnicity	1980	1985	1990	1995	2000
Latina/o	7.7	11.1	8.2	8.9	9.6
Latino Male	8.5	10.9	7.3	7.8	8.3
Latina Female	7.0	11.2	9.1	10.1	11.0

Source: NCES, 2002a, 2002b.

duction is mirrored across all ethnic groups, but it is strongest among African Americans and then Latina/os.

Other data we have collected (see Gándara, O'Hara, & Gutierréz, 2004) show the discrepancies in educational aspirations between Latinos and Latinas, as well as others, in high school that lead to these differences in bachelor degree production. However, why males are so much less motivated to pursue higher education remains a seriously understudied, but increasingly urgent, question.

Institutional Effects: The Double-Edged Sword

There are two primary pathways through college for Latina/o students. The first and most common is through a nonselective institution—often a community college—that may be located near their place of residence, is easily accessible, and costs relatively little. In fact, the majority of Latina/o college students are enrolled in two-year colleges. Nationwide, 58% of Latina/os who go to college attend two-year colleges (NCES, 2002a, 2002b). In California, the state with the largest proportion of Latina/os in the nation, and an extensive two-year college system, almost 75% of Latina/os attend two-year institutions. Since they cannot earn a college degree in a two-year institution, students must transfer to four-year colleges. Transfer rates, especially for minority students, however, are notoriously low. A recent study showed that in California, only about 3% of students enrolled in community college actually transfer to four-year colleges annually, in spite of the fact that approximately one-third report intending to transfer when they enroll (Hardy, 2000).

Almost half (about 45%) of all Latina/o students attend one of the 230 Hispanic Serving Institutions (HSIs) in the United States. To qualify as Hispanic Serving Institutions, colleges and universities must enroll at least 25% Latina/o students, thus these institutions have a critical mass of such students who can help to provide a supportive, and more familiar, environment. There is also an assumption that schools with large numbers of Latina/o students are more familiar with their needs and concerns and provide services that address these needs. However, there is little evidence to confirm or refute this claim. More than half of all HSIs, however, are two-year colleges where students are unable to complete a college degree and, therefore, must transfer to a four-year college. Moreover, HSIs tend to be nonselective institutions with relatively low graduation rates, and only 2% actually offer the doctorate, meaning that few Ph.D.s are produced in HSIs (Santiago, Andrade, & Brown, 2004; Stearns & Watanabe, 2002). In sum, while the common route of entering a local college or nonselective institution of higher education provides accessibility, low cost, and probably a better sense of comfort and belonging than do large, impersonal colleges and universities, it does not appear to be a very fruitful means of maximizing college degree production.

The second pathway is to go directly to a more selective, four-year college or university, where the chances of degree completion are considerably enhanced (Carnevale & Rose, 2003). However, apart from the greater difficulty of being accepted to one of these institutions, the higher costs involved, and their limited accessibility, selective four-year colleges can also be very isolating for Latina/o students. With few other Latina/os enrolled, such students often feel marginalized and lonely (Hurtado, 1994).

In a study examining the positive effects of racial diversity, Chang (2001) found that diversity had a positive effect on student socialization and participation in discourse on racial issues. Using student data from the Cooperative Institutional Research Program (CIRP) and the Higher Education Research Institute (HERI) at the University of California-Los Angeles (UCLA), Chang (2001) assessed the impact of college environment on student outcomes with respect to (1) socializing with students from different racial/ethnic groups and (2) discussing race issues. Chang found that multiracial diversity is significant in predicting the likelihood of increased interracial interaction as well as contributing to students' social self-confidence, academic self-concept, persistence, and overall college satisfaction. Diversity at multiple levels, or the willingness to promote diversity, may therefore be a contributing factor toward creating a positive cultural climate for Latina/o students and better cognitive outcomes for students with respect to academic, intellectual, and critical thinking skills (Gurin, Dey, Hurtado, & Gurin, 2002; Hurtado, 1994).

Although student diversity is important, Milem (2001) contends that simply increasing the number of students of color does not produce considerable changes in pedagogical practices or content. In a study on the effects of different levels of student diversity using the 1992–1993 Survey of College and University Faculty of 344 institutions by HERI, The Carnegie Foundation, and the Higher Education Governance Institutions Survey (HEGIS) of 244 institutions, Milem (2001) found that increased faculty diversity and leadership alters the campus climate because these individuals contribute to the institution's ability to adapt to a changing student body. For example, Milem (2001) found that faculty of color and female faculty members are more likely to engage in research on race, class, and gender and use more interactive learning methods to engage a diverse student body. Milem suggests that realizing the full value of diversity is contingent on the institution's ability to respond and adapt to the pedagogical needs of its students. Thus, while selective institutions may seek students of color to build a diverse campus, they fall short of realizing the full benefits of a changing student body if the teaching methods and composition of the faculty remain static.

Despite selective colleges and universities' apparent flaws in faculty composition and unchanging pedagogical practices, it has been well documented that college selectivity plays an important role in postgraduate access, success, and completion (Bowen & Bok, 1998, Carnevale & Rose, 2003). Students who attend selective colleges tend to have higher graduation rates and go on to graduate and professional education at much higher rates (Carnevale & Rose, 2003). In addition, selective schools may offer students access to brighter and more ambitious classmates and valuable learning experiences that reduce the likelihood of dropping out of college (Kane & Dickens, 1996) and expand social networks that will be valuable for future employment.

There also appear to be financial rewards associated with college selectivity in addition to the support and resources while in college. In a study that looked at the *National Longitudinal Study of the High School Class of 1972* and *High School and Beyond*, Brewer, Eide, and Ehrenberg (1996) examined the effects of college selectivity on wages and annual earnings 6, 10, and 14 years after high school. They found that students experienced significant economic returns in earnings for attending elite private institutions. They also found that there was a smaller labor market premium for attending a moderately selective private institution. A highly selective college or university therefore appears to be associated with higher earnings later in a student's professional life, even after holding constant several key variables routinely used to predict college completion and success, including high school grades, standardized exam scores, and parent income and education level (Brewer, Eide, & Ehrenberg, 1996; Kane & Dickens, 1996).

Because college selectivity plays an important role in successful undergraduate completion, postgraduate success, and earnings over the long term, it is problematic that the majority of Latina/os are disproportionately enrolled in institutions that do not impart these advantages. More than one-third (36%) of all doctorates earned by Latina/os in 2000 were given by 20 institutions, and more than one in five were awarded by only 10 institutions. The data in Table 6.6 show that Latina/o doctoral students, like their undergraduate peers, are concentrated in very few universities. And at the doctoral level, these institutions are among the most selective in the country.

TABLE 6.6
Top 10 Doctoral-Granting Institutions for Latina/os

Institution	Number	Percent of Latina/os Earning Doctorates
University of Texas, Austin	202	4.0
University of Puerto Rico-Rio Piedras Campus	193	3.5
Carlos Albizu University-Puerto Rico	160	2.9
University of California, Berkeley	146	2.6
Texas A & M University	112	2.0
Harvard University	89	1.6
University of New Mexico	84	1.5
Stanford University	84	1.5
University of Michigan-Ann Arbor	83	1.5
University of Arizona	80	1.4

Source: Survey of Earned Doctorates, 2000.

In addition to the top 10 doctoral-granting institutions for Latina/os, it is important to note that the combined nine campuses of the University of California (UC) system awarded close to 13% of all doctoral degrees in the United States in 2000 (UCOP, 2001), representing a tremendous opportunity to increase the production of Latina/o Ph.Ds. This is particularly relevant as the UC system has struggled in recent years to maintain a reasonable representation of Latina/o students in the face of a ban on affirmative action that extends to funding scholarships and other financial aid. Very dramatic declines in Latina/o undergraduate representation at the flagship campuses—UC-Berkeley and UCLA—are almost certain to have an impact on doctoral production down the line (Gándara & Chavez, 2003), thereby affecting the pool of Latina/o Ph.Ds for the nation. Of course, not all of these students are lost to academe. A recent study by Geiser (in press) demonstrates that highly qualified graduate students of color are more likely to enroll in private institutions that can offer them targeted financial aid than they are to accept the offer of study from places like UC-Berkeley that cannot provide such aid under existing law. Thus, while we can celebrate the fact that very talented Latina/os may find an institution to train them, one must worry what their allegiance to public institutions will be when they do not earn degrees from them.

Cost as a Consideration

While the economic returns to higher education are clear (Brewer, Eide, & Ehrenberg, 1996; Datcher-Loury & Garman, 1995; Kane, 1994), these returns come at a price with respect to time and indebtedness, and the cost and indebtedness often weigh more on those students with fewer resources and heavier responsibilities to families that may be struggling economically—a common fact of life for many Latina/os. Table 6.7 reveals the median number of years students stay in graduate school by ethnic group. Several factors can affect length of time to degree: the need to work part time or take time off for family responsibilities, less access to graduate advisors, and the need to "backfill" coursework that may have not been provided in undergraduate institutions are among the factors that can slow degree completion. Moreover, Latina/os are clustered in fields in which it generally takes longer to earn a degree (Survey of Earned Doctorates, 2002). The opportunity cost of so many years of study is likely to be at the forefront of many Latina/os' decision to pursue the Ph.D.

In addition to opportunity costs associated with the number of years needed to earn a doctoral degree, Latina/os must reconcile the debt they are likely to accrue in graduate school. Table 6.8 demonstrates that Latina/os and African Americans, and Native Americans—the last of which is the most under-represented of all ethnic groups in graduate education—are also the most likely to incur more than $30,000 in debt in the process of earning their Ph.Ds. For example, more than 23% of Latina/os complete their degrees with this level of debt, compared to only 16.6% of Whites. As Latina/os come from the least economically well off families, this level of debt almost certainly imposes a greater burden on them and their families than it does on their White counterparts.

College choice, therefore, is a double-edged sword. If Latina/os attend highly selective colleges, they risk social and academic isolation, the absence of role models and supporters in the form of Latina/o faculty and administrators, higher costs, and less accessibility. However, their overall chances of completing a degree and going on to graduate school are significantly enhanced (Bowen & Bok, 1998). On the other hand, if they attend less selective institutions, they may experience a more positive cultural climate, feel a greater sense of belonging among peers like themselves, and usually will find themselves in less debt as a result. But their likelihood of academic success and enrollment in graduate and doctoral programs is significantly diminished. This presents a substantial dilemma.

The Absence of Latina/o Faculty and Administrators

Because the pool of Latina/o students moving through the educational pipeline is so diminished at each stage of education, Latina/os with doctoral de-

TABLE 6.7

Median Number of Years in Graduate School, by Demographic Group and Broad Field of Study, 2002

Race/Ethnicity	All Fields	Physical Sciences	Engineering	Life Sciences	Social Sciences	Humanities	Education	Professional/ Other
Asian	7.1	6.5	6.5	7.0	7.5	8.9	7.9	8.5
Black	8.0	6.9	7.2	7.2	8.0	8.8	8.2	9.0
Latina/o	8.0	6.9	6.6	7.1	8.0	8.7	8.7	7.9
American Indian	8.7	6.3	6.2	7.3	8.4	10.0	9.8	11.3
White	7.7	6.5	6.4	7.0	7.7	9.0	8.6	8.2

Source: Survey of Earned Doctorates, 2002.

TABLE 6.8
Cumulative Debt Related to the Doctoral Education, by Race/Ethnicity 2000
(percent)

Cumulative Debt	Asian	African American	Latina/o	American Indian	White
$5,000 or less	7.1	9.7	8.8	6.2	8.4
$5,001–$10,000	7.9	8.1	8.6	8.6	8.3
$10,001–$15,000	6.7	7.3	6.2	2.5	7.0
$15,001–$20,000	5.2	6.7	6.3	8.6	6.4
$20,001–$25,000	3.9	4.8	7.2	6.8	4.8
$25,001–$30,000	2.5	7.5	6.2	4.9	4.1
$30,000 +	11.1	30.0	23.2	23.5	16.6
No Debt	55.6	25.9	33.7	38.9	44.3

Source: Survey of Earned Doctorates, 2000.

grees are in many ways an anomaly, and those who enter academia are even more distinct. According to the National Center for Education Statistics, Latina/os represented approximately 3% of full-time instructional faculty, half of whom were assistant professors or instructors—the lowest ranks of the academic hierarchy (NCES, 2002a, 2002b). Such limited representation leaves Latina/o students who aspire to these positions with very few role models within postsecondary institutions. Faculty members provide mentorship to students (Jacobi, 1991; Cole & Barber, 2003). A study on increasing faculty diversity explored the role that interaction with faculty role models plays in influencing career aspirations to become faculty members. One key finding was related to the role that historically Black colleges and universities (HBCUs) played in providing role models to African American students. Eighty-five percent of students attending an HBCU reported having at least one role model in graduate school. In addition, this study reported higher levels of contact between students and faculty at HBCUs. Having a role model also had a small positive effect on grade point average (GPA) and increased the self-confidence of African American males (Cole & Barber, 2003).

Perhaps the most important contribution that faculty members may provide to students of color is an environment that supports their research efforts. In the Cole and Barber (2003) study for example, higher percentages of Latina/os and African Americans conducted their own independent research (17% for each group, compared to 15% for Whites), which suggests that a climate of collaboration may not exist to the same degree at selective institutions and in doctoral programs in general for students of color.

The HBCU data confirm that faculty of color do play an important role in student achievement through mentoring (Cole & Barber, 2003). The Cole and Barber study also suggests that faculty of color may be more likely to provide opportunities to their students, at least at HBCUs. In a study conducted on faculty views of diversity (Maruyama & Moreno, 2000), a representative sample of faculty from the social sciences, humanities, education, and business at Carnegie Research-I institutions were asked several questions about their views on diversity in the classroom and its role in improving the educational environment and faculty learning. Among other key findings, the study found that faculty of color in particular viewed the climate of diversity at their respective institutions as less positive than their White peers perceived the climate. In addition, faculty of color asserted the benefits of diversity on classrooms, students, pedagogy, and research more positively than did White respondents (Maruyama & Moreno, 2000). Faculty of color respondents also conveyed a greater level of preparedness to deal with diversity and asserted that they were more likely to address diversity issues (Maruyama & Moreno, 2000). These findings support the assertion that faculty of color are more inclined to mentor and support diverse cohorts of students, because their comfort level with issues of diversity and their own value for diversity translate into pedagogical practices that validate the presence of students of color.

Moreover, we know that faculty produce faculty and that individuals are more likely to select a protégé from among others like themselves. That is human nature. In a study conducted on the pathway to graduate education for minority students, a consistent finding was that the biggest hurdles for minority graduate students were not academic ones but, rather, the problem of being taken seriously as scholars by faculty who had rather narrow views of what a future academic should look like (Gándara & Maxwell-Jolly, 1999). It is also true that apprenticeship in the academy plays a vital role in a student's decision to become a faculty member. With few Latina/o faculty, it is less likely that Latina/o graduate students will be mentored into faculty positions themselves. This creates a vicious cycle: few mentors in the academy who are likely to tap Latina/o graduate students for training as faculty members, and therefore few new Latina/o faculty and administrators.

Table 6.9 demonstrates that Latina/os are the least well represented of all ethnic groups among faculty in the United States, in spite of the fact that they are the largest minority in the country. Moreover, the majority of Latina/o faculty fall within the lower levels of academic rank; they are dispro-

TABLE 6.9
Latina/o Faculty Members in the United States by Race/Ethnicity and Academic Rank, Fall 1999

Academic Rank	Percent White	Percent African American	Percent Chicano/ Latina/o	Percent Asian American/ Pacific Islander	N
Men & Women					
All Ranks	82.8	5.0	3.0	6.0	590,937
Professors	88.6	3.0	2.0	5.5	161,309
Associate Professors	84.6	5.0	2.5	6.0	128,826
Assistant Professors	77.7	6.3	3.1	7.2	134,791
Instructors	80.9	6.7	4.6	4.3	80,089
Lecturers	80.7	5.5	4.1	4.3	16,057
Other Faculty	78.5	4.7	2.6	5.4	69,865

Note: American Indian professors across all categories were less than 1%.

portionately represented among the "instructor" and "lecturer" categories. This level of academic rank gives them little voice in university policies and practices, makes it difficult for them to mentor doctoral students (because of tenure pressures and lack of status), and places them in a vulnerable status and/or off the tenure-track path to the professorate. Given that Latina/os account for only 2% of all full professors in the academy, they are a scarce resource for Latina/o graduate students.

Similar trends exist for Latina/o administrators. In a study conducted on Latina/os in academic leadership, Haro and Lara (2003) indicate that the limited number of Latina/o faculty in liberal arts campuses helps to explain why opportunities to be promoted to administrative positions such as chair of department or academic dean are sparse. The dearth of Latina/os in key administrative roles, such as college presidencies, provosts, deans, and department chairs, may be considered a ripple effect from the very small number of Latina/o academics, because Latina/o administrators in executive positions are primarily selected from faculty ranks.

University administrators are also key in that they often have more decision-making power than do faculty, and they have access to budgets, which enables them to have a direct impact on minority student recruitment, retention, and well-being. Hence, the hiring of high-level Latina/o administrators must be viewed as an important priority in raising the profile of Latina/o issues within academe. However, the barriers to such hiring are substantial, as reflected in the data in Table 6.10.

While HSIs actually have relatively high numbers of Latina/os in executive positions (more than one-third), representation of Latina/o executives and other administrators in mainstream institutions is as low as it is for faculty. Haro (1995) provides us with some insight into why this is. In a study of university CEO hiring practices, he found that, although the popular perception was that Latina/o candidates were sought after, they actually fared significantly more poorly in the hiring process than did Whites. The reason most often given by hiring committees for not making offers to highly qualified Latina/o applicants was a difference in "style" that did not fit with the expectations of the committee. Among the components of style that were especially significant to respondents in this study were appearance and access to important networks, two attributes that almost certainly were affected by the candidates' ethnicity.

Conclusion

The dearth of Latina/os in the Ph.D. pipeline is a serious concern for the Latina/o community as academicians play an important role within higher education and the community as mentors, scholars, industry leaders, and leading researchers on issues pertinent to the Latina/o community as well as the society as a whole. Hayes-Bautista, Hsu, Beltran, and Villagomez (2004) points out that Latina/o medical researchers have found that Latina/os suffer from much less heart disease than do other groups, and that research into this area can potentially benefit thousands of non-Latina/os if the causes and a cure can come out of this Latina/o-specific research. Because Latina/os are the nation's largest minority group, unless they are able to achieve at the same levels as other groups, not only they, but the society as a whole, will suffer. The pathway to the doctorate, however, begins before kindergarten, and the whole of the education system that has failed these students so woefully must be addressed. There are interventions that institutions of higher education (IHEs) can incorporate to stimulate and retain the small pool of Latina/o students who can now aspire to doctoral-level education. IHEs must find ways to capitalize on the strengths of local, nonselective—and often Hispanic-serving—institutions while mitigating their disadvantages. Greater attention to the kinds of characteristics and practices that attract Latina/o students to these institutions could help increase the number of

TABLE 6.10

Employees in Hispanic Serving Institutions Compared to Employees in All Degree-granting Institutions, by Primary Occupation and Race/Ethnicity, 1999 (percent)

Type of Institution & Race/Ethnicity of Staff	Total		Executive/ Administration		Faculty (Instruction & Research)		Instruction & Research Assistants		Nonfaculty professionals		Non-professional staff	
	HSI	All	HSI	All	HSI	All	HSI	All	HSI	All	HSI	All
Total	5.6	100.0	5.0	100.0	7.2	100.0	2.6	100.0	3.7	100.0	5.9	100.0
White	4.2	74.5	3.7	84.5	6.1	81.6	1.9	56.4	2.6	77.1	3.1	68.2
African American	5.7	10.0	5.7	8.8	10.5	5.2	4.0	3.7	3.7	9.1	4.8	17.7
Latina/o	30.3	4.7	35.5	3.1	32.2	3.0	16.1	3.2	25.6	3.8	31.9	7.6
Asian/Pacific Islander	6.3	4.5	8.0	2.1	8.5	4.8	3.3	7.7	3.9	5.0	6.6	3.4

Note: American Indian, other, and nonresident categories are not shown.

Source: NCES, 2002a, 2002b.

selective IHEs becoming more hospitable places for Latina/o students to attend. Certainly, lower cost and easier accessibility are factors that weigh heavily for Latina/o families. More selective IHEs need to find ways to make themselves more transparently affordable (e.g., send clear messages about the ready availability of financial aid and increase the proportion of grant money available so that low-income students do not have to be unduly burdened with debt) and to increase the perception that they welcome Latina/o students. One way to do this is to increase the number of Latina/o faculty and administrators with whom the students come into contact and who present themselves as ready role models and mentors for these students. Borrowing from the findings of Hurtado (1994), these IHEs would also find that if they were to increase the representation of Latina/os in important positions on their campuses, a more hospitable campus climate would ensue.

Even if selective IHEs make bold moves to increase their attractiveness and success with Latina/o students, many, if not most, of these students will continue to choose local, easily accessible, and inexpensive institutions—often community colleges. So these institutions, too, must find ways to ensure that students are retained and that they successfully transfer to four-year colleges and universities where they earn degrees. Although the climate at many of these colleges may be more hospitable than at other larger, more impersonal institutions, evidence suggests that these institutions are not as challenging and that their expectations for students in general may be lower (Clark, 1960). HSIs and other nonselective institutions may need to re-examine their role in the higher education marketplace and in society as a whole. If they are the institutions first sought after by Latina/os, what is their social responsibility to enhance these students' chances of academic success? We think it is a great responsibility and perhaps one that has been taken too lightly. If Latina/os are to make the social and economic contributions to this society that are so urgently needed of them, all institutions of higher education must re-examine the role they can and must play in turning around the dismal educational statistics for this group.

Perhaps the best approach for increasing doctoral student representation is a twofold effort that works to raise achievement levels within HSIs while at the same time holding selective universities accountable for providing greater access for Latina/o students. In addition, selective colleges and state higher education systems should revisit the issue of affirmative action in light of the U.S. Supreme Court *Grutter v. Bollinger* (2003) decision. For example, institutions may want to consider how their internal efforts may better facilitate access and achievement among students of color. It is through this dual approach that institutions that traditionally serve Latina/os and those that have historically excluded our community may become more actively engaged in producing a critical mass of Latina/o scholars in the academy.

While developing a cadre of Latina/os with doctoral degrees is but one step toward creating a healthy cycle of sustainability and economic integration, it is an important effort that has the potential to inspire an entire generation of emerging scholars. These institutional and intellectual leaders will have the ability to help create a more seamless continuum for Latina/os as they navigate through postsecondary and postgraduate education, and the continued charge of redefining the academy for future generations of Latina/o students.

References

Bowen, W., & Bok, D. (1998). *The shape of the river.* New York: Basic Books.

Brewer, D., Eide, E., & Ehrenberg, R. (1996). *Does it pay to attend an elite private college? Cross cohort evidence on the effects of college quality on earnings.* Paper prepared for the National Bureau of Economic Research, Working Paper 5613.

Carnevale, A. P., & Rose, S. J. (2003). *Socioeconomic status, race/ethnicity, and selective college admissions.* Report prepared for the Century Foundation. New York: The Century Foundation.

Chang, M. (2001). The positive educational effects of racial diversity on campus. In G. Orfield, *Diversity challenged* (pp. 175–186). Cambridge, MA: Harvard Education Publishing Group.

Clark, B. R. (1960). The cooling-out function in higher education. *The American Journal of Sociology, 65*(6), 569–576.

Cohn, E. (1979). *The economics of education.* Cambridge, MA: Ballinger Press.

Cole, S., & Barber, E. (2003). *Increasing faculty diversity.* Cambridge, MA: Harvard University Press.

Datcher-Loury, L., & Garman, D. (1995). College selectivity and earnings. *Journal of Labor Economics, 13* (2), 289–308.

Gándara, P. (2005). *Latino achievement: Identifying models that foster success.* Storrs, CT: National Center for Research on the Gifted and Talented, University of Connecticut.

Gándara, P., & Chávez, L. (2003). Putting the cart before the horse: Latinos in higher education. In D. López & A. Jiménez (Eds.), *Latinos and public policy in California: An agenda for opportunity* (pp. 87–120). Berkeley, CA: Institute of Governmental Studies, Regents of the University of California.

Gándara, P., & Maxwell-Jolly, J. (1999). *Priming the pump: Strategies for increasing the achievement of underrepresented undergraduates.* New York: The College Board.

Gándara, P., O'Hara, S., & Gutierréz, D. (2004). The changing shape of aspirations: Peer influence on academic achievement. In M. Gibson, P. Gándara, & J.

Koyama (Eds.), *School connections: U.S. Mexican youth, peers, and school achievement* (pp. 39–62). New York: Teachers College Press.

Geiser, S. (in press). Who goes where? *Journal of Educational Policy.*

Grogger, J., & Trejo, S. (2002). *Falling behind or moving up? The intergenerational progress of Mexican Americans.* San Francisco: Public Policy Institute of California.

Grutter v. Bollinger (2003) (02-241). 288 F.3d 732.

Gurin, P., Dey, E., Hurtado, S., & Gurin, G. (2002). Diversity and higher education: Theory and impact on educational outcomes. *Harvard Educational Review, 72*(3).

Guzman, B. (2001). *The Hispanic population in the United States.* Washington, DC: U.S. Census Bureau.

Hardy, T. (2000, March 27). Fewer community college students make leap to UC, CSU. *Sacramento Bee,* B-1.

Haro, R. (1995). Held to a higher standard: Latino executive selection in higher education. In R. Padilla & R. Chávez (Eds.), *The Leaning Ivory Tower* (pp. 189–207). Albany, NY: State University of New York Press.

Haro, R., & Lara, J. (2003). Latinos and administrative positions in American higher education. In J. Castellanos & L. Jones (Eds.), *The Majority in the minority: Expanding the representation of Latina/o faculty, administrators and students in higher education* (pp. 153–165). Sterling, VA: Stylus Publishing.

Hayes-Bautista, D., Hsu, P., Beltran, R., & Villagomez, J. (1999). *The Latino physician shortage in California, 1999.* Los Angeles: Center for the Study of Latino Health, UCLA.

Hurtado, S. (1994). The institutional climate for talented Latino students. *Research in Higher Education, 35*(1), 21–41.

Jacobi, M. (1991). Mentoring and undergraduate academic success: A literature review. *Review of Educational Research, 61*(4), 505–532.

Kane, T. (1994). College attendance by Blacks since 1970: The role of college cost, family background and the returns to education. *Journal of Political Economy, 102,* 878–911.

Knapp, L., Kelly, J., & Broyles, S. (2002). *Enrollment in postsecondary institutions, fall 2000 and financial statistics fiscal year 2000.* Washington, DC: National Center for Education Statistics, U.S. Department of Education.

Maruyama, G., & Moreno, J. (2000). University faculty views about the value of diversity on campus and in the classroom. In American Council on Education & American Association of University Professors, *Does diversity make a difference? Three research studies on diversity in college classrooms* (pp. 1–95). Washington, DC: American Council on Education.

McCarthy, K., & Burciaga, R. (1985). *Current and future effects of Mexican immigration in California.* Santa Monica, CA: RAND Corp.

Milem, J. (2001). Increasing diversity benefits: How campus climate and teaching methods affect student outcomes. In G. Orfield, *Diversity Challenged* (pp. 233–249). Cambridge, MA: Harvard Education Publishing Group.

National Center for Education Statistics (NCES) (2002a). *Hispanic serving institutions: Statistical trends from 1990–1999.* Washington, DC: U.S. Department of Education.

National Center for Education Statistics (2002b). *Student financing of graduate and first-professional education, 1999–2000.* Washington, DC: U.S. Department of Education.

Olsen, L. (1997). *Made in America: American immigrants in our public schools.* New York: The New Press.

Orfield, G. (2003). *Latino dropouts.* Cambridge, MA: Harvard Civil Rights Project.

Pascarella, E., & Terenzini, P. (1991). *How college affects students.* San Francisco: Jossey-Bass.

Perlmann, J. (1987) A piece of the educational pie: Reflections and new evidence on Black and immigrant schooling since 1880. *Sociology of Education, 60,* 54–61.

Rumbaut, R. (1995). The new Californians: Comparative research findings on the educational progress of immigrant children. In R. Rumbaut & W. Cornelius (Eds.), *California's immigrant children. Theory, research, and implications for educational policy* (pp. 17–70). San Diego, CA: Center for U.S.-Mexican Studies, University of California, San Diego.

Santiago, D., Andrade, S., & Brown, S. (2004). *Latino student success at Hispanic-serving institutions.* Report prepared for the U.S. Department of Education.

Stearns, C., & Watanabe, S. (2002). Hispanic serving institutions: Statistical trends from 1990–1999. *Educational Statistics Quarterly, 4* (4),39–62.

Survey of Earned Doctorates (2000). *Doctorate recipients from United States universities: Summary report 2000.* Report sponsored by the National Science Foundation, National Institutes of Health, U.S. Department of Education, National Endowment for the Humanities, U.S. Department of Agriculture, and National Aeronautics and Space Administration. Chicago: National Opinion Research Center, University of Chicago.

Survey of Earned Doctorates (2002). *Doctorate recipients from United States universities: Summary report 2002.* Report sponsored by the National Science Foundation, National Institutes of Health, U.S. Department of Education, National Endowment for the Humanities, U.S. Department of Agriculture, and National Aeronautics and Space Administration. Chicago: National Opinion Research Center, University of Chicago.

U.S. Census Bureau (2003). *Current population survey, annual social and economic supplement.* Washington, DC: Author.

Tara Watford

Tara Watford is a doctoral student at UCLA's Graduate School of Education and Information Studies. Her research focuses on the experiences of students of color and women in graduate programs, anti-racist and feminist pedagogies, and the politics of institutional change. To uncover perspectives that are often silenced or invalidated by the academy, Ms. Watford is committed to critical feminist policy analysis and participatory action methodological designs.

Martha A. Rivas

Martha A. Rivas is a doctoral student at UCLA's School of Education in the Social Science and Comparative Education division, specializing in race and ethnic studies. She earned her master's degree in race and ethnic studies in education from UCLA (2003) and her bachelor's degree in comparative literature and Chicana/Chicano studies with a minor in education from UCLA (2002). Her current work includes documenting how issues of race, class, gender, age, citizenship status, and inequity affect educational experiences of students of color pursuing higher education in general, but Chicanas and Chicanos specifically. Ms. Rivas is originally from Michoacan, Mexico, but she was raised in Indio, California.

Rebeca Burciaga

Rebeca Burciaga has a B.A. in Latin American and Latina/o studies from the University of California at Santa Cruz and an Ed.M. from the Harvard Graduate School of Education. She is a doctoral candidate in education at UCLA. Her interests include Chicana feminist theories, methodologies, and epistemologies in education. Her dissertation research focuses on the personal and professional aspirations of Chicanas beyond the doctorate and explores racialized gender discrimination, *testimonio* as method, and *nepantla* as theory.

Daniel G. Solorzano

Dr. Daniel Solorzano is a professor in the Education Department in the Graduate School of Education and Information Studies at UCLA. His faculty appointment is in the Division of Social Sciences and Comparative Education; he has a joint appointment as professor in the Chicana and Chicano Studies Department at UCLA. His teaching and research interests include race and gender studies on the educational access, persistence, and graduation of under-represented minority students in the United States. Dr. Solorzano earned his bachelor's and master's degrees from Loyola University in 1972 and 1974, respectively. He received a master's and a doctorate in the sociology of education from the Claremont Graduate School in 1986.

7

LATINAS AND THE DOCTORATE

The "Status" of Attainment and Experiences from the Margin

Tara Watford
Martha A. Rivas
Rebeca Burciaga
Daniel G. Solorzano

As the U.S. Latina/o[1] population experiences tremendous growth[2], the educational attainment of Latina/os continues to lag far behind the national average. Traditional research has tended to describe the disparities Latinas/os face in schooling collectively, with little attention given to the distinctive ways in which gender dynamics affect Latinas' educational trajectories.[3] While Latina/os face many of the same challenges, studies are needed to uncover the sexist structures and social expectations that create additional barriers for Latinas' educational attainment.

To fully understand the disparities Latinas face in U.S. schools, their trajectories throughout the educational pipeline (K–12–higher education) must be examined. Figure 7.1 compares the educational pipeline for females in the five major racial/ethnic groups in the United States.

[1] In this chapter, Latina/o is defined as females and males of Latin American ancestry living in the United States. It should be noted that the political, historical, and social dimensions of these identity labels are not addressed in this chapter. For a more in-depth discussion of identity terminology see Martinez, 1998.

[2] Latinas/os comprise the largest and fastest-growing ethnic minority group in the United States, representing 12.5% of the population, with an estimated growth to 18% by 2025 (U.S. Census, 2000).

[3] Although the ways in which gender expectations and dynamics specifically affect Latino educational trajectories is not the topic of this chapter, research is also needed in this area.

FIGURE 7.1
Latinas' Attainment Rates at Each Stage of the U.S. Female Educational Pipeline

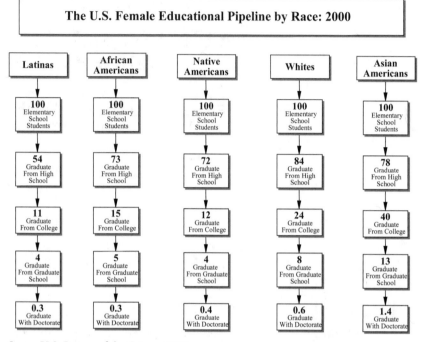

The U.S. Female Educational Pipeline by Race: 2000

Latinas	African Americans	Native Americans	Whites	Asian Americans
100 Elementary School Students	**100** Elementary School Students	**100** Elementary School Students	**100** Elementary School Students	**100** Elementary School Students
54 Graduate From High School	**73** Graduate From High School	**72** Graduate From High School	**84** Graduate From High School	**78** Graduate From High School
11 Graduate From College	**15** Graduate From College	**12** Graduate From College	**24** Graduate From College	**40** Graduate From College
4 Graduate From Graduate School	**5** Graduate From Graduate School	**4** Graduate From Graduate School	**8** Graduate From Graduate School	**13** Graduate From Graduate School
0.3 Graduate With Doctorate	**0.3** Graduate With Doctorate	**0.4** Graduate With Doctorate	**0.6** Graduate With Doctorate	**1.4** Graduate With Doctorate

Source: U.S. Bureau of the Census, 2000.

Beginning with 100 elementary students, Figure 7.1 reveals the number of females in each racial/ethnic group that move through the pipeline to achieve various levels of educational attainment. For example, among the 100 Latinas who begin elementary school, a little more than half will graduate from high school, and only 11 will receive a college degree. Eventually, less than one of the original 100 Latinas will complete a doctoral degree. A critical finding in Figure 7.1 is the fact that Latinas have the lowest levels of attainment at every stage of the educational pipeline. Consequently, if current population and education trends continue, a large constituent of the U.S. population will be severely undereducated.

In this chapter we focus on Latinas' last stop in the educational pipeline—the doctorate. Few studies focus solely on the experiences of Latinas in graduate education (Gándara, 1982, 1995, 1996), and even fewer specifically examine Latinas in doctoral programs (Achor & Morales, 1990; Flores, 1988). Building on these studies, the intention of this chapter is to present an overview of the status of Latina doctorate education. This overview will meet two objectives. The first is to provide baseline information on female doctorate production from 1990 to 2000 in U.S. universities. Within this objective, we provide a racial/ethnic analysis of female doctorate production in the United States. Additionally, we compare doctorate production of females and males within racial/ethnic groups. Our second objective is to highlight Latina doctoral students' experiences of marginality that production data do not address. To meet this objective we examine the different themes of marginality found within the literature on Latina doctoral education. In the end, by presenting production records and a review of literature, it is our aim to provide a heuristic overview of the status of attainment for Latina doctorates.

Methodology

Doctorate Production

For our doctorate records analysis, the National Opinion Research Center's (NORC, 1990–2000) Survey of Earned Doctorates (SED) data are used to provide a national overview of female doctorate production in U.S. universities. The SED is a yearly survey completed by all doctoral recipients in the United States. Data are collected in the seven broad fields of physical science, engineering, life science, social science, humanities, education, and professional. In addition to general demographic data, the SED generates such information as recipients' baccalaureate and master's degree origins, fields of study, financial support, time to degree, and postdoctoral plans.

For the purposes of our analysis, we examine overall doctorate production in the 11-year period of 1990 to 2000. Although the SED data set for this period includes more than 440,000 cases, our study includes only those that self-identify in the survey as U.S. citizens or permanent U.S. residents. The exclusion of foreign doctoral recipients reduces the data set for our study to 325,573 cases (72.6% of overall doctorates earned). Of these doctorates, 148,337 (45.6%) were earned by women during the 11-year period. In our analysis, we compare female doctorate production among the five major racial/ethnic groups in the United States (Latinas, African Americans, Native Americans, Whites, and Asian Americans)[4]. To provide more in-depth infor-

[4] SED racial categories are listed as (1) American Indian or Alaskan Native, (2) Asian, 3) African American, (4) Puerto Rican, (5) Mexican American/Chicano, (6) Other Hispanic, and (7) White. For our analysis that compares the five major racial/ethnic groups in the United States, we use the term, Native American, to represent those who self-identified in the SED as American Indian or Alaska Native; the term, Asian American, to represent those who checked the categories of Asian as well as Native Hawaiian or Pacific Islanders; and Latina/o for those who identified as Mexican American/Chicano, Puerto Rican, Cuban, or Other Hispanic.

mation on Latina origin doctorates, we also present data on three sub-groups[5]: Chicanas[6], Puerto Ricans, and Other Latinas. In addition to our comparison of female doctorate production across racial/ethnic lines, we include a gender analysis within each of the five major racial/ethnic groups and Latina/o subgroups. Both the racial/ethnic and gender analyses are generated using the combined data from all seven broad fields identified by the SED. In addition to providing a broad overview of Latina doctorate production, we highlight gender disparities among the Latina/o subgroups within the seven broad fields. Thus, our study serves as a broad overview of Latina doctorate production and does not reflect racial/ethnic or gender disparities within the specific SED-defined fine fields.

Doctoral Parity

To determine if parity is occurring in doctorate production, the number of doctorates produced must be compared to a baseline figure. Using 1990 and 2000 U.S. Census data[7], we employ the 30- to 34-year-old age cohort (hereafter, age cohort) population as a comparative baseline (see Berryman, 1983; Leggon, 1987, Solorzano, 1995). In her work on science production, Berryman (1983) argues that this age cohort represents the median age at which a doctorate is awarded (i.e., age 32). Therefore, this age cohort is a baseline that allows doctoral recipients to be compared with an age-relevant population. Although age cohort data create a broad figure and therefore might underestimate doctorate production, they do provide a helpful comparative base of population representation (see Solorzano, 1995).

In our analysis, U.S. Census 30- to 34-year-old population figures for the years 1990 and 2000 are averaged to generate decade-wide age cohort percentages for each of the racial/ethnic groups we examine. To determine parity, the median doctorate production is found for the years 1990–2000 and compared to decade-wide age cohort averages for each racial/ethnic group. If these decade-wide figures are equal, parity occurs. If a group's age cohort figures are higher than their earned doctorate percentages, then they are under-represented within doctorate production. Similarly, over-represen-

---

[5] The Latina/o subgroups within the SED are listed as (1) Mexican American, (2) Puerto Rican, (3) Cuban, (4) Hispanic, and (5) Other Hispanic. The selection of Cuban as a Hispanic subgroup has only been available since 2001. Thus, for our study, we use the term, Other Latina, to represent the combined Cuban, Hispanic, and Other Hispanic SED data.

[6] The term, Chicana, describes women of Mexican ancestry living in the United States. It should be noted that the political, historical, and social dimensions of these identity labels are not addressed in this chapter.

[7] It should be noted that the population within the age cohort includes those who may not be U.S. citizens or permanent residents.

tation occurs when age cohort figures are lower than doctoral recipient percentages. Finally, we use age cohort data to determine parity in our gender comparison within each racial/ethnic group analysis.

Literature Review Analysis

In addition to our analysis of doctorate records, we review the literature to highlight important themes of marginality that emerge from studies on Latinas' experiences in pursuing doctoral education.[8] In our review, we share specific examples of Latina doctoral students' experiences cited in the literature. In this sense, one voice provides a powerful representation of re-occurring narratives found in multiple studies. Because very little research focuses specifically on Latinas in doctoral programs, our review incorporates several sources that include the experiences of both Latina and Latino students. We also review a few studies that examine graduate schooling in general, including M.A. and J.D. programs. Studies that examine the aggregated experiences of graduate students of color are not included in our review. While we recognize that such work is valuable and contributes greatly to our understanding of racial equity in higher education, it is our intention to highlight issues particular to Latina doctoral students.

Doctorate Production in U.S. Universities

Overall Female Doctorate Production

From 1990 to 2000, women accounted for 45.6% of doctoral recipients, receiving 148,337 doctorates. In Table 7.1, the percentages of women earning doctorates within the five major racial/ethnic groups in the United States are presented during the 11-year period, 1990–2000. This table demonstrates that the number of women of color receiving doctorates is increasing slowly. For example, Latinas increased from 3.5% of female doctoral recipients in 1990 to 5.0% in 2000. Similarly, African American, Native American, and Asian American women experienced gains in doctorates earned during the 11-year period.

However, to determine if equitable representation occurs, female doctorate production for each racial/ethnic group must be compared to its average age cohort population baseline.[9] Parity occurs when the average percentage

---

[8] The majority of research we review examines Latina students enrolled in doctoral programs in the humanities, social sciences, and education.

[9] In 1990, the overall U.S. female population consisted of: 8.9% Latinas, 12.7% African Americans, .7% Native Americans, 74.2% Whites, and 3.3% Asian Americans; in 2000, the U.S. female population included: 14.5% Latinas, 13.1% African Americans, .8% Native Americans, 64.8% Whites, and 4.9% Asian Americans (see U.S. Census Data, 1990 & 2000).

TABLE 7.1
Percent of Female-earned Doctorates, by Group, 1990–2000

Percent of Female Earned Doctorates in the United States

Year	Latina	African American	Native American	White	Asian American
1990	3.5	5.1	0.4	86.5	4.1
1991	3.6	5.1	0.5	85.5	4.8
1992	3.4	5.3	0.6	85.2	5.3
1993	3.9	5.4	0.5	83.2	6.7
1994	3.6	5.6	0.5	80.4	9.5
1995	3.9	5.9	0.5	79.4	9.8
1996	3.8	5.7	0.6	79.9	8.9
1997	4.4	6.3	0.7	79.5	7.7
1998	4.8	7.3	0.6	78.5	7.6
1999	4.9	7.5	0.8	78.9	6.8
2000	5.0	7.6	0.6	78.2	7.3
1990–2000 Doctorate Production Average	4.1	6.1	0.6	81.1	7.2
1990–2000 Age Cohort Average	11.6	12.9	0.8	69.7	4.1

Note: Doctorates shown in data are U.S. citizens or permanent U.S. residents. Census data includes those who may not be U.S. citizens or permanent U.S. residents.

Sources: NORC, 1990–2000; U.S. Bureau of the Census, 1992; U.S. Bureau of the Census, 2000.

of doctorate production for each racial/ethnic group is equal to its average age cohort percentage. In comparing these data, one sees that Latina and African American women doctorates were significantly under-represented in female doctorate production for the 11-year period. For example, the 1990–2000 average doctorate production for Latinas was 4.1%, whereas their age cohort for the same period was 11.6%. Therefore, although Latina doctorates progressively increased within the 11-year period, their representation would need to grow almost 300% to reach parity in doctorate production. Similarly, the number of African American women earning doctorates would need to approximately double for parity to occur. In decade-wide comparisons, Native American women doctorates are only slightly under-represented. However, it should be noted that Native American women earning doctorates is an extremely small base. In contrast, White women doctorates are considerably over-represented in doctorate production for the entire 1990–2000 period. And Asian American women doctorates reach parity in 1990 (4.1%) and for all subsequent years are over-represented in doctorate production.

To fully comprehend the under-representation of Latinas, we now turn to an examination of the doctorate production of Latina subgroups.

Latina Subgroup Doctorate Production

Within the Latina subgroups, Table 7.2 demonstrates that a very gradual increase in doctorate production occurs for Chicanas, Puerto Rican women, and Other Latinas from 1990 to 2000. It should be noted, however, that the doctoral gains for these groups are relative to a very small starting base.

Moreover, the average doctorate production percentages are almost

TABLE 7.2
Percent of Female-earned Doctorates, by Latina Subgroup, 1990–2000

Year	Chicana	Puerto Rican	Other Latina*
1990	0.8	0.8	1.9
1991	0.8	1.1	1.7
1992	0.9	0.8	1.7
1993	1.1	1.0	1.8
1994	1.0	1.0	1.6
1995	0.9	1.0	2.0
1996	0.9	1.0	1.9
1997	1.3	1.3	1.9
1998	1.4	1.2	2.2
1999	1.2	1.4	2.2
2000	1.6	1.2	2.2
1990–2000 Doctorate Production Average	1.1	1.1	1.9
1990–2000 Age Cohort Average	6.7	1.3	3.5

*Other Latina category includes recipients that self-identified as Cuban, Hispanic, or Other Hispanic within the SED survey.

Note: Doctorates shown in data are U.S. citizens or permanent U.S. residents.

Sources: NORC, 1990–2000; U.S. Bureau of the Census, 1992; U.S. Bureau of the Census, 2000.

equivalent across the subgroups for the 11-year period. While the Latina subgroups' percentages of doctorate production are similar, when compared to their age cohort averages, various patterns of under-representation appear.

As the largest population of the Latina subgroups, Chicanas have an age cohort average for 1990–2000[10] of 6.7%, yet their average doctoral production is 1.1%. Thus, to achieve parity, Chicana doctorate production would need to increase by over 600%. In contrast to the consistent under-representation of Chicana doctorates, in decade-wide comparisons, Puerto Rican women doctorates are only slightly under-represented in doctoral production. It is important to note that our data include doctorate production records from universities on the island of Puerto Rico. Further analysis should be conducted to compare island and U.S. mainland doctorate production. Similar to Chicanas, women earning doctorates within the Other Latina subgroup also remain under-represented throughout the 11-year period. For parity to be achieved for this subgroup, Other Latina doctorate production would need to increase by almost 200%.

In general, all of the Latina subgroups are under-represented within doctorate production, with Chicanas experiencing the largest disparity in representation. Furthermore, even though all three subgroups show an increase in doctorate production, these gains are small, especially in comparison to the population growth of Latinas in the United States from 1990 to 2000.

Gender Analysis within Racial/Ethnic Groups

After uncovering the racial/ethnic disparities that occur among those females obtaining doctorates, we examine the gender differences that existed within racial/ethnic groups between 1990 and 2000. Table 7.3 presents the average female and male age cohort percentages as well as the doctorate production percentages within each of the five major racial/ethnic groups in the United States. For equitable gender representation to occur, the percentages of female and male doctorates should match their respective average age cohort percentages.

Table 7.3 reveals that Latina and African American females generally earned more doctorates throughout 1990–2000 than did males within their respective racial/ethnic groups. For example, Latina doctorates only fell below their average age cohort percentage (47.4%) in 1990 (46.6%) and 1992 (45.3%). In contrast, Latinos were slightly under-represented in doctorate

---

[10] In 1990, the overall U.S. female population consisted of: 5.2% Chicanas, 1.1%, Puerto Rican women, and 2.7% Other Latinas. In comparison, in 2000, Chicanas accounted for 8.3%, Puerto Rican women 1.5%, and Other Latinas 4.3% of the U.S. female population.

TABLE 7.3
Gender Comparison of Earned Doctorates within Racial/Ethnic Groups, 1990–2000

Gender Comparison of Earned Doctorates within Racial/Ethnic Groups (Percent)

Age Cohort	Latina/o		African American		Native American		White		Asian American	
	Female	*Male*	*Female*	*Male*	*Female*	*Male*	*Female*	*Male*	*Female*	*Male*
Average 1990–2000	47.4	52.6	53.2	46.8	51.1	48.9	49.9	50.1	51.7	48.3
Doctorate Production	*Female*	*Male*	*Female*	*Male*	*Female*	*Male*	*Female*	*Male*	*Female*	*Male*
1990	46.6	53.4	53.9	46.1	38.7	61.3	42.8	57.2	34.3	65.7
1991	48.7	51.3	51.9	48.1	46.7	53.3	43.8	56.2	34.5	65.5
1992	45.3	54.7	54.3	45.7	47.6	52.4	44.0	56.0	35.7	64.3
1993	50.5	49.5	56.4	43.6	51.6	48.4	44.4	55.6	34.9	65.1
1994	47.8	52.2	57.4	42.6	45.0	55.0	45.3	54.7	30.0	70.0
1995	49.6	50.4	57.7	42.3	44.0	56.0	45.7	54.3	34.9	65.1
1996	47.4	52.6	55.7	44.3	53.3	46.7	46.5	53.5	37.1	62.9
1997	49.0	51.0	57.9	42.1	52.1	47.9	46.1	53.9	38.9	61.1
1998	53.0	47.0	61.1	38.9	46.9	53.1	47.0	53.0	41.4	58.6
1999	54.2	45.8	61.4	38.6	52.9	47.1	47.2	52.8	42.5	57.5
2000	54.7	45.3	63.5	36.5	55.7	44.3	48.6	51.4	45.7	54.3

Note: The doctoral cohort age is 30–34 years old. Doctorates shown in data are U.S. citizens or permanent U.S. residents. Census data used for age cohort figures include those who may not be U.S. citizens or permanent U.S. residents

Sources: NORC, 1990–2000; U.S. Bureau of the Census, 1992; U.S. Bureau of the Census, 2000.

production from 1994 to 2000. Likewise, African American female doctorates only fell below their average age cohort percentage (53.2%) in 1991 (51.9%). However, African American men were under-represented in doctorate production throughout the 11-year period. Native American doctorate production reflected an inconsistent pattern of gender representation. Here, Native American women doctorates fell below their age cohort percentage six years (1990–92, 1994–95, 1998), and Native American men were slightly under-represented for five years (1993, 1996–97, 1999–2000) of the 11-year period. In comparison, White women earned fewer doctorates than did White men throughout 1990–2000, but came closer to parity within the last several years of the period. Similarly, Asian American women made gains toward parity, but even at their peak in 2000 (45.7%) they were still somewhat less than their average age cohort (51.7%). Finally, when compared to their average age cohort, White and Asian American men are over-represented in doctorate production throughout 1990–2000.

Gender Analysis within Latina/o Subgroups

When one examines the gender differences in doctorate production within each of the Latina/o subgroups, inconsistent patterns of representation emerge. In Table 7.4, the 1990–2000 average age cohort percentages for females and males are compared to doctoral recipient percentages within each Latina/o subgroup.

For Chicanas, doctorate production fell below their age cohort (45.7%) in five (1990–92, 1995–96) of the 11 years. Thus, parity was either achieved or Chicanas were slightly over-represented within Chicana/o doctorate production for the remaining years within the period (1993–94, 1997–2000). Puerto Rican women, in comparison to their age cohort (51.6%) were slightly under-represented only three years in the period (1990, 1992, 1996). Additionally, within the Other Latina/o category, Latinas were slightly under-represented in doctorate production in comparison to their age cohort (47.8%) for five years (1991–92, 1994, 1996–97) in the 11-year period. Therefore, for Chicanos, Puerto Rican men, and Other Latinos there seems to emerge a pattern of under-representation near the end of the 11-year period (after 1997). However, because these disparities are slight, it will take investigation of doctorate production into the next decade to see if this gender pattern remains consistent.

In general, gender disparities within overall doctorate production for the different Latina/o subgroups are extremely small. However, subgroup gender differences do occur when comparing female- and male-earned doctorates

TABLE 7.4
Gender Comparison of Earned Doctorates within Latina/o Subgroups, 1990–2000

Gender Comparison of Earned Doctorates within Latina/o Subgroups (Percent)						
	Chicana/o		*Puerto Rican*		*Other Latina/o*	
Age Cohort Average	*Female*	*Male*	*Female*	*Male*	*Female*	*Male*
1990–2000	45.7	54.3	51.6	48.4	47.8	52.2
Doctorate Production	*Female*	*Male*	*Female*	*Male*	*Female*	*Male*
1990	40.8	59.2	49.2	50.8	48.3	51.7
1991	42.9	57.1	58.8	41.2	46.4	53.6
1992	45.4	54.6	46.2	53.8	44.8	55.2
1993	48.1	51.9	52.6	47.4	50.8	49.2
1994	46.2	53.8	54.7	45.3	45.2	54.8
1995	44.4	55.6	52.8	47.2	50.9	49.1
1996	45.6	54.4	50.3	49.7	46.8	53.2
1997	47.4	52.6	57.4	42.6	45.4	54.6
1998	51.1	48.9	58.3	41.7	51.6	48.4
1999	48.1	51.9	60.9	39.1	53.9	46.1
2000	54.3	45.7	55.2	44.8	54.6	45.4

Note: The doctoral cohort age is 30–34 years old. Doctorates shown in data are U.S. citizens or permanent U.S. residents. Census data used for age cohort figures include those who may not be U.S. citizens or permanent U.S. residents.

Sources: NORC, 1990–2000; U.S. Census Bureau of the Census, 1992; U.S. Bureau of the Census, 2000.

within the seven broad fields. Table 7.5 demonstrates the percentage of earned doctorates for Latina/o subgroups within each of the seven broad fields.

Within the Chicana/o subgroup, both women and men earn the majority of doctorates in education and social sciences. For Chicanas, these two fields tend to dominate their production, accounting for 60.2% of their earned doctorates. In comparison, Chicanos earn 42.6% of their doctorates in education and social sciences. The greatest gender disparities between Chicanas and Chicanos exist in physical science and engineering. When combining Chicana/o doctorate production in physical science and engineering, Chicanos are almost four times more likely to earn doctorates than are Chicanas. Similar to Chicanas, Puerto Rican women earn the majority of doctorates (59.1%) in education and social sciences, whereas, Puerto Rican

TABLE 7.5
Percentage of Latina/o Subgroup Earned Doctorates by Broad Field, 1990–2000

Broad Field of Earned Doctorate	Chicana/o		Puerto Rican		Other Latina/o	
	Female	*Male*	*Female*	*Male*	*Female*	*Male*
Physical Sciences	4.1	13.7	5.5	15.4	6.1	15.7
Engineering	1.7	9.6	2.0	10.1	3.3	14.2
Life Sciences	15.4	15.4	14.7	17.9	17.2	19.0
Social Sciences	24.9	19.6	26.8	18.4	26.1	18.4
Humanities	14.5	14.0	14.1	14.3	21.0	17.4
Education	35.3	23.0	32.3	18.4	22.0	11.1
Professional	4.2	4.7	4.7	5.6	4.3	4.3
All Fields	100.1	100.0	100.1	100.1	100.0	100.1

Note: Doctorates shown in data are U.S. citizens or permanent U.S. residents.
Source: NORC, 1990–2000.

men earn the majority of doctorates (54.7%) in education, life science, and social sciences. Yet, again, significant gender disparities occur in physical science and engineering for Puerto Ricans. In comparison, the majority of earned doctorates (69.1%) for Other Latinas are across the social sciences, education, and humanities. Other Latinos' degrees are distributed more evenly across the seven broad fields, whereas the majority of earned doctorates (54.8%) are in life sciences, social sciences, and humanities. In physical science and engineering, significant gender disparities occur again as Other Latinos are more than three times more likely to earn doctorates in these fields than are Other Latinas. Finally, it is also important to note that women and men from all three Latina/o subgroups are poorly represented within the professional disciplines.

Overall, when using a racial and gender comparison analysis, several important patterns emerge regarding Latina doctorate production from 1990 to 2000. First, Latinas made small but steady gains in earning doctorates during the 11-year period. Second, although gains have been made, Latina doctorates are the most under-represented within female doctoral recipients from the five major racial/ethnic groups in the United States. Third, within Latina subgroups, Chicanas experience the greatest disparities in doctorate production. Fourth, within Latina/o doctorate production, gender differences between the number of Latinas and Latinos earning doctorates tend to cluster within the education/social sciences and physical sciences/engineering.

Latina Graduate Students' Experiences of Marginality: A Literature Review

Without considering daily experiences in graduate school, doctorate production records provide only a glimpse into doctoral education for Latinas. Thus, to better understand Latinas' experiences during their enrollment in doctoral programs, we now discuss the theme of marginality that emerges from the literature review. This theme brings to light the various challenges Latina graduate students confront as well as the resistance strategies they use to defy barriers and succeed.

Within our study, marginality is defined as a complex and contentious status of subordination. The process of marginality occurs as dominant structures, practices, and/or beliefs are used to push women of color out of the mainstream into the margins of society (see Collins, 1990; hooks, 1990). For Latina doctoral students, experiences of marginality arise as they confront multiple, intersecting, and ever-shifting power dynamics, including (but not limited to) race, gender, and class, on college campuses.[11]

In our review, several forms of marginality emerge within Latinas' experiences in graduate school. These forms include overt marginality, covert marginality, and resistance from the margins. Overt marginality occurs as one experiences actions that intend to discriminate in ways that are public, conscious, and direct. In comparison, covert marginality occurs through the experience of actions that discriminate through a more subtle and indirect manner. It is important to note that the processes of overt and covert marginality can manifest via individual acts, institutional structures, and/or societal norms and beliefs. In contrast to these two forms, as Latinas struggle to challenge and change their subordinated status, they use strategies of resistance from the margin. In this sense, the experience of living in the margin nurtures ways of being and communicating that are counterhegemonic. Therefore, resistance to marginality offers "the possibility of [a] radical perspective from which to see and create, to imagine alternatives, [and] new worlds" (hooks, 1990, p. 150).

---

[11] In addition to the dynamics of race, gender, and class, other forms of domination that may contribute to Latinas' marginalization include ethnicity, language, immigration or citizenship status, sexuality, religion, age, or nationality.

Overt Marginality

Multiple studies document how Latinas experience overt forms of marginality such as facing blatant acts of racism and sexist attitudes as graduate students. These overt forms include Latinas overhearing or being targeted by racial/ethnic/sexist jokes and stereotypes in academic environments, having their merit questioned, or told they do not belong in academia (Cuádraz & Pierce, 1994; Flores, 1988; González et al., 2001; Nieves-Squires, 1991; Solorzano, 1998; Williamson, 1994). For example, in Madeline Williamson's study (1994), a Chicana doctoral student is sexually harassed by a professor, after which he tells her that she will not graduate from the department. Other examples included verbal abuse from professors. For instance, a Chicana student recounts how a professor made jokes about being Chicana in the classroom (Williamson, 1994). She also recalls how this professor insisted on calling on her to respond whenever issues regarding people of color arose in the classroom, despite the fact that she had reminded the teacher that she was capable of commenting on topics beyond "minority issues" (Williamson, 1994). Although universities generally have policies against such blatant discrimination, research demonstrates that Latinas continue to experience these forms of overt marginality within higher education (Nieves-Squires, 1991).

Covert Marginality

With policies that prohibit forms of overt marginality, and public opinion that generally admonishes it as socially unacceptable, marginality for Latinas in graduate programs tends to occur in more covert manners.[12] Covert forms of marginality are often perpetuated in doctoral education via stereotypes and may be sanctioned within classrooms, curricula, and overall program policies. These covert forms are manifested in ways that are not explicitly discriminatory; instead, they are masked or explained in "neutral" ways that society finds more acceptable.

Covert marginality often stems from racial/ethnic stereotypes. A common example of a covert form of marginality is the accusation by colleagues and professors that Latinas and Chicanas gain their entrance into graduate programs as "affirmative action charity cases" (Achor & Morales, 1990, p. 278; see also Cuádraz & Pierce, 1994; Nieves-Squires, 1991; Williamson, 1994). Such perceptions contain racist overtones, especially considering recent research that reveals "that most Students of Color are admitted [to uni-

---

[12] For more discussion of how racism has shifted from more overt to covert policies and behaviors in the United States since the 1960s, see Bonilla-Silva (2003).

versities] based on the same criteria and standards as majority students" (Solorzano & Villalpando, 1998, p. 216). Similarly, a Chicana doctoral student in Madeline Williamson's research (1994) describes being categorized as a foreign student and told by faculty and staff that they were amazed she did not speak with an accent. Furthermore, in a study of Chicana/o Ford Foundation Minority Fellows, Daniel Solorzano (1998) documents similar patterns of covert marginalization that he calls racial and gender microaggressions. Racial and gender microaggressions are forms of systemic, everyday racism and sexism used to keep those at the racial and gender margins in their place (adapted from Solorzano, 1998). An example Solorzano (1998) highlights as a gender microaggression occurs as a Chicana participant describes her experience after she has a baby. She states, "My advisor, other department faculty, and some of my fellow students felt that I wasn't serious about graduate school or my professional career since I brought this 'burden' on myself" (Solorzano, 1998, p. 130).

In the classroom, Latina graduate students report various experiences of covert marginality. Many students recount how faculty and colleagues prompt them to speak on behalf of all communities of color when discussions regarding race and ethnicity arise. Yet, in discussions not centered on race and ethnicity, Latina students' input is neither encouraged nor affirmed (González et al., 2001; Nieves-Squires, 1991; Solorzano & Yosso, 2001; Williamson, 1994). Having one's presence rendered invisible in classrooms except in rare moments when discussions of race occur creates a sense of tokenism (Nieves-Squires, 1991). The paradox of experiencing both invisibility and tokenism is exacerbated as Latinas often find that they are the only persons of color, or Latina/os, in their graduate program. Furthermore, during classroom dialogue and curricula, Latinas frequently confront common misperceptions that race is constructed through notions of a Black-White binary (Solorzano, 1998; Solorzano & Yosso, 2001). One common way this binary is reproduced is in course curriculum that presents race only through the historical relationships between African Americans and Whites, thus, ignoring how race is constructed through issues such as immigration, language, and culture for Latina/os (Solorzano & Yosso, 2001).

Covert marginalization also occurs through mentorship relationships and academic structures that evaluate scholarly work. For instance, Latina graduate students describe being dissuaded from pursuing research interests on communities of color (Alvarez, 2001; González et al., 2002). Doctoral students report being told that such research is "too ethnic," lacks prestige within academia, and, thus, will hinder their future employment opportunities (Cuádraz & Pierce, 1994; González et al., 2002; Nieves-Squires, 1991).

Overall, experiences of overt and covert marginality create additional weight for Latina students who already face the immense pressures of graduate school requirements. Their under-representation and marginalization in graduate school create an environment where few are able to share with others who would understand their fears and challenges (Alvarez, 2001; Cantú, 2001; González et al., 2001; Williamson, 1994). Scholars note that many Latinas experience "survivor's guilt" because they survived and succeeded within the educational pipeline while friends and family members have not (González et al., 2001; Solorzano & Yosso, 2001). Such guilt, combined with other experiences of marginality, may cause Latinas to doubt their skills and question whether their pursuit of graduate education is worth the effort (González et al., 2001; Nieves-Squires, 1991; Solorzano, 1998; Solorzano & Yosso, 2001). Moreover, the toll of carrying this load creates stress, emotional burden, and self-doubt for Latinas, all of which can prolong or deter completion of students' graduate school careers (Cuádraz & Pierce, 1994; González et al., 2001).

Resistance from the Margins

The absence of policies to support Latinas in doctoral programs has resulted in self-reliance and, ultimately, the development of resistance strategies[13] to help them navigate the rocky terrain of graduate school. These strategies are grounded in Latina doctoral students' drive to succeed and their determination to challenge hierarchical power dynamics. In this sense, Latinas and Chicanas use knowledge gained from their position within the margin to challenge structures that negate their existence in the academy.[14]

Scholars report various resistance strategies used by Latina and Chicana graduate students (Gándara, 1982, 1995, 1996; González et al., 2002; Solorzano, 1993, 1998; Solorzano & Yosso, 2001). Such strategies enable Latinas to develop what Sylvia Alva (1995) calls "academic invulnerability" or a determination to succeed in spite of facing what may seem like insurmountable barriers. Gloria Cuádraz and Jennifer Pierce (1994) define their persistence to complete their doctoral program in sociology at UC-Berkeley as "endurance labor." The authors note that their determination to endure the racist, classist, and sexist assaults that they experienced in their Ph.D. program was fueled by an emotional desire to beat the system that worked to alienate them. Similarly, scholars note Latina students' willingness "to fight back"

[13] For a more in-depth discussion of resistance, see Solorzano & Delgado Bernal, 2001.
[14] For a discussion of how the experiences of marginality provide epistemological insight for resisting dominant structures, see Delgado Bernal, 1998, and hooks, 1990.

and succeed despite their feelings of being "out of place" within the academy (González et al., 2001; Williamson, 1994). Scholars (Solorzano & Yosso, 2001) also assert that an important component in Chicanas' will to resist is their anger at campus environments that render them "invisible." They posit, "For Chicanas within the university setting, anger is necessary and good. It is often our anger that fuels our spirit, gives voice and direction to silence, and provides the energy to go on" (p. 483).

Resistance strategies also help promote Latinas' academic success in graduate school. In their study of 100 Chicana doctorates, Shirley Achor and Aida Morales (1990) argue that an important factor in their participants' success is the ability to develop what they call "resistance with accommodation." The authors contend that Chicanas were able to succeed in their programs by constructing ways to challenge and reject dominant discourses while simultaneously embracing institutional means of academic attainment, such as working hard and completing quality scholarly work.

Denise Segura (2003) states that one way Chicanas have resisted within the walls of the academy is through the type of intellectual work they produce. Engagement in work that challenges Eurocentric and masculine paradigms is one expression of Chicanas' participation in a "community of praxis" that helps broaden their respective disciplines while simultaneously contributing to better understandings of their communities of origin (Segura, 2003). In addition, González et al. (2002) emphasize the importance of Latina/os participating in scholarly work that connects to issues of empowerment for their communities of origin. Latina/o scholars' narratives describe how involvement within their communities of origin is what tended to ground and retain many of them in academia (González et al., 2002; López, 2001; Revilla, 2003).

Overall, developing resistance from their place at the margin helps to position Latina doctoral students as outsiders within the academy[15] (Collins, 1990). This status allows Latina doctoral students to challenge (and transform) institutions that claim to value diversity, but do little to create or maintain environments that are welcoming for students of color.

Conclusion

Researching the status of attainment for Latina doctoral recipients remains complex. When combining our analysis of doctorate production records and

[15] For a more in-depth discussion of how Women of Color academics experience the outsider-within phenomena, see Collins, 1990.

overview of Latinas' experiences in graduate school, several layers of important findings arise. On the surface, it is important to note that the number of Latina doctoral recipients increased over the 1990–2000 period; however, they remain the most under-represented in doctorate production among their female peers. Looking closer at Latinas' under-representation, we note that, of the three Latina subgroups, Chicanas overwhelmingly experience the greatest disparities in doctorate production for the 11-year period. Furthermore, gender disparities between Latina and Latino doctorate recipients for 1990–2000 are insignificant within overall doctorate production, but they do occur between the seven broad fields. These disparities between Latina and Latino doctorate awards tend to occur most acutely in education, social sciences, physical science, and engineering.

While their numbers are increasing on college campuses, Latina students continue to experience multiple forms of marginality in doctoral programs. As universities adopt policies prohibiting discrimination, the process of marginalization tends to occur more in subtle, covert forms that work to cultivate a hostile campus climate for Latina doctoral students. For Latinas, this climate adds an additional burden on top of the already demanding load of graduate education. Here, we should note, the absence of national data on attrition rates for doctoral students means that we are unable to fully understand the effects of overt and covert marginality for Latinas who are unable to complete the doctoral process. For those who do succeed, research highlights how Latinas have used resistance strategies to combat overt and covert marginality on their route to the doctorate. Thus, research that documents the ways in which Latinas challenge dominant discourses and norms of graduate education is extremely important for us to understand the day-to-day realties of doctorate production.

While the data reveal that Latinas are making small gains in doctorate production, a closer examination of the numbers signals problems that can only be uncovered fully through in-depth qualitative research. Therefore, research is needed to examine the environments of disciplines and specific programs that nurture (and impede) promotion of Latina doctorates. For instance, what are the campus climate differences for Latinas in physical science and engineering programs in comparison to education and social sciences? And how do Latinas' experiences in these climates differ from Latinos'? Such inquiry would serve as an important reminder that the goal of building a critical mass of Latina doctoral students requires far more effort than just increasing enrollment percentages.

Considering the current complexities involved in understanding the experiences of Latina doctoral students, what can be learned to aid the next generation of Latinas in doctoral programs? We believe that our overview points to several areas in which future scholarship on Latina doctoral education should be explored further. First, an area of research that requires more attention is Latinas' experiences of covert marginality within their doctoral education. Aside from Latinas' overlapping experiences of race, class, and gender, scholars must examine issues such as nationality, language, sexuality, citizenship status, and religion, all of which merit attention if we are to address the multiple factors contributing to the under-representation of Latinas in doctoral programs. Second, there is very little known about the experiences of Latinas with families in doctoral programs. This is especially critical given that the median age of doctorate attainment coincides with childbearing years. Research that examines these issues and how they influence recruitment and retention of Latina doctoral students is especially timely. Finally, much of the literature we review addresses coping mechanisms or resistance strategies used by Latina doctoral students. The current research suggests that Latinas develop strategies that adapt to institutional norms of progress while at the same time challenging racist and sexist practices. Thus, an important research question is, how does the development of such strategies affect students' emotional health and influence their career plans within the academy?

Our overview of Latina doctoral education reveals macro and micro inequities that scholars, policy makers, and universities must address to better understand the current context of higher education. The commitment to such research and policy is extremely important for us to promote more equitable conditions in which future Latina doctoral students will thrive. Our next generation of scholars depends on our level of commitment.

References

Achor, S., & Morales, A. (1990). Chicanas holding doctorates: Social reproduction and cultural ecological approaches. *Anthropology and Education Quarterly, 21,* 269–287.

Alva, S. (1995). Academic invulnerability among Mexican American students: The importance of protective resources and appraisals. In A. Padilla (Ed.), *Hispanic psychology: Critical issues in theory and research* (pp. 288–302). Thousand Oaks, CA: Sage.

Alvarez, C. (2001). Snapshots from my daze in school. In Latina Feminist Group (Ed.). *Telling to live: Latina feminist testimonios* (pp. 177–184). Durham, NC: Duke University Press.

Berryman, S. (1983). *Who will do science? Minority and female attainment of science and mathematics degrees: Trends and causes.* New York: Rockefeller Foundation.

Bonilla-Silva, E. (2003). *Racism without racists: Color-blind racism and the persistence of racial inequality in the United States.* New York: Rowman & Littlefield.

Cantú, N. (2001). Getting there *cuando no hay camino.* In The Latina Feminist Group, *Telling to live: Latina feminist testimonios* (pp. 60–68). Durham, NC: Duke University Press.

Collins, P. (1990). *Black feminist thought: Knowledge, consciousness, and the politics of empowerment.* New York: Routledge.

Cuádraz, G., & Pierce, J. (1994). From scholarship girls to scholarship women: Surviving the contradictions of class and race in academe. *Explorations in Ethnic Studies: Race, Class, and Gender, 17*(1), 21–44.

Delgado Bernal, D. (1998). Using a Chicana feminist epistemology in educational research. *Harvard Educational Review, 68*(4) 555–582.

Flores, J. (1988). Chicana doctoral students: Another look at educational equity. In H. S. Garcia & R. Chavez (Eds.), *Ethnolinguistic issues in education* (pp. 90–99). Lubbock, TX: College of Education, Texas Tech University.

Gándara, P. (1982). Passing through the eye of the needle: High-achieving Chicanas. *Hispanic Journal of Behavioral Sciences, 4*(2), 167–179,

Gándara, P. (1995). *Over the ivy walls: The educational mobility of low-income Chicanos.* New York: State University of New York Press.

Gándara, P. (1996). Chicanas in higher education: Implications for policy. In A. Hurtado, R. Figueroa, & E. García (Eds.), *Strategic interventions in education: Expanding the Latina/Latino pipeline* (pp. 167–213). Santa Cruz, CA: University of California, Santa Cruz, Latino Eligibility Study.

González, K., Marín, P., Figueroa, M., Moreno, J., & Navia, C. (2002). Inside doctoral education in America: Voices of Latinas/os in pursuit of the Ph.D. *Journal of College Student Development, 43*(4), 540–557.

González, K., Marín, P., Peréz, L., Figueroa, M., Moreno, J., & Navia, C. (2001). Understanding the nature and context of Latina/o doctoral student experiences. *Journal of College Student Development, 42*(6), 563–580.

hooks, b. (1990). Choosing the margin as a space of radical openness. In b. hooks, *Yearning: Race, gender, and cultural politics* (pp. 145–153). Boston: South End Press.

Leggon, C. (1987). Minority underrepresentation in science and engineering graduate education and careers: A critique. In L. Dix (Ed.). *Minorities: Their underrepresentation and career differentials in science and engineering.* (pp. 151–157). Washington, DC: National Academy Press.

López, I. (2001). Reflection and rebirth: The evolving life of a Latina academic. In The Latina Feminist Group, *Telling to live: Latina feminist testimonios* (pp. 69–85). Durham, NC: Duke University Press.

Martinez, E. (1998). *De colores means all of us: Latina views for a multi-colored century.* Cambridge, MA: South End Press.

National Opinion Research Center (NORC) (1990–2000). *Survey of earned doctorates* (Unpublished raw data). Chicago, IL: National Science Foundation, National Institutes of Health, U.S. Department of Education, National Endowment for the Humanities, U.S. Department of Agriculture, and National Aeronautics and Space Administration.

Nieves-Squires, S. (1991). *Hispanic women: Making their presence on campus less tenuous.* Washington, DC: Association of American Colleges, Project on the Status and Education of Women.

Revilla, A. (2003). *Inmensa fe en la victoria*: Social justice through education. *Frontiers, 24*(3), 282–301,

Segura, D. (2003). Navigating between two worlds: The labyrinth of Chicana intellectual production in the academy. *Journal of Black Studies, 34*(1), 28–51.

Solorzano, D. (1993). *The career paths of Chicana and Chicano doctorates: A study of Ford Foundation Minority Fellows in California.* Berkeley, CA: California Policy Seminar.

Solorzano, D. (1995). The baccalaureate origins of Chicana and Chicano doctorates in the social sciences. *Hispanic Journal of Behavioral Sciences, 17*(1), 3–32.

Solorzano, D. (1998). Critical race theory, race and gender microaggressions, and the experience of Chicana and Chicano scholars. *Qualitative Studies in Education, 11*(1), 121–136.

Solorzano, D. & Delgado Bernal, D. (2001). Examining transformational resistance through a critical race and LatCrit theory framework: Chicana and Chicano students in an urban context. *Urban Education, 36,* 308–342.

Solorzano, D., & Villalpando, O. (1998). Critical race theory, marginality, and the experience of students of color in higher education. In C. Torres & T. Mitchell (Eds.), *Sociology of education: Emerging perspectives* (pp. 211–224). New York: State University of New York Press, Albany.

Solorzano, D., & Yosso, T. (2001). Critical race and LatCrit theory and method: Counter-storytelling Chicana and Chicano Graduate School Experiences. *Qualitative Studies in Education, 14*(4), 471–495.

U.S. Bureau of the Census. (1992). 1990 Census of population: *General population characteristics, United States summary* (1990 CP-1-1). Washington, DC: U.S. Government Printing Office.

U.S. Bureau of Census. (2000). *American Fact Finder*, U.S. Census 2000, Summary File 4 (SF4) Retrieved on June 5, 2004 from http://www.census.gov/.

Williamson, M. (1994, April). *Strengthening the seamless web: Fostering minority doctoral student success with Mexican American and American Indian doctoral students in their doctoral programs.* Paper presented at the meeting of the American Educational Research Association, New Orleans, LA.

Vasti Torres

Dr. Vasti Torres is associate professor of higher education and student affairs administration in the W.W. Wright School of Education at Indiana University. Before going to Indiana University in 2003, she was a faculty member at The George Washington University Graduate School of Education and Human Development in Washington, D.C. Dr. Torres teaches classes in student affairs administration and related topics. Before joining the faculty, she had 16 years' experience in administrative positions, most recently serving as associate vice provost and dean for enrollment and student services at Portland State University in Portland, Oregon. Dr. Torres' research focuses on how the ethnic identity of Latina/o students influences their college experience. She has written numerous articles on Latina/o college students, survey development and use, and other diversity issues. Dr. Torres is the principal investigator for a grant investigating Latina/o students' choice to stay in college. She is active in several student affairs and higher education associations, and she has been honored as an Emerging Scholar and a Diamond Honoree by the American College Personnel Association, as program associate for the National Center for Policy in Higher Education, and as a SACSA Scholar by the Southern Association of College Student Affairs. Dr. Torres has a Ph.D. in counseling and student affairs administration from The University of Georgia.

8

BRIDGING TWO WORLDS
Academia and Latina/o Identity

Vasti Torres

In the end . . . he must choose between the two worlds: if he intends to succeed as a student, he must, literally and figuratively, separate himself from his family . . . (Rodriguez, 1975, p. 17)

Unfortunately, the sentiment Richard Rodriguez experienced in the 1970s continues to be expressed by Latina/o doctoral students (Gonzalez et al., 2001; Ibarra, 2001; Rendón, 1992). The achievement of a doctoral degree brings social and intellectual status, but the journey is wrought with difficult cultural choices that can affect an individual's identity. An integral aspect of doctoral work is the socialization of the student into the academic program. Academic departments have both formal and informal activities that define how individuals are socialized into the institution (Tierney, 1997). This socialization process is particularly visible to doctoral students, who are aware that the goal of doctoral work is to create an identity as scholars in the discipline, while having little regard for the salience of a person's previous identity. Ibarra referred to this process as the metamorphosis of the individual "from one ethnic culture into another" (2001, p. 89). The doctoral experience in most disciplines repeatedly requires the individual to leave behind his or her previous identity and assume the characteristics of a scholar in the chosen field or risk being marginalized within the department. This sentiment is often articulated as choosing between two worlds.

The personal choices individuals make about how they define themselves and function within a given environment is at the crux of what identity development theories attempt to explain. These choices become more complicated when an individual is part of an ethnic or racial minority group and must simultaneously negotiate the expectations of both mainstream and native cultures. The resolution of the conflicting negotiation process between two cultures is how an individual creates and understands his or her own ethnic or racial identity (Cross, 1991; Helms, 1994; Phinney, 1993; Torres, 1999). Marcia (2002) referred to this process as reformulation of identity as one resolves the disequilibrium involved in a particular developmental era. Although the disequilibrium Rodriguez describes seems dichotomous, in fact it is not. Instead, Latina/o doctoral students must face complex decisions to determine their own orientation and balance the expectations of academia and their Latina/o identity. These choices in the disequilibrium between two worlds can be even more difficult during doctoral study because of the environmental pressures and lack of control graduate students feel during their training.

Much of the research on Latina/os in doctoral education focuses on describing experiences, barriers, or environmental pressures. Little research focuses on the developmental processes Latina/o graduate students encounter that affect their identity development and, more specifically, their ethnic identity. This chapter takes existing research on the doctoral experience of Latina/os and infers how these experiences can be interpreted within the framework of Latina/o identity development. A short review is presented on identity development research, including the concept of detouring from the linear progression of development. This review is followed by a discussion of operational definitions of bicultural orientation and the four conditions that describe how Latina/o college students negotiate their identity as well as the potential application of these models to the developmental process of doctoral students. These conditions are illustrated using the issues consistently identified in the literature as major influences on the Latina/o doctoral experience. As mentioned above, little research considers the developmental process doctoral students encounter, and for this reason the chapter ends with future research recommendations.

Identity Development Maps Do Not Always Have a Straight Route

Early developmental theorists, such as Erickson, Loevinger, and Kohlberg, considered development occurring in an orderly manner, with stages building on each other. Although this orderly development may occur in some individuals, more recent theorists view development as a complex process that considers the use of suppositions from multiple stages to create a desired solution (Chickering & Reisser, 1993; King, 1990). In contrast, some scholars changed from stages to statuses to highlight the nature of change while not focusing on orderly progression through the developmental process (Helms, 1994). These changes in developmental theories reflect a clearer understanding of the process that occurs when identity changes as a result of experiences or time. Beginning a doctoral program is a situation that promotes change in identity; this experience can be a substantial challenge for Latina/o students, and their response to change can divert them or cause them to revisit previous statuses of their identity. This developmental recycling can explain some of the experiences described in the literature on Latina/o doctoral students and provides the impetus to consider ethnic identity frameworks developed with college students.

The following models focus on the notion of choosing between two cultures to create bicultural identity. These studies validate the existence of a bicultural orientation in which individuals must make choices between two distinct cultures.

Bicultural Orientation

Biculturalism represents the potential ending status that results from the choices made by an individual navigating two distinct cultures. Managing two distinct cultures is a phenomenon for Latina/o students who maintain a strong ethnic identity when they enter a primarily Anglo-oriented world. These individuals need to make choices about the two cultures, and, out of these choices, their cultural orientation is defined.

Researchers have used various operational definitions to describe this notion of bicultural orientation. For example, Ramirez (1983) identified four bicultural/multicultural identities among clinical patients and used these identity categories to explain culturally based behaviors among the patients. Féliz-Ortiz de la Garza, Newcomb, and Myers (1995) considered familiarity with culture and cultural identity to determine their four cultural identities. More recently, Torres (1999) validated the Bicultural Orientation Model (BOM) from data on the choices Latina/o college students make between the majority Anglo culture and their cultural origin.

The BOM was created using measures of acculturation (Marín et al., 1987) to represent the majority Anglo culture and ethnic identity (Phinney, 1992) to represent the Latina/o culture of origin. There are four categories of bicultural orientation in the BOM. In particular, a student with a high level of ethnic identity and acculturation would be Bicultural Oriented, whereas, a student with a high level of ethnic identity and low level of acculturation would be Latina/o Oriented. A student with a low level of ethnic identity and a high level of acculturation would be Anglo Oriented. Finally, a student with low levels of both ethnic identity and acculturation would be Marginally Oriented. Although the operational definitions of these bicultural models differ, each endorses the notion that individuals from Latina/o cultures make choices between two different worlds and in turn create their own identity based on those decisions. "A simplistic definition would involve a synthesis of two cultures and languages out of which a third arises that was previously not present" (Torres, 1999, p. 288).

The two worlds Rodriguez (1975) and Rendón (1992) have described in the past are defined in the present day as "wrestling with the reality of living on the margins of two worlds: their [doctoral students'] communities of origin, and their new academic environment" (Gonzalez et al., 2001, p. 574). The conflicts between these two worlds prompt questions that include self-worth, ability to adapt, and future career aspirations. Cultural conflict occurs when educational values clash with cultural values. Latina/o students experience cultural conflict when they are encouraged to advance in their education, but are also pressured to spend more time with family or are questioned about assuming new roles outside of the family (Torres, 2004). Students are prompted to act differently depending on which culture they have contact with, thus switching behaviors (i.e., code switching) to survive in both worlds. The margins of these worlds are created when Latina/o doctoral students feel the need to downplay their ethnicity to absorb the academic values their faculty exhibit or because faculty perceive "ethnic values and perspectives as injecting bias into the learning-knowledge process within the discipline" (Ibarra, 2001, p. 91).

These experiences illustrate the informal and perhaps unintentional pressures doctoral students experience about the choices they must make in doctoral programs. Previous research illustrates that college students and, more often, college graduates, have higher levels of acculturation (Sánchez & Fernández, 1993; Torres, 1999), which *might* provide students with the coping mechanisms to manage the conflicts between these two worlds. Yet, research indicates that previous coping mechanisms and level of acculturation are not always sufficient in the elite environment of doctoral studies (Gonzalez et al., 2001; Ibarra, 2001).

One of the reasons previous coping mechanisms may not be effective is that a bicultural orientation also supports high levels of ethnic identity. While Latina/o college students who attend predominantly White institutions (PWIs) have significantly higher levels of acculturation than do students in areas where Latina/os are a critical mass, they maintain similar levels of ethnic identity (Torres, Winston, & Cooper, 2003). Hence, fitting into a

PWI environment does not necessitate losing a sense of pride in one's ethnicity.

Doctoral students learn "to play the game" even when they disagree with the institutional values the faculty represent (Gonzalez et al., 2002). Latina/o students' experiences in PWIs may challenge doctoral students to rethink their Bicultural Orientations toward a more Anglo-Oriented value system, thereby becoming more consistent with their new academic environment. This challenge can further affect the ethnic identity formation process at the doctoral level because of students' desire to be mentored and guided by faculty. The need for guidance prompts Latina/o doctoral students to believe they need to transform themselves into the scholar their faculty members want or leave; this need to transform can be even more intense for students in elite research programs (Ibarra, 2001). The lack of Latina/o faculty, combined with the influential nature of doctoral work, creates power issues that perpetuate a majority White cultural stronghold on doctoral education. Ultimately, the changes and adaptations necessary to survive the doctoral experience vary according to how Latina/o graduate students situate their identities on entering the graduate program.

Environmental Factors

The less dissonance students experience between their home environment and the new academic environment, the more likely they will adapt to new expectations (Torres & DeSawal, 2004). Unfortunately, most graduate programs are located in predominantly White institutions, so students who come from areas where their culture is represented and respected are likely to experience dissonance when they enter graduate programs. As a result of moving between their home and academic environments, students experience culture shock that can cause feelings of doubt and influence their self-esteem (Rendón, 1992). Additional environmental dissonance can occur in the classroom when the curriculum is inconsistent with these students' cultural values. The continuous dissonance and need to make alternative interpretations in the classroom can be exhausting for Latina/o doctoral students.

A qualitative study was conducted recently to illustrate the issues of dissonance, cultural conflict, and lack of support for ethnic issues. Using an autoethnographic technique and dialogical research methods, a group of doctoral students presented a collective understanding of their doctoral experiences (González et al., 2002). This group described the academic environment in their doctoral programs as "conservative, restrictive, and racist" (p.

545), and this negative environment required them to expend energy address-ing the restrictive ideologies and traditions both inside and outside of the classroom setting. Part of this restrictive and racist environment stems from inattention to ethnic-related research topics. In particular, lack of faculty in-terest in exploring ethnic-related research was considered to be racist in na-ture as opposed to being grounded in constructive critique (González et al. 2002; Ibarra, 2001).

Additional environmental issues were related to tokenism, where unin-formed public views about affirmative action prompted feelings of marginali-zation. As a result, doctoral students exposed to these types of cultural aggressions may question their individual perceptions about their ability to participate and complete a doctoral degree. These negative cultural aggres-sions can create inner conflict for Latina/o doctoral students that are unwel-come aspects of the academic discussion within their departments. Students experiencing marginalizing tensions may not feel they can or should discuss these tensions with their advisor, who is likely to be White. They might want to seek support from other Latina/o doctoral students or faculty; however, students attending PWIs may not have this option. Thus, faculty should be aware of the potential isolation Latina/o doctoral students can experience in the presence of substantial environmental dissonance.

The level of dissonance felt between the environment individuals come from and the academic environment they enter influences how they situate themselves as Latina/os. Doctoral students' negotiation of dissonance can af-fect their response to faculty, student peers, and their own views of their discipline. Depending on the level of dissonance, students can respond by: (1) being cautious and not taking any risks in the environment, (2) integrat-ing themselves within the new environment and taking their previous values for granted, or (3) exploring the environment and expanding their definitions of diversity within the academic community (Torres, 2003; Torres & De-Sawal, 2004). The possible outcomes of how students situate their Latina/o identity depends to a large extent on their dissonance level and individual choices. For example, some students rely on e-mail to quickly and instanta-neously maintain contact with others who understand their perspectives and cultural values. Further, culturally based, discipline-oriented listservs also provide information and resources to students who lack the needed support on campus. Although these communication methods are not always desir-able, they allow students to create their culturally congruent environment regardless of location.

Familial Influences

Within Latina/o culture, the importance of family and the desire to please family members is central. The dimensions of this practice are often associated with generational and acculturation status (Torres, 2004). U.S.-born students who have more acculturated parents are likely to fuse White and native cultures, creating a more prominent bicultural identity. In contrast, students with less-acculturated parents are more likely to struggle with this balance. Similarly, the few students who have acculturated parents who are also familiar with graduate education in the United States (which can be different from Latina/o countries) are more likely to intermingle the two worlds they experience. When looking at the doctoral student experiences of Latina/os, familial support is important but is difficult as well.

The high proportion of first-generation Latina/os college students contributes to the issues doctoral students feel about familial support. Although family members support their adult children's aspirations, they seldom understand the experiences and struggles these students encounter. For example, some students are conflicted in that they can no longer turn to their parents for advice about their educational concerns. Their internal conflict stems from knowing "that those who knew them and loved them the most were unable to offer advice to them during one of the most challenging times in their lives" (González et al., 2001, p. 569).

The majority of Latina/o doctoral students encounter cultural conflict and a level of disequilibrium that can prompt them to question their identity and reformulated self-perception. For example, students' guilt is often associated with educational advancement or living a privileged life while recognizing the hardships and sacrifices their families and previous generations endured (Comas-Díaz, 1997). In addition, there is guilt associated with a sense of obligation to assist family. Another source of guilt and stress for students is spending the majority of their time in academic departments and conducting independent work. As a result, they might feel isolated from campus and the real world. Unfortunately, doctoral students "learn that new values are rewarded here: specialization, fragmentation, attention to minute detail, and accuracy" (p.90)—not the real-world happenings where culture and identity matter (Ibarra, 2001). At some point, while maintaining family connections, doctoral students have to resolve the dissonance to redirect personal energy to academic challenges and avoid risking their career aspirations by not completing the doctoral degree. The changes and dissonance involved in doctoral education can cause students to question their status as minority students and thus their self-perceptions as Latina/os.

Self-Perception of Personal Status within the Academic Environment

The ability to recognize racist behavior and not internalize negative messages is critical to situating an individual's Latina/o identity (Torres, Howard-Hamilton, & Cooper, 2003), particularly because Latina/o and Black doctoral students are more likely to experience and have heightened feelings of racial discrimination. These students of color are also more likely to receive lower doctoral grade point averages (Nettles, 1990). The cultural aggressions, combined with the feelings of tokenism, promote an environment where social status is questioned and dysfunctional behaviors are seldom addressed (Comas-Díaz, 1997).

Experiencing a culturally exclusive environment can prompt students to question their role in the academy and doubt their perceptions of their environment. An advisor or faculty mentor is critical in combating potentially negative reactions. In a study of graduate students, the relationship with faculty and mentors was considered to be the single most important aspect in determining satisfaction with the graduate program (Nettles, 1990). Faculty advisors and mentors are key to research opportunities in and guidance through the academic field. Without these relationships, Latina/o doctoral students can feel marginalized by and isolated from departmental culture.

In some instances the process of developing a mentoring relationship with a faculty advisor requires that students gain the right to participate in the faculty member's research or writing. At times, participation in the research team often means that a student "must bend to the faculty's definitions of what constitutes hard work and success" (Ibarra, 2001, p. 87). Bending to expectations ultimately can mean that students lessen or lose their ethnic identification to please the faculty mentor. Latina/o doctoral students might fear pointing out that this process is discriminatory; respect is an important cultural value in Latina/o culture (Delgado-Romero et al., 2003). Confronting such an injustice can also raise feelings of putting one's academic future at jeopardy. Again, these stressors affect how Latina/o students perceive their status and how they manage their identity to survive the doctoral process.

The most severe potential outcome of this self-perception condition is that Latina/o doctoral students can experience stereotype threat (Steele & Aronson, 1995) and believe negative messages about their ethnicity. Stereotype threat occurs when a negative stereotype about a social group, like women or Latina/os, is internalized and believed to be true. Students who experience stereotype threat can perceive their ethnicity as a negative aspect of being a doctoral student. For example, faculty members who believe that ethnicity biases research could create negative feelings about one's ethnicity during doctoral work. Students who must expend energy to work through these negative images and incongruent messages are vulnerable to stereotype threat. Working through this level of dissonance requires positive role models and alternative explanations for the negative messages received (Torres & Baxter Magolda, 2004). For example, if a doctoral student works with a faculty advisor who believes ethnicity creates bias in research, the student would need an equally powerful alternative message to counteract that belief. Alternative messages that reinforce positive images of Latina/o ethnicity are likely to come from Latina/o faculty advisors. Unfortunately, the lack of Latina/o mentors in academic departments, combined with family members' limited understanding, creates a critical identity issue.

Implications for Higher Education and Future Research

It is not the intent of this chapter or of the supporting literature to say that doctoral work and maintaining a Latina/o identity are incompatible. However, this interpretation does need to be addressed. As part of the emphasis on increasing the number of Latina/o doctoral degree recipients, one must recognize the conflicts as well as the mechanisms available to manage the conflicts. The present expectation within the literature, and one that is often endorsed by faculty, is that doctoral students will adapt and acculturate to the academic culture. Is this expectation, however, realistic and necessary?

There is significant criticism of doctoral education, and several reforms have been suggested (Boyer, 1990; Tierney, 1997). These reforms have not substantially changed the perpetuation of academia or the impact of the socialization process for doctoral students. The notion that students should be socialized into static norms seems peculiar when deconstructed, yet this custom continues to occur in doctoral programs. With these realities in mind, the major changes needed in doctoral education are associated with the socialization process of students into the disciplines. If higher education is truly a learning organization, then it should strive to expand the definition of organization to fit diverse students rather than seek out students who fit the organization (Tierney, 1997).

Tierney and Bensimon (1996) advocate reforming higher education into organizations in which two-way interaction rather than one-way socialization occurs. For example, a bidirectional process would include individuals influencing the organizations while organizations influence the individual. A bidirectional learning organization would be contrary to the present mode that requires an individual either to assume the values of the organization or leave the organization. Changing how socialization into different disciplines occurs would allow Latina/o doctoral students to develop and maintain healthy ethnic identities while growing as scholars.

The individualistic nature of doctoral work can be misunderstood within Latina/o cultures. Although some research must be undertaken individually, there is room to explore possibilities for collaborative research and writing opportunities for students. For example, the use of oral histories and personal narratives in the research design allows for expressions of culture. Other examples include alternative lenses within the research process that would acknowledge and appreciate the worldview of those who do not espouse White cultural values. In considering the individualistic nature of doctoral work, programs must recognize the importance of family instead of creating barriers for students who have family responsibilities. The expectation that students must be full time to be good doctoral students may not be realistic for Latina/os with family responsibilities. Expanding the context and manner in which doctoral education is delivered is important to expanding the diversity of doctoral candidates.

The compilation of research and application of identity frameworks presented make a compelling case for research on the developmental aspects of the doctoral experience for Latina/o students. To increase the pool of Latina/o doctoral graduates, the impact of the doctoral process on the individual must be understood. The level of identity reconfiguration for Latina/o doctoral students' experiences merits examination. In addition, it is assumed that doctoral students have minimal familial influences, but this assumption is inconsistent with existing research on Latina/o cultural values and behaviors. While more research is needed to understand familial influence, to ignore its impact could alienate Latina/o doctoral students. By understanding these developmental processes, institutions can better prepare Latina/o students for graduate studies through orientation programs that address both the technical and personal aspects of graduate education. Preparing doctoral students for intellectual *and* personal challenges can help them to understand the potential dissonance that can occur, while also letting them know that support is available. These ideas require that faculty advisors are open to this developmental process and are informed about Latina/o doctoral student issues.

Additional research is needed to investigate how racism, tokenism, and prejudice influence various developmental aspects of Latina/o doctoral students. These are difficult constructs to consider, but they clearly affect the doctoral experience. The impact of mentors on the doctoral process is also an important and related area of research. Specifically, what are the benefits of having Latina/o mentors? How would Latina/o mentors promote greater gains than non-Latina/o mentors for Latina/o doctoral students?

Examining the experiences of Latina/o doctoral students through an identity framework can dismantle the development issues for mental health and student affairs practitioners as well as faculty who are invested in helping Latina/o students adjust to the doctoral experience. The conditions presented throughout the chapter lend insight into how Latina/o students situate their identity and the factors that affect both their identity and doctoral work. Understanding how students situate their identity is critical for a successful doctoral experience. Although inferences made in this chapter are plausible, further research on Latina/o doctoral students and subsequent models and theories are needed. Without these data and this knowledge about student development, the under-representation of Latina/o doctoral graduates can be perpetuated.

The evidence provided in this chapter indicates that doctoral students can be more focused on their academic department rather than the broader university community. The importance of socialization into a discipline and faculty advisor mentorship makes an academic program's environment the most influential source of support for Latina/o doctoral students (Williams, 2000). If an academic program is serious about attracting Latina/o doctoral students, faculty in the discipline must expand their definitions of what it takes to fit in and attempt to understand that culture does not exist in a vacuum—it is intricately integrated into the identity of Latina/o doctoral students.

References

Boyer, E. L. (1990). *Scholarship reconsidered: Priorities of the professoriate*. Princeton, NJ: Carnegie Foundation for the Advancement of Teaching.

Chickering, A. W., & Reisser, L. (1993). *Education and identity* (2nd ed.). San Francisco: Jossey-Bass.

Comas-Díaz, L. (1997). Mental health needs of Latinos with professional status. In J. G. García & M. C. Zea (Eds.), *Psychological interventions and research with Latino populations* (pp. 142–165). Needham Heights, MA: Allyn & Bacon.

Cross, W. E. (1991). *Shades of Black*. Philadelphia: Temple University Press.

Delgado-Romero, E. A., Flores, L. Y., Gloria, A. M., Arredondo, P., & Castellanos, J. (2003). Developmental career challenges for Latina/o faculty in higher education. In J. Castellanos & L. Jones (Eds.), *The majority in the minority: Expanding* the representation of Latina/o faculty, administrators and students in higher education* (pp. 257–283). Sterling, VA: Stylus.

Féliz-Ortiz de la Garza, M., Newcomb, M. D., & Myers, H. F. (1995). A Multidimensional measure of cultural identity for Latino and Latina adolescents. In A.M. Padilla (Ed.), *Hispanic psychology critical issues in theory and research* (pp. 26–42). Thousand Oaks, CA: Sage Publications.

González, K. P., Marín, P., with Figueroa, M. A., Moreno, J. F., & Navia, C. N. (2002). Inside doctoral education in America: Voices of Latina/os in pursuit of the Ph.D. *Journal of College Student Development, 43,* 540–557.

González, K. P., Marín, P., Xóchiti Pérez, L., Figueroa, M. A., Moreno, J. F., & Navia, C. N. (2001). Understanding the nature and context of Latina/o doctoral student experiences. *Journal of College Student Development, 42,* 563–580.

Helms, J. E. (1994). The conceptualization of racial identity and other racial constructs. In E. J. Trickett, R. J. Watts, & D. Birman (Eds.), *Human diversity: Perspectives on people in context* (pp. 285–311). San Francisco: Jossey-Bass.

Ibarra, R. A. (2001). *Beyond affirmative action reframing the context of higher education.* Madison, WI: The University of Wisconsin Press.

King, P. M. (1990) Assessing development from a cognitive developmental perspective. In D. G. Creamer (Ed.), *College student development: Theory and practice for the 1990s* (pp. 81–98). Alexandria, VA: American College Personnel Association.

Marcia, J. (2002). Identity and psychosocial development in adulthood. *Identity: An International Journal of Theory and Research, 2*(1), 7–28.

Marín, G., Sabogal, F., Marín, B. V., Otero-Sabogal, R., & Perez-Stable, E. J. (1987). Development of a short acculturation scale for Hispanics. *Hispanic Journal of Behavioral Sciences, 9*(2), 183–205.

Nettles, M. T. (1990). Success in doctoral programs: Experiences of minority and white students. *American Journal of Education, 98*(4), 494–522.

Phinney, J. S. (1992). The multigroup ethnic identity measure. *Journal of Adolescent Research, 7*(2), 156–176.

Phinney, J. S. (1993). A three-stage model of ethnic identity development in adolescents. In M. E. Bernal & G. P. Knight (Eds.), *Ethnic identity formation and transmission among Hispanics and other minorities,* (pp. 61–79). Albany, NY: State University of New York Press.

Ramírez, M. III (1983). *Psychology of the Americas mestizos perspective on personality and mental health.* New York: Pergamon Press.

Rendón, L. I. (1992). From the barrio to the academy: Revelations of a Mexican American "scholarship girl." In L. S. Zwerling & H. B. London (Eds.), *First-generation students: Confronting the cultural issues* (pp. 55–64). San Francisco: Jossey-Bass.

Rodriguez, R. (1975) Going home again: The new American scholarship boy. *American Scholar, 44,* 15–28.

Sánchez, J. L., & Fernández, D. M. (1993). Acculturative stress among Hispanics: A bidimensional model of ethnic identification. *Journal of Applied Social Psychology, 23*(8), 654–688.

Steele, C. M., & Aronson, J. (1995). Stereotype threat and the intellectual test per-formance of African Americans. *Journal of Personality and Social Psychology, 69*(5), 797–811.

Tierney, W. G. (1997). Organizational socialization in higher education. *The Journal of Higher Education, 68*, 1–16.

Tierney, W. G., & Bensimon, E. M. (1996). *Promotion and tenure: Community and socialization in academe.* Albany, NY: State University of New York Press.

Torres, V. (1999). Validation of a bicultural orientation model for Hispanic College students. *Journal of College Student Development, 40*, 285–298.

Torres, V. (2003). Influences on ethnic identity development of Latino college stu-dents in the first two years of college. *Journal of College Student Development, 44*, 532–547.

Torres, V. (2004). Familial influences on the identity development of Latino first year students. *Journal of College Student Development, 45*(4), 457–469.

Torres, V., & Baxter Magolda, M. (2004). Reconstructing Latino identity: The in-fluence of cognitive development on the ethnic identity process of Latino stu-dents. *Journal of College Student Development, 45*(3), 333–347.

Torres, V., & DeSawal, D. (2004, March). *The role environment plays in retaining Latino students at urban universities.* Paper presented at the annual meeting of the National Association of Student Personnel Administrators, Denver, CO.

Torres, V., Howard-Hamilton, M. F., & Cooper, D. L. (2003). Identity develop-ment of diverse populations: Implications for teaching and administration in higher education. *ASHE-ERIC Higher Education Report, 29*(6). San Francisco: Jossey-Bass.

Torres, V., Winston, R. B., Jr., & Cooper, D. L. (2003). The effects of geographic location, institutional type, and stress on Hispanic students' cultural orientation. *NASPA Journal, 40*(2), Article 10. Retrieved on July 22, 2004, from http://publi-cations.naspa.org/naspajournal/vol40/iss2/art10.

Williams, K. B. (2000). Perceptions of social support in doctoral programs among minority students. *Psychological Reports, 86*, 1003–1010.

Aída Hurtado

Aída Hurtado is professor of psychology at the University of California, Santa Cruz. She received her B.A. in psychology and sociology from the University of Texas, Pan American, and her M.A. and Ph.D. in social psychology from the University of Michigan. Her main areas of expertise are in the study of social identity (including ethnic identity), Latino educational issues, and feminist theory. Her books include *The color of privilege: Three blasphemies on race and feminism* (University of Michigan Press, 1996); *Voicing feminisms: Young Chicanas speak out on sexuality and identity* (New York University Press, 2003, Honorable mention for the 2003 Myers Outstanding Book Awards given by The Gustavus Myers Center for the Study of Bigotry and Human Rights in North America); *Chicana feminisms: A critical reader* (co-edited with Gabriela Arredondo, Norma Klahn, Olga Nájera-Ramirez, and Patricia Zavella, Duke University Press, 2003). Her latest book is *Chicana/o Identity in a changing U.S. society. Quien soy? Quienes somos?* (co-authored with Patricia Gurin, The University of Arizona Press, 2004).

Mrinal Sinha

Mrinal Sinha is a doctoral student in the social psychology program at the University of California, Santa Cruz. His research interests include racialized masculinities, feminist theory, and social identity. Mr. Sinha's dissertation examines gender consciousness with men of color and the implications thereof for building coalitions with other oppressed groups. He received his B.A. in social and behavioral sciences from California State University, Monterey Bay, and his M.A. from UC Santa Cruz.

9

DIFFERENCES AND SIMILARITIES

Latina and Latino Doctoral Students
Navigating the Gender Divide

Aída Hurtado
Mrinal Sinha

A recent study by the American Association of University Women Educational Foundation made national headlines as it documented that Hispanic[1] women and men had a higher high school dropout rate (30%) than Blacks (11.1% for males and 12.9% for females) and Whites (9.0% for males and 8.2% for females). These findings captured the attention of media as the results of this study appeared in numerous newspapers around the United States (reports appeared in the following newspapers: *The Monitor* [McAllen, Texas], *USA Today, Houston Chronicle, Santa Cruz Sentinel, Los Angeles Times, New York Times*). The newspapers attributed the high dropout rates of Latinas (not Latinos) to "cultural values."

> Schools must do more to recognize cultural values that saddle Hispanic girls with family responsibilities, such as caring for younger siblings after school, that take away from educational endeavors . . . "Many Latinas face pressure about going to college from boyfriends and fiancés who expect their girlfriends or future wives not to be 'too educated' and from peers who accuse them of 'acting white' when they attempt to become better educated or spend time on academics," the study said. (Gamboa, 2001, p. 1A)

[1] For purposes of clarity, we use the ethnic labels used in the reports we cite. Otherwise we use the ethnic label, Latina/os, which refers to individuals with ancestry in Latin America.

149

The reports of this study failed to mention or recognize in their analysis of Latinas' "school failure" the poverty conditions in which many families live, the inferior school facilities, the overcrowded classrooms, the inferior teaching in many minority schools, and the constant threat of violence many poor students have to negotiate daily. By relying on a cultural explanation for Latinas' school failure, the reports fell prey to what anthropologist Virginia Dominguez (1992) calls "culturalism," that is, the over-reliance on "cultural" factors in attributing causation and ignoring powerful structural influences like poverty on Latinas' behavior. Furthermore, because the cultural explanation the report uses to interpret its results cannot be applied to Latino men, newspaper reports simply ignore the fact that Latinos are also not graduating from high school and deserve an equal analysis as Latinas. In addition, early marriage for young women indeed can be detrimental to educational achievement, but the same holds true for young men.

This report also inadvertently blames Latino parents for their children's school failure and does not distinguish among different parenting styles within poor, Latino communities. In rushing to judgment and blaming Latino culture as transmitted by parents, it does not allow for the examination of educational success even among this country's poorest Latino residents. In short, reports of this study fail to acknowledge similarities and differences in gender, diversity in the enactment of Latino culture, and structural factors such as poverty that may influence the schooling outcome of poor Latino students. The only viable solution for educational success for students is to assimilate into White culture or risk school failure, condemning Latina/os to a lifetime of poverty.

An alternative lens for examination of school "failure" is to focus on the schooling process of the most educationally successful Latino students, that is, students who have reached the highest levels of educational achievement. In this chapter we examine the educational and gender socialization of 17 Mexican-descent Latinas and 10 Latino men in doctoral programs through qualitative interviews to examine the messages these individuals received about education from their parents. We assume that there are similarities as well as differences in their socialization around education as influenced by their gender. We also assume that Latino families enforce, question, and modify "cultural values," as all ethnic groups do, as they encounter new environments and as they develop as parents and human beings. Therefore, "Latino culture" is not static or immune to influence and change. Indeed, when Latino culture does change, the change is not necessarily in linear ways to emulate "White culture," but, rather, in intricate and complicated ways to accommodate parents' history, language, social class, and social environments. As such, we expect messages about education to reflect Latino parents' complex social contexts rather than simply being for or against educational achievement.

Different Forms of Support and Knowledge to Facilitate Educational Success

Several researchers (Apple, 1978; Oakes, 1985; Rendón, 1992; Skemp, 1978) have emphasized the importance of instrumental knowledge, such as knowing the factual and procedural information to enter and succeed in higher education, as essential to students' educational success. For students to succeed, instrumental knowledge, or know-how is essential, especially as they attend higher education, where a large portion of what students accomplish includes negotiating the bureaucratic structures necessary to design courses of study, approach professors, and gain access to resources such as the library, computer labs, and financial aid. Scholarly work has emphasized the role of parents in providing instrumental knowledge to their children so they can do well in higher education. It is not surprising, therefore, that most students who succeed in higher education come from households where one or both parents attended college. It is also implied that the instrumental knowledge provided by educated parents leads to other kinds of resources such as social support as well as financial help. In other words, parents' educational attainment has been examined as a whole, and the research generally is in agreement that educated parents are best equipped to instruct, support, and otherwise encourage their offspring to succeed in higher education.

The effects educated parents have on their offspring's educational success are so powerful that the mostly undocumented assumption is that less-educated parents are not very helpful to successful students, and, in fact, may even hinder their children's educational success. This assumption is even stronger for students of color in general, and for Latinos specifically. Latino parents with low educational levels not only lack instrumental knowledge, but they also have rigid views of gender that favor sons in every way, including encouraging them to succeed educationally, while they encourage their daughters to stay at home and marry early and view raising a family as more important than accomplishing educationally. In our studies, we ask doctoral students their parents' views on their educational success, and we outline the resources that parents provide, which at times include instrumental knowledge—especially if the parents attended college—but also other types of knowledge and assets like encouragement, social support, economic support (no matter how limited), affirmation, and emphasis on valuing education.

Method

The data presented here come from one study already conducted by Hurtado (2003) with young Latinas (who had at least one parent of Mexican descent) and a second study now in progress (Hurtado & Sinha, 2004) conducted to mirror the Hurtado study with young Latinos (with at least one parent of Latin American ancestry). Hurtado (2003) interviewed 101 Mexican-descent Latinas who had some education beyond high school and who were between the ages of 20 and 30. The respondents were contacted mainly through networks in institutions of higher education in various cities in the five southwestern states of Arizona, California, Colorado, New Mexico, and Texas. Respondents were also interviewed in Massachusetts, Michigan, New York, and Washington, D.C. The Hurtado and Sinha study (2004) expanded the ethnicity requirement to include all Latinos with ancestry in Latin America, not just Mexico, but followed all of the other procedures used in the Hurtado study. The Hurtado and Sinha study (2004) has already interviewed 75 respondents in California, Michigan, New Mexico, New York, and Texas. The goal is to interview 100 young Latinos. Respondents in both studies were interviewed in focus groups of two and three, and, when necessary, respondents were interviewed individually. The interviews were audio- and videotaped, transcribed, and coded by bilingual/bicultural research assistants. We conducted both quantitative and qualitative analysis of the transcripts. Whenever we quantified responses, we present them in percentages. Most of our analysis, however, was based on a qualitative approach where we identified major themes and did not calculate percentages.

We gave all of our respondents the option of using their own names or pseudonyms. A majority of respondents chose to use their own names, others chose only their first names, and still others chose either a first name pseudonym or a first and last name pseudonym. We only indicate when respondents chose to use their own names; the rest are chosen pseudonyms.

In this chapter we focus on only the 17 female respondents in the Hurtado (2003) study and the 10 male respondents in the Hurtado and Sinha study (2004) who were attending doctoral programs. The remaining respondents (84 females and 65 males) were not doctoral students. None of the respondents in either study at the time of the interview had yet obtained his or her doctorate. Below we examine the data from both sets of interviews to discuss differences and similarities among these young Latina/os' educational trajectories as they navigate their doctoral programs.

Sample Characteristics

Table 9.1 lists the doctoral programs and institutions the respondents were attending at the time of the interview. Most Latinas were enrolled in doctoral programs in sociology ($n = 8$), and most Latinos were enrolled in doctoral programs in sociology and in literature ($n = 3$ in each field). Of the 17 female respondents who were in doctoral programs, 71% ($n = 12$) were their families' first generation in college. The remaining 24% ($n = 4$) of respon-

TABLE 9.1
Doctoral Programs and Institutions Respondents Were Attending at the Time of the Interview

Doctoral programs in:	Women Respondents (N = 17)	Male Respondents (N = 10)
American Culture, University of Michigan	1	
Anthropology, New York University	1	
Chemistry, UC-Berkeley		1
Education, UC-Berkeley, UCLA, University of Michigan	4	
Engineering, UC-Santa Cruz		1
Literature, Stanford University, UC-Berkeley		3
Political Science University of New Mexico	1	
Psychology CUNY, UC-Santa Cruz,	1	1
Sociology, Columbia University, Harvard University, UC-Berkeley, UC-Santa Cruz, University of Michigan	8	3
Urban Planning, UC-Berkeley	1	
Zoology, UC-Berkeley		1
Total	17	10

dents had one or two parents who had graduated from college, although in two instances the parents were divorced and the respondents lived with the mother who did not have a college education. Also, all five respondents with college-educated parents were of mixed heritage—Mexican and White. Of the 12 respondents who were their families' first generation in college, both parents were of Mexican origin. Of the 10 male respondents who were in doctoral programs, 80% ($n = 8$) were first generation in college. The remaining 20% ($n = 2$) of respondents had parents who had attended college. In these two instances, both parents had some college; one father, who was Puerto Rican, had attended college but had not obtained a degree. His wife, who was also Puerto Rican, had a master's degree. In the second instance, the mother, who was White, had an associate's degree, and the father, who was Mexican, had a bachelor's degree.

Table 9.2 summarizes the sociodemographic characteristics for the respondents. Most respondents grew up in two-parent households (Latinas,

TABLE 9.2
Respondents' Sociodemographic Characteristics

Social Characteristics	Latina Respondents (N = 17)	Latino Respondents (N = 10)
Respondent Grew Up in Single-head-of-household Family	5	3
First Generation in College*	12	8
Mixed Heritage		
White and Latino Descent	5	1
Salvadorian and Panamanian		1
Respondents' Class Identification While Growing Up		
Poor	6	4
Working Class	8	4
Middle Class	3	2
Upper Middle Class		
Wealthy		
Marital Status		
Married (no children)	2	2
Married (with children)	1	
Single (no children)	13	8
Single (with children)	1	

*Neither parent had attended college.

n = 11; Latinos, n = 7), and most came from families where both parents were of Latino ancestry (Latinas, n = 12; Latinos, n = 9). Most respondents identified their social class while they were growing up as either poor or working class (Latinas, n = 14; Latinos, n = 8). Only a few respondents considered their backgrounds as middle class (Latinas, n = 3; Latinos, n = 2), and none of the respondents considered themselves as upper middle class or wealthy. Most respondents were not married (Latinas, n = 13; Latinos, n = 8) and did not have children (Latinas, n = 15; Latinos, n = 10).

Most respondents were born in the United States (Latinas, n = 16; Latinos, n = 8), or if they were born outside this country, they had been raised in largely Latina/o communities. They fully acknowledged their Latina/o background but claimed their rights and privileges as U.S. citizens.

Results

As indicated in our introduction, educators and researchers have argued that the difference in educational achievement between Latinas and Latinos is due to differences in gender socialization, where women are highly restricted, both socially and sexually, whereas boys are given freedom and male privilege. This difference in gender socialization leads to different expectations of success where Latinas are socialized to marry, have children, and care for a family as the primary basis for a successful life. In contrast, Latinos are socialized to have freedom and male privilege and succeed outside the home and are not expected to perform household chores. In presenting the results of our interviews, we first examine differences in gender socialization, specifically examining the differences in terms of sexual and social restriction and household responsibilities. We follow these results by examining whether potential differences in socialization lead to different parental educational expectations for Latinas and Latinos or whether, in spite of differences in gender socialization, respondents received similar parental messages about the importance of educational success.

Differences in Gender Socialization: Boys Will Be Boys, and Girls Will Be Virgins

The Latina respondents uniformly reported, regardless of other sociodemographic differences (such as whether they lived in two-parent or single-parent households), being heavily supervised by their parents, primarily by their mothers. There were well-specified curfews and explicit consequences if the rules were violated. Furthermore, parents, primarily mothers, monitored the Latinas' friendships and peer networks to protect them from "hanging out" with inappropriate people. While they were growing up, most Latinas were not allowed to "date" in the sense of having a boy come and pick them up at home and leaving unsupervised with them. Even when they went away to college (and in some instances, even when they went away to graduate school), upon returning home, they were expected to abide by a curfew or at least "check in" if they were going to be out beyond a certain time.

In many instances familial proscriptions regarding dating served to ensure that respondents' sexuality developed according to a culturally sanctioned framework. Furthermore, many of the respondents described themselves as "late bloomers" and not particularly popular in high school. It was unclear whether respondents' lack of one-to-one dating was because of their parents' unusual strictness or because of their academic inclinations and disinterest in boys, compared to their peers. Also, their socializing took the form of strong friendship networks and going out with groups of friends.

Most Latinas raised under these social restrictions did not perceive them as particularly punitive, as most of their female friends had similar rules. A few also saw their parents' socialization practices as reflecting cultural differences between their families and those of White students in their high schools. Most did not admire White students' freedom to come and go as they pleased and preferred their parents' concern about their whereabouts.

Valuing Virginity

As part of the restrictions on dating, the majority of Latinas stated that their parents valued virginity until marriage. Sometimes there was an explicit discussion of these values, but most simply "knew" their parents' preference without having had an outright conversation about it. The preservation of virginity was to increase the probability of securing husbands and happy futures but, just as important, to avoid pregnancy outside of marriage at all costs. Several mothers had gotten pregnant before marriage and felt that their lives "ended" once they had to get married. Monitoring their daughters and avoiding getting pregnant were also seen as essential for their daughters' educational achievement. Once pregnant, according to most mothers, the daughters had to refocus on raising the child.

Even in situations where Latinas were engaged to be married, premarital cohabitation was generally taboo. The only exception, for the most part, was with mixed-heritage families. For example, Sonya Smith, who chose to use her own name, was a 24-year-old doctoral student in the American culture

(Chicano studies/Asian American history) program at the University of Michigan whose father was White and whose mother was of Mexican descent. She received a bouquet of yellow roses from her mother when she found out that Sonya had "lost her virginity" by "finding condoms in the garbage."

> I was in high school, and I was petrified because I thought, what is she [her mother] going to think of me? I'm not a virgin. I was very nervous about it, but then it turns out everything I feared that she would do, it was completely the opposite. She was like, "I just want to make sure you are safe. I'm glad you are using condoms. Let's get you on the pill." The next day I woke up in the morning and I had a dozen yellow roses from her. I was just like, "Oh, okay. Why didn't I tell her earlier?" But in terms of telling my dad, he has never been told, but I think by now he knows.

Although her father was White and had a master's degree in business administration from the University of California-Berkeley—which supposedly made him more open-minded about sexual issues—Sonya was very reluctant to speak to him about her sexual behavior.

Latinas did not necessarily follow their mothers' admonishments, and some did have premarital sex. However, they had to maneuver so that their families would not find out. Most Latinas eventually told their mothers, but not their fathers, about their sexual activity. Although most mothers did not approve, they did not threaten to disown them. The mothers, however, did express sadness and loss when their daughters did not follow what they considered the proper way to conduct themselves sexually.

Family Responsibilities

Most Latinas had specific household chores that started with age-appropriate tasks when the respondents were relatively young. As they grew older, their responsibilities increased. Several Latinas stated that every Saturday was "cleaning day." They, their sisters, and their mothers cleaned the entire house. Soledad, who was 27 years old and a graduate student in the doctoral program in education at the University of Michigan, stated, "We'd wake up very early on Saturdays. We thought we were the only family in America that woke up at 6:30 to clean house."

Only a few of the Latinas did not have any chores or had parents who were lax about enforcing compliance with their duties. Several of these mothers wanted their daughters to focus on their schoolwork, and others felt that they were going to be saddled with housework when they married, so they wanted to spare them from the burden of "women's work." Sara, who was 29 years old and a doctoral student in sociology at the University of Michigan, stated that her mother "cleaned and cleaned. She made my bed, she washed dishes. I didn't wash dishes." Her mother's rationale was, "Your day will come, when you are going to have to do this for the rest of your life. So as long as I'm alive and I can do this, I will." Sara was well aware that her mother was providing a "privilege" that would be short-lived, although Sara's mother was only partially right because Sara's "husband [now] does all the housework."

In the majority of families, however, the only viable excuse for not doing housework was having homework. Most mothers deferred or suspended household chores for the sake of their daughters' schoolwork. So Soledad could escape the Saturday morning cleaning rituals if she said, "I had lots of homework; that was the tactic I came up with."

Most Latina respondents who had brothers reported that the brothers were exempt from household chores as they were from curfews. In the most extreme cases, economic resources were distributed unfairly according to the children's gender. Soledad's brother, Ben, was an extreme example, albeit not the only one, of the privileges males had in these families. Ben was allowed to come and go as he pleased, he did not have a job during the school year, and he was not required to perform household chores. During the Saturday morning cleanings, Soledad's mother told her daughters, "Hush, [because] your brother is asleep," and not to "run the vacuum yet." After Ben got up and left his bedroom for the living room to watch television, by now clean and tidy, his sisters would enter his room and clean it for him. Soledad recognized that "the freedom that my brother has, even as a 20-year-old, is incredible to me." Through high school, Ben simply announced, "Mom, I'm doing this," not "Mom, may I do this?" Everybody in the family indulged Ben, "the baby," including Soledad's father who routinely gave him spending money because he empathized with a young man "wanting to go do things and not having money." When Soledad jokingly challenged her father, "What about me and Julie [her sister]? When we ask for money you didn't say, 'Here's fifty bucks.' You said, 'Go get a job!'" He replied, "Well, you're going to end up taking care of Ben anyway, so I need to groom you to be independent 'cause someone's going to have to take care of him."

The privileged position of Latinas' brothers was also present in ethnically mixed families. Mariposa was 30 years old and a doctoral candidate in sociology at the University of Michigan. Her father was of Mexican descent, but her White mother in San Francisco raised her. Mariposa recalled that her brother had all the "privileges that my father would have had if he lived in our house. My mom surrendered everything to my brother." Mariposa was well aware that "it definitely had to do with the fact that he was a boy and I was a girl." Similar to Ben above, Mariposa's brother's privileges extended to not "having a curfew that stuck. He pretty much had freedom." Mariposa picked up the slack by doing chores usually assigned to boys and "mowed the lawn out of embarrassment. He had his own room—the works."

Most respondents' perceptions about their brothers recognized their brothers' privileges and vulnerabilities. They tried to be patient with their brothers' shortcomings and worried about them, but they also were perfectly capable of getting "pissed off" at them when they acted irresponsibly. Several respondents worried about their brothers' educational prospects. For example, Valerie, a 29-year-old doctoral student in education at the University of California-Los Angeles (UCLA), stated that her mother had worked several jobs so Valerie could attend Catholic school. Valerie's mother reasoned that a Catholic education would maximize Valerie's educational achievement. However, by the time Valerie's much younger brother graduated from eighth grade, her mother wanted him to attend Catholic high school. Valerie's father disagreed because he wanted his son to be "streetwise" and go to public school. Valerie wanted her brother to have the same educational benefits she had received. She also recognized her brother's vulnerability as a man when he later served in the armed forces in operation Desert Storm and participated in combat.

Latinas gave several justifications for gender differences in privileges: brothers were the youngest in the family, or the oldest, or the only boys in the family, or there were all boys in the family, and the respondent was the only female. Whatever the justification, male privilege often went unchallenged. Other respondents, however, did not accept gender differences within their families. After years of struggle, many of them succeeded in changing the family dynamics, making their brothers accountable to more equitable standards.

Several Latinas reported much more egalitarian treatment in their families. For example, Ruth N. Lopez Turley, who chose to use her own name, was 24 years old and a doctoral student in sociology at Harvard University. Her parents were of Mexican descent, and Ruth was raised by her mother in Laredo, Texas. Ruth was allowed to date boys, although her mother questioned her extensively after she went out by probing, "*¿Y qué hicieron? ¿Y a dónde fueron?*" [What did you do? Where did you go?], which resulted in Ruth "rarely coming home past 11." However, unlike in other families, her brothers were also treated the same way in terms of curfew and household chores. According to Ruth, "The expectations were pretty much the same for all of us as far as the household work. My mother had this cause that she was going to fight against *machismo*. She was very into not going along with the typical Mexican practice of expecting the women to do the housework from a very young age. My mother kept insisting that her boys were not going to grow up like that."

It was a similar situation for Valerie, whose mother "was the oldest and so . . . she didn't have a childhood because she was too busy raising her brothers and sisters and changing the diapers and stuff. So she wanted me and my brother to have one." Valerie felt that both she and her brother "were given a lot of freedom" and that "things were pretty equal between them."

The egalitarian families were not necessarily the most educated. Ruth's mother, for example, was an orphan who had lived in the streets of Mexico until she was nine, when she walked across the bridge connecting Mexico and the United States and ended up in an orphanage in Laredo, Texas, where she remained until she got married at the age of 15. Similarly, both of Valerie's parents were born in El Paso, Texas, and her mother had been raised in Compton and her father in Florence, predominantly poor areas in Los Angeles. Valerie's father had a sixth-grade education and worked as a cabinetmaker, and her mother graduated from high school and had been a homemaker most of her life, eventually working as a secretary to help pay for Valerie's Catholic school tuition.

Boys Will Be Boys

These socialization patterns described for Latinas were reversed for the Latino respondents. All of the Latinos ($n = 10$) reported being allowed to date and having very little supervision and few curfews as they entered their teenage years. Of the 10 Latinos, 8 had sisters and 7 reported that their sisters had different rules than the boys in the family (one Latino respondent did not live with his sister). Jorge Morales, who was 27 years old and a doctoral student in comparative literature at UC-Berkeley, stated that while he was growing up his parents never had to tell him when he could start dating, "I was never given an age, where I was allowed . . . I never really asked for permission . . . I never felt like there was a prohibition on dating." Unlike him and his brother, however, his sisters "weren't allowed to date by my father throughout high school." Jorge's response was very similar to the rest of the Latino respondents.

Similarly, while Latinas reported that their parents emphasized virginity until marriage, (with the exception of two mixed-heritage respondents),

Latinos received a similar message, but the understanding was that more than likely they would violate such a restriction. Nava, who was 30 years old and a doctoral student in sociology at UC-Santa Cruz, stated that although his parents preferred that he abstain from sex until marriage, he was "from an early age . . . given a lot of freedom . . . in the ninth or tenth grade when my parents let me stay out . . . until two or three in the morning . . . I had a lot of freedom to move around." When Nava went out on dates, his father would simply say to "wear a raincoat" to avoid pregnancy.

Even though most parents did not discuss sex directly with Latinas or Latinos, they did communicate the importance of virginity until marriage, especially for women. As Jorge Morales stated:

> It was implied, you know, that you don't have sex until you get married because it's supposed to be like the traditional Mexican family. But, I mean, there was certainly a more implied stigma towards women, you know, having sex before marriage than for men. I think for men, for us, for the males in the family, the big fear was "what if you get your girlfriend pregnant," then you're going to have a lot of responsibilities and troubles, and you may not end up going to college for those reasons. The emphasis was more on how that would possibly hinder your future. Although sex doesn't imply having a child, but that was sort of like the fear that my parents had.

Parents would use the occurrence of pregnancy in the family or community to emphasize the importance of avoiding the problem to secure an educational future:

> They would just express a lot of disapproval when someone, a friend, a family's son, got his girlfriend pregnant, and they would point out and emphasize that that was really bad and how we should be careful about that. Also, I guess, at least in the Mexican American community, abortion wasn't really an option. It was not something that people even really thought about. You got pregnant, you had the kid. That's just the way it was.

Latino Cultural Values and Educational Achievement

Most of the educational literature has assumed that differences in gender socialization will lead to a lack of emphasis on education for Latinas in our study and a privileging of Latinos' educational achievement. Obviously, the Latinas had already excelled educationally beyond what would be expected, given the national rates of educational success for Latinas and Latinos. So the question was whether the Latinas in our sample had overcome their gender socialization, or were their parents providing other messages and resources besides the values expressed above? Furthermore, how did these messages compare to what parents were providing for equally successful Latinos? We address these questions next.

Similarities in the Educational Pathways of Latinas and Latinos

Lack of Instrumental Knowledge; Other Multiple Sources of Support

Most respondents were the first generation in their families to attend college (Latinas, $n = 12$; Latinos, $n = 8$), and therefore their parents did not have the instrumental knowledge to help them navigate higher education. For example Nava stated,

> I think my parents, even though they didn't understand the whole college thing in the beginning, they were always supportive and wanting us to do well in school. It's just that they didn't necessarily have the skills to help us. Like my dad couldn't really help me with my writing; he couldn't even write himself. So, yeah, there are certain things that we had to do for ourselves, but the fact that our parents put value on education was important—they valued education, they just didn't understand what it's all about.

Even though Nava reported differences in gender socialization between him and his younger sister around curfews and valuing virginity, his parents wanted an education for his sister as well.

Similarly, Soledad's family demanded less from her brother, Ben, in terms of chores at home and curfews—even providing him with spending money unlike the girls in the family. Soledad was encouraged by her mother and her father to value educational achievement. For example, Soledad's family didn't have a lot of money growing up, so her father gave her a choice when she turned 15, the age at which everybody in her family had had a *quinceañera* celebration. He said, "You can have a *quinceañera* or we can take the money and do something else." Soledad said her parents were very "focused on us going to college. They had sent me to a very expensive private school." So instead of a *quinceañera*, Soledad's parents suggested that she apply the money "toward a Stanley Kaplan SAT prep course." Soledad's extended family, including "my aunts, my uncles, and my grandma, said 'She's got to have a *quinceañera*; everyone's got to have one.'" Her father did not bow to the pressure, however, replying, "That's not the way she's going to enter society. I want her to enter society with a degree. That's more important." In fact, Soledad's parents were so invested in their children's educational achievement that they worked extra jobs to send them all to private school from kindergarten through 12th grade and even contributed to Soledad and her sister's education at private colleges. It was her brother who went to a public college:

> My parents really scraped and saved and did everything they could to make sure that we went to a private Catholic grammar school. We all went to private high schools. . . . Ben goes to a public college, but Julie and I went to private colleges. . . . Sometimes my dad had three jobs. Most times he had two. He was always doing something. We'd call them his "side jobs." And mom has always worked—she's been working since she was 17. Her mom died when she was very young. She was the oldest in her family and had to take care of them. She's a secretary for an insurance company in Chicago. My dad is a sergeant in the Chicago Police Department.

For the parents who had attended college, the amount of involvement in providing guidance for their children varied. In fact, some parents discussed the respondents' career choices and requirements extensively. Gabriella Gonzalez, who chose to use her own name, was 26 years old and in the sociology doctoral program at Harvard University. Her father was a biophysicist and read her papers in graduate school and talked to her about her research interests. Others, however, were not involved in the respondents' career and research choices, even though they had instrumental knowledge about higher education.

The area where most parents, especially mothers, provided the most support was in the form of what various respondents called "moral support" and "affirmation" for their life choices. There was no gender difference between Latinas and Latinos in their closeness with their mothers, the main providers of this type of support. There was much more variation in respondents' reported closeness to their fathers, and, again, there was no gender difference between Latinas and Latinos. The type of support mothers provided for respondents also did not vary. As Soledad stated, even though her mother was in Chicago, and she was attending the University of Michigan in Ann Arbor:

> I speak to my mom almost every day and we're very close. It's the kind of intimacy where, she'll know the minute I'm on the phone what kind of

day I'm having. Do you know what I mean? There's nobody in the world that knows me like she does. I can go weeks without talking to my father, you know? But his thing is always like, "Have you talked to Soledad, have you talked to Julie?" And she says, "yes," so she's kind of like our filter.

The communication patterns in most of these families consisted of mothers speaking directly to children, especially daughters, and then reporting back to fathers. Fathers rarely spoke directly to children about sensitive topics, especially sex or menstruation, or about the day-to-day details of their children's lives.

Fathers also provided support, but it was not as intimate as the support provided by mothers. For example, Marie, who was 28 years old and a doctoral student in sociology at the University of Michigan, compared her relationship with her father to the one she had with her mother:

> I mean there's certain topics you cannot talk to Dad about. But I think he's a very loving and tender and caring man. So there are things you can do with Dad that are actually fun, like you can go and have ice cream. . . . I think that makes it kind of close, or we can take walks together. But you know you can't talk to him about sex or anything like that. I mean, it's just different; it's a different kind of closeness.

Regardless of most parents' lack of knowledge about the intricacies of higher education, overall, parents were extremely supportive of both Latinas' and Latinos' educational achievement. The support many parents expressed was unconditional, even when they didn't fully understand their children's career choices. For example, Jorge Morales reported that his father was extremely supportive of his career choice to become an academic in literature even if that wasn't the best-paying job, and when his father, who had not finished high school and worked as a laborer in a seed company, did not fully understand what being a professor entailed:

> I admire my father, for many things, for pushing college, you know, being supportive of me going to college when a lot of members of my family didn't really see the value of education. They did see it, but it was the kind of thing where you go to college and you get a good job and you make good money. My father has been very supportive of me pursuing an academic career and going to college for the sake of learning, for the sake of getting an education itself. That's something that a lot of members of my family, they're somewhat supportive, but somehow they're also puzzled by it. Like they're always asking me, "Why so many years of college? Isn't it bad for you to study so much? Why don't you stop school now and just

get a job and make money?" As you know, academia is not the place to make money. My father is certainly someone I really admire for really being supportive.

Only one Latina reported her father, when they lived in Mexico, not supporting her educational aspirations. However, her mother fought with him about his closed-mindedness and won. At the time of the interview, Sandra Saenz, who was 30 and attending UCLA, was writing her dissertation to complete her doctorate in higher education.

Discussion

Many Latino parents want what is best for their children, including education. However, the majority of Latino students are the first in their families to attend college and often the only ones to finish high school, so parents are at a loss about how exactly to enforce their commitment to educational achievement.

Our interviews revealed some important clues to what contributes to the educational achievement of Latina/o doctoral students. While some of the gender socialization documented for Latinos was indeed practiced by many of our respondents' families, especially around the gender division of household labor and women's restrictions of sexuality, *at the same time* both Latinos and Latinas were being told that education was important, not only for gaining better employment but for living a fulfilling life as well. The emphasis on getting married and having children was true for Latinas but also for Latinos. In fact, all of the respondents had internalized these values as their own when they expressed a desire to be married, if they were not married already, and with the exception of one Latino respondent, all wanted to have children. However, these personal goals did not detract from their commitment to finish their doctoral programs.

Our studies also indicate that, although the majority of Latino parents do not have direct experience with higher education and, therefore, lack much of the instrumental knowledge necessary to succeed in college and graduate school, as a group they provided other kinds of support, such as small amounts of money; affirmation whenever their children succeeded educationally; babysitting when respondents had children; moral support, especially mothers; and working extra jobs to provide extra money for private schools.

Another important contribution of our studies is refuting that "cultural values" alone are responsible for Latinas' educational failure. The description at the beginning of this chapter of what was reported in numerous newspapers across the country, was similar to what Latinas in the Hurtado (2003) study reported, but they were not high school dropouts. In fact, they were among the most educationally successful Latinas in this country, attending some of the top doctoral programs in the most prestigious universities in the world. How to explain the discrepancy? The cultural values outlined at the beginning of this chapter were not the only values their parents were imparting—they were embedded within other messages of achievement and academic discipline. The discipline many Latinas learned from doing "chores" and taking care of siblings was later applied to structuring their academic courses of study. Many of the Latinas in the Hurtado (2003) study reported having brothers who were less academically successful than they were, regardless of their "male privilege" within their families. Lack of structure and discipline did not help these young men succeed. Of course, among the 101 respondents in Hurtado's study (2003) there were also many successful brothers, because family socialization around achievement is not the only determinant of success.

Reflections and Future Directions for Research

The purpose of the Hurtado (2003) and Hurtado and Sinha studies (2004) was not to explore the determinants of educational experience. Both studies were conducted to examine successful Latinas' and Latinos' views on feminism. As part of this exploration, we asked them about growing up in their families and about their gender socialization. Education was such a central part of their family lives that the interviews inevitably led to discussions of attribution for their educational success as well as their parents' views on education. We are now in the process of conducting a second wave of interviews with the same respondents focusing on their educational trajectories and their explanations for their educational success. However, we offer below a few of the insights respondents mentioned about their educational success as potential avenues for future research on Latina/os' educational achievement.

The importance of institutional programs: recruitment programs, mentorship, and financial aid. Most of our respondents, including those with college-educated parents, admitted having had the benefits of recruitment programs, special summer programs, and affirmative action policies directed at students of color. In spite of their families' commitment and support for their children's academic achievement, it is unlikely that the respondents would have been so successful without structural interventions directed at under-represented students. For example, Ruth N. Lopez Turley, the doctoral student discussed earlier, had one of the most egalitarian mothers in our sample, who took it upon herself to directly contradict cultural messages of *machismo*. However, Ruth attributed her educational success to a combination of factors that included her mother's encouragement and sacrifices as well as educational programs designed for students of color (such as the one Ruth attended in the summer during high school at Harvard University), mentorship by teachers and peers who knew more about college than she did, and, most important, financial assistance directed at students of color and students from lower socioeconomic status. In other words, academic success is dependent on a variety of factors, including but not limited to parents. In fact, several of the respondents commented that if their parents had been born later rather than earlier and had had the educational benefits they experienced, they perceived their parents were capable and disciplined enough to have succeeded as much as, if not more than, the respondents had succeeded.

The respondents' stories of educational achievement also indicate that higher education institutions can have a proactive role in attracting talented students of color and can help them overcome structural barriers such as poverty and geographic isolation.

The overemphasis on gender socialization to the exclusion of other factors. Respondents did not isolate their ethnicity or culture as explanatory factors for their academic failures or successes. In other words, they did not objectify themselves as being "Mexican" or "Latino" and then make attributions about their educational experiences solely based on ethnicity. From a social psychological perspective, this makes perfect sense. People think of themselves as integrated human beings, and they take all of their life circumstances into account in making sense of their lives. Respondents mentioned poor schools, underprepared teachers, and poor curriculum as school characteristics associated with being poor and Latina/o. None of the respondents discussed having difficulty in school because of their Latino "culture" or because of "culture conflict." Also, none of the respondents mentioned distancing from their families as a result of their experiences in higher education. In fact, many of the respondents reported including their families in school activities once they arrived at the university, bringing home books and other resources to educate their families as well as relatives, and many times inspiring their parents to pursue degrees. The educational experiences of many of the respondents spilled over to their families and communities.

Future studies of Latino and Latina academic achievement will have to provide deeper analysis that takes into account culture, language, structural opportunities, and family socialization to provide a more complete picture of what makes Latino and Latina students succeed even when the odds are against them. The respondents' stories show that poverty is not destiny and even though "*querer es poder*" [where there's a will there's a way], such values have to be undergirded by special programs and by proactive institutions of higher education.

References

Apple, M. (1978). Ideology, reproduction, and educational reform. *Comparative Educational Review, 22*, 367–387.

Dominguez, V. (1992). Invoking culture: The messy side of "cultural politics." *South Atlantic Quarterly, 91*(1), 19–42.

Gamboa, S. (2001, January 25). Diploma deficit: Fewer caps, gowns for Hispanic girls. *Monitor*, 1A, 8A.

Hurtado, A. (2003). *Voicing Chicana feminisms: Young women speak out on identity and sexuality.* New York: New York University Press.

Hurtado, A., & Sinha, M. (2004, March). *Restriction and freedom in the construction of sexuality: Young Chicanas and Chicanos speak out.* Paper presented at the annual meeting of the National Association of Chicana/Chicano Studies, Albuquerque, NM.

Oakes, J. (1985). *Keeping track: How schools structure inequality.* New Haven, CT: Yale University Press.

Rendón, L. I. (1992). Eyes on the prize: Students of color and the bachelor's degree. *Community College Review, 21*(2), 3–13.

Skemp, R. R. (1978). Relational understanding and instrumental understanding. *Arithmetic Teacher, 26*(3), 9–15.

10

Sustaining Latina/o Doctoral Students

A Psychosociocultural Approach for Faculty

Alberta M. Gloria
Jeanett Castellanos

Given the growing graduate student population and the influence of educational progress in the United States, it is critical to thoroughly examine Latina/os' doctoral experiences. Although a large portion of the research on graduate education focuses on White students' experiences, the literature addressing racial and ethnic minority students' unique journeys and challenges is limited. In particular, there is a dearth of literature addressing the graduate experience that encompasses academic, psychological, social, cultural, and environmental variables; the interaction of these variables with the graduate environment; and their subsequent effects on student experiences. Extensive literature addresses the social context of the graduate process, and more recent literature has incorporated race and ethnicity; yet, incorporation of psychological, social, cultural, and environmental aspects internal to Latina/o doctoral experiences warrants further examination.

Acknowledging the complexities and interrelatedness of the person and the environment to gain a contextualized and holistic understanding of Latina/o doctoral student experiences is warranted. In doing so, this chapter briefly discusses common doctoral student experiences and then discusses more extensively those additional issues and experiences that Latina/o doctoral students contend with and negotiate in their training processes. Next, areas of particular educational concern for Latina/o students, including managing doctoral life roles and familial expectations, negotiating relationships with faculty and peers, establishing self within academic culture, and integrating personal and professional identities are discussed. Next, operationalization and application of a *psychosociocultural* (PSC) approach (Gloria & Rodriguez, 2000) to working (e.g., advising, mentoring, retaining), within the previously discussed context for Latina/o doctoral students is presented. Vignettes (based on real-life experiences in working with Latina/o doctoral students in formal and informal capacities) and a table identifying attitudes and beliefs, knowledge, and skills when working with Latina/os students elucidate the application of the PSC approach.

Commonalities of Graduate School Experiences

It is not surprising that life as a graduate student is simultaneously an invigorating and stressful experience. Literature (i.e., anecdotal, theoretical, and empirical) on the graduate school experience suggests that students must manage personal, cultural, environmental, and social issues concurrently, within the context of a rigorous academic structure designed to expand and challenge one's thinking and knowledge (Ülkü-Steiner, Kurtz-Costes, & Kinlaw, 2000). Due to a "lack of status, competition, financial duress, high workload, performance anxiety, and continuous evaluation" (p. 297), graduate students contend with high levels of stress (Bowman, Hatley, & Bowman, 1995; Rocha-Singh, 1994). Regardless of the discipline area (e.g., "hard" versus "soft" sciences), doctoral students experience difficulties of managing expectations and responsibilities in their training processes equally (Hodgson & Simoni, 1995).

Students' stress or anxiety relative to doctoral programs is a commonly discussed issue as entry into a graduate program brings new life roles and transitions (Bowman & Bowman, 1990), heightened performance expectations, need to balance personal and professional (Adams, 1993), and negotiation of academic culture and climate. Given the intensity and stress associated with graduate school, literature has indicated that students are often at risk for moderate to major psychological and/or physical concerns (Bowman & Bowman, 1990), with females reporting higher levels of psychological distress than males (Hodgson & Simoni, 1995).

A substantial amount of stress and distress experienced by doctoral students results from a host of general and specific life changes. For example, doctoral students often change residence, shift work hours, return to school after having worked in different or respective fields, feel pressure for outstanding personal achievement, and experience a decrease in finances and subsequent living conditions. Each of these changes in personal and physical settings reflects high-stress events (Holmes & Rahe, 1967). Fear of the unknown (e.g., expectations of faculty), anxieties about the size and complexity of research institutions, and unease regarding competition inherent to graduate education, may cause students to inadvertently spend more time managing personal and professional concerns to the detriment of their academics (Adams, 1993), which may, in turn, elevate stress levels.

Balancing the personal (e.g., insecurities or uncertainties) and the professional (e.g., rigorous demands on abilities) dimensions is a common and continuous process for doctoral students. Unfortunately, graduate school curricula, research responsibilities, and even faculty advisors often overlook "having a life beyond school." Although students are encouraged to practice self-care by negotiating a working, school, and home-life balance; taking time for themselves; and "living their lives," the reality of research and academic roles and responsibilities often precludes a balanced approach (Adams, 1993). Despite encouragement, students are readily dismissed and frequently deemed as unacceptable students when they are unable to meet or exceed faculty expectations of academic requirements (Gloria & Pope-Davis, 1997).

As a result, all graduate students must negotiate the academic culture by learning formal and informal rules, norms, and expectations (e.g., student-faculty interactions); institutional considerations warrant survival. For example, students need to know where to find resources and opportunities or from whom they can receive "insider information" to get their doctoral needs met—known as "learning the ropes"—to negotiate their training experiences. In short, doctoral training experiences are challenging (yet manageable) experiences.

Differentiated Experience of Latina/os Doctoral Students

It is well established that Latina/o students' educational experiences are steeped in a cultural context that differs from the current educational system's (Castellanos & Jones, 2003); understanding those differentiated experiences beyond the common doctoral students' experiences is necessary (Adams, 1993; Herrera, 2003). Specifically, explicating the subtle cultural values and mores and their impact on Latina/o students' action, interactions, and reactions within the training setting lends insight into their culture-specific concerns, challenges, and considerations (Adams, 1993; Castellanos & Jones, 2003; Trevino, 1996).

Managing Doctoral Life Roles and Familial Expectations

As is the case with other doctoral students, graduate education introduces significant life changes for Latina/o students who enter an often unknown and unfamiliar process. For Latina/os, a fundamental component of managing all life roles, in addition to academic life roles (e.g., Gloria & Segura-Herrera, 2004), family is fundamental (Santiago-Rivera, Arredondo, & Gallardo-Cooper, 2002). Serving as a central support source and venue for growth, Latina/o families are rooted in *familismo*, which is characterized by closeness, cooperation, and interdependence in problem solving (Marín & Triandis, 1985; Santiago-Rivera et al., 2002). Socialized by familial loyalty, cohesiveness, and consistent connections with family networks, Latina/o doctoral students often struggle to maintain consistent and strong family ties, share family tasks, and respond to familial needs.

Due to the heavy workloads of all doctoral students, Latina/os often struggle with being away from family, unable to meet daily family obligations inherent in core cultural values as *personalismo* (i.e., interactional style of collaboration, connection, and personalism) (Levine & Padilla, 1980), *familismo* (familism), and *respeto* (respect for others) (Gloria & Segura-Herrera, 2004). For example, manifestation of these values is evident in *compartiendo tiempo* for many Latina/os. *Compartiendo tiempo* means to share one's time with others to build personal relationships with immediate (e.g., siblings) and extended family (e.g., *prima/os*—cousins), often through attendance at life events (e.g., birthdays or family functions) and lending support when called upon (e.g., helping family members move, taking care of nieces/nephews).

Valuing group interdependence, Latina/o graduate students often feel guilty for not fulfilling family expectations and are affected by the incongruence between program and family demands (Gloria & Rodriguez, 2000). Attempting to keep a balance at home (e.g., family misinterpreting an absence), Latina/o students make concerted efforts to be home on weekends and academic breaks, in addition to maintaining weekly contact with family members. Despite living in close proximity to family (Hurtado, 1994), many Latina/o doctoral students struggle to determine the amount of time they can "afford" to be away from their studies academically and/or away from family culturally. When familial difficulties arise (e.g., health of parent or grandparent, financial difficulties), values hold that Latina/os provide support (e.g., emotional, financial, physical) during the family's time of need despite other demands. Placing group needs before those of the individual can create unique challenges for retention of Latina/o students. For example, Latina/o students may question whether their individual academic endeavors and resulting losses (e.g., being away from family, missing out on life events) are worth the pursuit of a doctoral degree.

Although Latina/o graduates experience pressure to keep cohesive family relations, the pressure to create family also affects their educational journeys (Gloria & Segura-Herrera, 2004). Similar to family formation demands that White women encounter in graduate school (Marshall & Jones, 1990; Ülkü-Steiner, Kurtz-Costes, & Kinlaw, 2000), Latina/os experience a cultural and social pressure to create family and maintain strong *familismo*. Although socially and culturally proscribed Latina/o gender roles have changed (Santiago-Rivera et al., 2002), Latina/os continue to face cultural pressures regarding family (see Hurtado & Sinna, ch. 9). As a result, the process of explaining, and often justifying, their educational decisions and reasons for attending graduate school often makes Latina/os feel disconnected from and misunderstood by family (Gloria & Segura-Herrera, 2004). Justifying continued educational pursuits, while putting family or the ability to provide for family on hold (Morales, 1996), is particularly difficult when families perceive Latina/o doctoral students as already having degrees (e.g., bachelor and/or master's degrees). Family friends and community members may also have expectations about the creation of family, which reflects on one's family (often questioning family's upbringing of their children), additional stresses for Latina/o students who may feel that they are not meeting a host of personal and cultural expectations.

Negotiating Relationships with Faculty and Peers

Graduate school offers an array of unique, culturally based challenges in addition to family and cultural obligations that affect Latina/o educational pursuits. Entering departments with primarily White middle- to upper-class male perspectives and faculty, Latina/o students are challenged to find advisors who are culturally aware and sensitive to their background (Poock, 1999). As a result, Latina/o students often have limited contact with advisors, awkward communication, and overall discomfort in their advisor-advisee and faculty-student interactions (Ibarra, 2001). Central to advising relationships is consideration of dissertation topics. For example, dissertation advisement and support for topic choice may be limited if faculty endorse the perspective that examination of racial and ethnic minority issues does not entail true scholarship. Further, faculty may question the merit and intellectual capability of students who pursue culture-based research agendas in addition to minimally directing or declining to direct such projects. It is not surprising that such beliefs and interactions with faculty discourage students from studying Latina/o issues (Gonzalez et al., 2002), devalue cultural differences, disenfranchise intellectual pursuits, hinder development of scholarship training, and, ultimately, affect student retention.

Stemming from advisor mismatch, limited research advisement, and often little general support for research interests, Latina/o graduate students must contend with assumptions of academic inferiority and misperceptions stemming from the environment and, occasionally, themselves (Grijalva & Holman Coombs, 1997). Often challenged to demonstrate their qualifications and admission (i.e., affirmation action admit) to their peers and sometimes faculty, Latina/o students (along with other students of color) must work harder to prove themselves (Gloria & Segura-Herrera, 2004; Grijalva & Holman Coombs, 1997). As doctoral students already experience self-doubt and uncertainty about admissions (e.g., imposter syndrome), the additional external questioning isolates, demoralizes, and sets Latina/o students apart. Instead of working to advance their knowledge and understanding of issues, students are providing evidence of their competence, feeling they are evaluated differently from their counterparts.

In the midst of proving themselves, Latina/o graduate students are often tokenized when asked by faculty or university personnel to serve as *cultural ambassadors* or university cultural representatives for on- and off-campus minority affairs efforts (Gonzalez et al., 2002). At the university and department level, for example, Latina/o doctoral students are expected to serve on multicultural committees, mentor Latina/o undergraduates, review student admission files, and assist with recruitment of other Latina/o students. At the national and local community levels, they are asked to represent departments and universities at national conferences, establish connections for the university with neighboring minority communities, and interpret the university culture for local communities (e.g., describe admission procedures for first-generation minority families). Although the culture-specific responsibilities and expectations serve as a support network for graduate retention (Herrera, 2003), these additional tasks can intensify the challenge to keep on track academically (e.g., develop research skills and agenda) and become involved in other scholarship skill-building opportunities (e.g., teaching assistantships). At the same time, declining to conduct community outreach can create guilt and distress for Latina/o students, knowing that their communities are not receiving information or advocacy.

Similar to the *cultural ambassador* effect, Latina/o students (and other students of color) are looked to as *cultural experts*, prompted to speak for entire racial or ethnic groups (Nieves-Squires, 1991). Expected to know their sociopolitical and cultural histories, students are unrealistically and inappropriately asked to lead the classroom discussion with "the minority perspective" (Gloria & Pope-Davis, 1997). Such tokenism fosters a hostile and separatist learning space in which responsibility for knowing and teaching others about diversity is imposed on Latina/os and other students of color, thus minimizing the importance of this issue for all students and faculty. Being placed in the cultural expert role also serves to marginalize and distance students from their peers, as Latina/o students are perceived as "special," holders of diversity, or only having knowledge and skills regarding their own culture.

Establishing Self within Academic Culture

Holding different cultural values and norms from those of most training programs, coupled with the expectations and assumptions discussed above, Latina/o students are challenged to negotiate their ethnic identity throughout the graduate school process. This transformative process involves (re)negotiation of ethnic identity (Ibarra, 2001)—coming to terms with what being Latina/o means and what value they find in being Latina/o. Unfortunately, Latina/o students (along with other students of color) find themselves hiding or repressing who they are culturally in their classroom and daily program interactions to retain themselves academically (Gloria & Castellanos, 2003). Depending on the degree to which they are willing or able to mask the cultural differentness (while being called out as *cultural experts*), Latina/o students have to navigate between their academic and native cultures.

As a result of negotiating the distinctively different values of the academy (e.g., individualism, competition, formal social exchange) and Latina/o cultural values (e.g., *familismo*, collectivism, *personalismo*), Latina/o students often experience cultural incongruity, ethnic identity conflict, and uncomfortable situations in which they may find themselves interacting in ways that are counter to their cultural values (Anzaldúa, 1987) and norms (Gloria & Castellanos, 2003; see Torres, ch. 8). Needing substantial "psychic energy" to hold and integrate diametrically opposing values (Anzaldvá, 1987), Latina/o students may feel culturally depleted. For example, in meeting the time demands for research, Latina/o students may distance themselves from their local and university Latina/o communities; however, doing so does not allow them the established community presence needed to conduct outreach and research activities central to their intellectual pursuits. As a result, Latina/o students often experience increased cultural tension, aggravated cultural distress, and intensified cultural disconnections from indigenous systems of support (e.g., local communities, family network, overall connection to culture) (Gloria & Castellanos, 2003).

As is the case with other doctoral students, establishing a mentoring relationship with faculty can facilitate the negotiation of the academic culture for Latina/o students (Menchaca et al., 2000; Williams, 2002). Along with providing financial, emotional/moral, mentorship, and technical support, Valverde and Rodriguez (2002) emphasize the importance of institutional support relative to a quality doctoral experience and ultimate persistence to completion. Mediating stressful educational experiences (Bowman & Bowman, 1990) and developing a mentoring relationship that allows Latina/os access to their professional lives and shapes students into "studious inquirers" (Brown et al., 1999, p. 116) promotes possibilities and increases efficacy for students.

Having an individual or group of individuals who can provide positive and supportive mentorship is ideal within graduate education; however, finding faculty who share similar research interests and/or similar cultural and ethnic backgrounds is often a challenge for Latina/o students (Gonzalez et al., 2002). The limited number of racial and ethnic minority faculty, much less those who are tenured or have full professorships, adds to the struggle of finding an individual through whom Latina/o students can see themselves personally and culturally (Delgado-Romero et al., 2003). Although some students complete their training with minimal to no mentorship from faculty or university personnel throughout their doctoral training, familial support (e.g., belief in the person regardless of academic outcome) is primary. Negotiating the subtle balance of self in relation to others within the academy (e.g., explaining cultural self to faculty) can make seeking help and support from faculty very stressful.

Integrating Personal and Professional Identities

Ultimately, striking a balance between personal and professional identities is fundamental for Latina/o doctoral student retention. Because enculturation to the climate and value of graduate training requires reshaping and values reconfiguration for many Latina/o students (Ibarra, 1996), staying connected to "life outside of academics" allows Latina/o students to remain culturally, spiritually, and personally revitalized. In particular, maintaining strong family ties, community relations, noncohort peer interactions, and even a reconnection to their *cultura* (via activity or celebration) keeps Latina/o students grounded in their educational pursuits—reminding them of their educational purpose and helping them to assess their development from a professional, personal, cultural, and community advocates' perspective.

Unfortunately, informal opportunities to connect and integrate within their communities are limited as Latina/os often move away from home to study and find themselves set apart and isolated from their families and friends. With most doctoral programs offered at large, research, predominantly White institutions and in rural towns with limited diversity, Latina/o graduate students are forced to be creative in developing a personal and professional balance. For example, Latina/os create opportunities for their own family weekend activities (e.g., mother-daughter weekends) by inviting *la familia* to school such that their family members and friends can understand and take part in their educational journey. However, family's involvement may be limited due to financial constraints, job demands, and other family obligations.

To bridge the cultural value of collectivism and family, many Latina/o graduate students create educational or university families with other Latina/o students who encounter similar educational experiences. Creating student support groups, retention committees, research or writing teams (e.g., creating Latina/o doctoral student anthology), and informal support network systems, Latina/o doctoral students again must negotiate their own personal commitments in concert with their professional responsibilities. Doing so can ease the tension of home and school cultures, allowing Latina/o students to move from an "either-or" to a "both-and" approach to their doctoral training. Negotiating the personal and professional within the context of relationships (e.g., family, peers, faculty); educational systems (e.g., classrooms and programs); and social networks (e.g., campus climate, university family) is likely to minimize isolation, marginalization, and separation and increase retention and overall satisfaction of Latina/o doctoral students.

Applying a Psychosociocultural Approach with Latina/o Doctoral Students

A framework originally developed for university counseling center staff who provide counseling services for Latina/o university students, a psychosociocultural approach emphasizes the dynamic and interdependent relationships of student dimensions (i.e., psychological concerns, social support systems, cultural factors, and university environmental contexts). Addressing the dimension's interactive confluence facilitates a comprehensive culture- and context-specific understanding of Latina/o personal, cultural, and educational concerns and needs (Gloria & Rodriguez, 2000; Gloria & Segura-Herrera, 2004). One of the few approaches that incorporates a multidimensional context for counseling Latina/o students (Constantine, Gloria, & Baron, in press), the psychosociocultural model can be extended to advanced Latina/o students (i.e., doctoral degree earners).

Gloria and Rodriguez (2000) argued that university counseling center staff are in primary positions to increase academic retention and persistence for Latina/o students given their

> (a) psychological training (e.g., multicultural awareness) and expertise to enhance student self-efficacy, (b) ability to provide outreach and consultative programming to a wide range of campus personnel, (c) familiarity with and interaction in the campus environment, (d) knowledge of available campus and community resources, and (e) accessibility to Latino students. (p. 146)

Given the amount of time doctoral students spend pursuing their degrees, potential for strong connection with one's faculty (in particular faculty advisor), and importance of having efficacious strategies to retain Latina/o students (along with all other doctoral students of color), the applicability of a PSC approach to recruit, retain, and train Latina/os doctoral students is presented. Parallel to counseling center staff working with Latina/o undergraduates, doctoral faculty can offer the strongest support and assistance to Latina/o doctoral students, given their (a) respective training and expertise in their fields to know and provide relevant student-efficacy opportunities (e.g., research and teaching); (b) ability to provide regular academic and professional development feedback; (c) first-hand knowledge of and interaction within the department climate and culture in which Latina/o students train; (d) knowledge of program, department, and university resources and opportunities; and (e) commitment to support all doctoral students, including Latina/os, to succeed. Because a PSC framework is psychoeducationally supportive, implementing this approach with students does not necessitate personal counseling or deep exploration of rationales, motives, or historical understanding of individual students. Instead, faculty can provide supportive assistance as advisors, advocates, or facilitators of systems (Constantine, Gloria, & Baron, in press) for Latina/o doctoral students without risk of inappropriate interactions or violation of faculty-student boundaries.

In working with Latina/o doctoral students, doctoral faculty (much like university counseling center staff) need to assess their multicultural counseling competencies (Sue, Arredondo, & McDavis, 1992), or in this case, their multicultural, educationally supportive competencies. The multicultural counseling competencies are conceptualized within a 3 x 3 (dimensions by characteristics) matrix. For purposes of this application, the dimensions of *Attitudes and Beliefs, Knowledge,* and *Skills* are discussed across the interrelated characteristics that encompass the *psychological, social,* and *cultural* for

Latina/os within the context (i.e., environment) of doctoral training programs (see Table 10.1). For a comprehensive discussion of the multicultural counseling competencies, readers are referred to Arredondo et al. (1996) and the American Psychological Association (2002). For purposes of presentation, select constructs are identified (i.e., well-being, mentorship, ethnic identity, and training context) to highlight the framework; however, doctoral faculty can identify and integrate additional interdependent and dynamic constructs (e.g., academic self-efficacy, competitive interactions, and enculturation) to support Latina/o students.

Application of PSC Approach with Latina/o Doctoral Students

Throughout our work with Latina/os, the number of Latina/o doctoral students who have substantially negative training experiences and struggles beyond those common to doctoral training far outweigh those who were able to follow relatively positive and uncomplicated paths. In compiling Latina/o doctoral student experiences, two composite vignettes reflecting the interrelated PSC issues are presented, followed by brief explanations and suggestions for providing integrative and supportive faculty interventions. Despite the mutual dependence and confluence of psychosociocultural elements, specific issues highlighted are not presented as stereotypical Latina/o doctoral student dilemmas, but as individual cases that illustrate salient Latina/o doctoral student issues.

Sonia, a 26-year-old, second-generation Chicana in the history department at a large Midwestern university, grew up in a close-knit family who values collaboration and interaction with immediate and extended family. Despite being a few hours away from home, her doctoral training is Sonia's first time away from family. She returns as often as possible (most weekends) and faithfully attends family socials and gatherings. Having been consistently surrounded by other Latina/os growing up and into her adulthood, she often finds herself in awkward and anxiety-producing situations when she is the only Latina/o and the only student of color in different situations (e.g., classroom, program social).

Despite having a strong sense of ethnic and cultural pride as a Chicana, Sonia has become confused and angry at having been continuously pointed out as different, asked to give the minority and/or Latina/o point of view, and expected to have multiple proficiencies of her program of study (i.e., history of women and gender) in addition to Latina/o, Mexican American, Chicana/o, and racial and ethnic minority histories. Given her focused academic energy and stellar work and academic record, Sonia has spent little time with the Latina/o student community and has been unable to provide leadership as a graduate student for the undergraduate Latina/o students. As a result, Sonia's cultural authenticity has been challenged within the student community. Feeling the duress of unrealistic expectations (from home, school, and community), Sonia feels heightened stress when she cannot complete an academic assignment in time to attend her niece's first birthday party at home. Sonia informs you, as her course instructor, that she will miss this week's class and turn in her assignment late.

As one of few Latina/o doctoral students within a program or department, students often and inadvertently are forced to reassess their ethnic identity. Looked to as Latina/o cultural ambassadors or being forced to "represent" an entire culture is unrealistic and often leads to resentment, alienation, or even self-distancing. Within the context of being away from a home in which they are supported as a group member (particularly for those Latina/o student who strongly value *familismo* [familialism]), Latina/o students' feelings of isolation frequently increase. Sonia is simultaneously expected to be the "Latina/o expert" within her doctoral program, yet she is questioned within community as about whether she is "being Latina/o enough." Doctoral faculty can intervene and provide support and challenge for Sonia. For example, Sonia's course instructor, having reflected on her biases regarding Sonia's priorities and capabilities (*Attitudes and Beliefs*), and knowing the importance of family for many Latina/os (*Knowledge*), can validate Sonia's feelings of anger and resentment while assessing the degree to which she has disconnected from the program to challenge Sonia firmly yet appropriately to re-engage in her learning processes (*Skills*). Without these integrative considerations, a faculty member may perceive Sonia as a complaining student who is overly dependent on family and unmotivated to earn a doctoral degree—a description that uses a deficit approach to working with students.

James, a first-generation Latino who self-identifies as *Mexicano*, is the first in his family to earn a high school, college, and advanced university degree. He is currently a second-year doctoral student in school psychology at a West Coast university's doctoral program. Despite having spent a year in the program, James missed the application for student funding (i.e., teaching fellowship) for the second consecutive year, which has resulted in his being in the department even less than he already is. Having school, family (wife, two children, and parents), community (volunteer staff at Latina/o immigrant social services center), and financial demands (a 30-hour-per-week position at a community mental health center), James has yet to establish connections with faculty or other students in his program. Having

TABLE 10.1

Attitudes and Beliefs, Knowledge, and Skills for Providing a Psychosociocultural Approach with Latina/o Doctoral Students

	Psychological	*Social*	*Cultural*	*Environmental*
	Well-being and Academic Adjustment	*Mentorship*	*Ethnic Identity and Cultural Values*	*Training Context*
Attitudes and Beliefs	*An awareness of one's own . . .*			
	understanding of what it means to be "well" or academically adjusted	definition and parameters of what constitutes mentorship	ethnic identity and biased assumptions about Latina/os	assumptions of what it means (attitudes and behaviors) to be a doctoral student
	assumptions about the impact of balancing home and school expectations	willingness and assumptions of ability to mentor students who are culturally different	willingness to explore continuously one's prejudices about Latina/os	assumptions of the extent to which Latina/o students should submit and/or change to fit into the established doctoral training system
Knowledge	*One's anecdotal, conceptual, theoretical, and empirical knowledge of . . .*			
	the dimensions of well-being for Latina/os (e.g., familial, spiritual, cultural)	mentoring frameworks for Latina/os and other students of color	ethnic identity models for Latina/os	academic myths and educational stereotypes about Latina/os
	the different stresses and distresses of Latina/o doctoral students	differential mentoring needs of Latina/os and other students of color	Latina/o core cultural values (general and ethnic subgroup specific) and resulting influence on interactions	racial and cultural climate of program, department, and university for Latina/o students

(continues)

TABLE 10.1 (Continued)

	Psychological *Well-being and Academic Adjustment*	*Social* *Mentorship*	*Cultural* *Ethnic Identity and Cultural Values*	*Environmental* *Training Context*
	the different expectations and responsibilities asked of Latina/o students' home and school contexts	collective mentoring practices for Latina/o students	how cultural differences from and similarities to Latina/os affect faculty-student and student-environment interactions	the equitable treatment and cultural integration of Latina/o students into the program and department
	One's abilities to accurately and effectively. . .			
Skills	assess the levels of stress and distress of Latina/o students and the impact on their personal and academic functioning	establish the necessary trust or *confianza* needed to develop strong working relationship with Latina/o students	assess Latina/o students ethnic identity and adherence to cultural values while responding with culturally efficiency	deconstruct inaccurate assumptions about and biases against Latina/o students within training context
	provide culturally integrative suggestions and feedback to facilitate Latina/o students' home-school balance	engage in faculty-student relationship that enacts *personalimo* and other core cultural values	understand the confluence of cultural values in conducting daily academic interactions	take responsibility for changing biased standards for Latina/os and other students of color

provide feedback regarding successes and areas for growth for personal and professional identities	become a genuine and supportive part of Latina/o students' university families	delineate culturally bound actions, interactions, and meanings from idiosyncratic behaviors and vice versa	reconnect Latina/o students back to their educational context when they disengage from their training process
encourage Latina/o students to expand their coping strategies to meet demands of home and school contexts (e.g., develop university family)	connect with other mentors with whom you can develop a collective mentoring network to support Latina/o students	challenge Latina/o students' value systems to negotiate their training contexts	intervene in classroom interactions in which Latina/os (or any students) are asked to serve as a cultural expert for others
support students through stressful and distressful situations and experiences (e.g., appropriate and timely referral to support and counseling services)	provide professional development activities that increase Latina/o students' efficacy (e.g., opportunities to present at national conferences or teach)	seek consultation about application and integration of cultural values	seek consultation with department faculty and university personnel to establish and maintain a culturally welcoming training environment

missed all but one of the faculty-student socials and departmental professional development trainings, he finds that students openly question his
commitment to his training, particularly because he rarely speaks in class.
More recently, James performed poorly on a class project, missing key elements of it by not having consulted during faculty office hours. During the
mid-year faculty review of students, James's performance in several of his
courses was questioned.

Often the first in their families to earn a college degree, many Latina/o
doctoral students do not have families who can help guide them through
their studies. Unaware of the expectations and norms inherent in doctoral
training, all students may have difficulty knowing the parameters of faculty-
student interactions. For those Latina/o students who reticently establish
connections without *confianza* (trust and confidence that the other has one's
best interest in mind), there may be additional issues with which to contend.
In helping James to succeed in his studies, his faculty advisor—having identified his biases regarding James's commitment to completing his program (*Attitudes and Beliefs*), and knowing how many Latina/os are often the first in
their families to attend college and the central role of *personalismo* and *confianza* to interactions (*Knowledge*)—can provide more concrete mentorship
with James to connect him to information (e.g., funding opportunities) and
teach him about program norms with faculty (e.g., use of office hours) and
classroom interactions (e.g., norms for participation) (*Skills*). Without these
integrative considerations, faculty may question James's academic capabilities and priorities, rather than try to identify how mentoring and culturally
based interactions could facilitate his academic experience. Further, identifying how James could integrate his family into his academic program and
maintain a balance that is beneficial to both his personal and professional
lives is essential to Latina/o doctoral graduate student progress. Ultimately,
application of a PSC approach addresses the holistic and culturally integrative means to retain Latina/o doctoral students.

References

Adams, H. G. (1993). *Focusing on the campus milieu: A guide for enhancing the graduate school climate* (Report No. ED381065). Notre Dame, IN: National Consortium for Graduate Degrees for Minorities in Engineering and Mathematics, Inc.
American Psychological Association (2002). Guidelines on multicultural education,
training, research, practice, and organizational change for psychologists. *American Psychologist, 58*(5), 377–402.

Anzaldúa, G. (1987). *Borderlands/La frontera: The new mestiza.* San Francisco: Aunt Lute.

Arredondo, P., Toporek, R., Brown, S., Jones, J., Locke, D. C., Sanchez, J., & Stadler, H. (1996). *Operationalization of the multicultural counseling competencies.* Alexandria, VA: American Counseling Association.

Bowman, R. L., & Bowman, V. E. (1990). Mentoring in a graduate counseling program: Students helping students. *Counselor Education and Supervision, 30*(1), 58–65.

Bowman, V.E., Hatley, L.D., & Bowman, R.L. (1995). Faculty-student relationships: The dual role controversy. *Counselor Education and Supervision, 34,* 232–242.

Brown, M.C., Jr., Davis, G.L., & McClendon, S.A. (1999). Mentoring graduate students of color: Myths, models, and modes. *Peabody Journal of Education, 74,* 105–118.

Castellanos, J., & Jones, L. (Eds.) (2003). *The majority in the minority: Expanding the representation of Latina/o faculty, administrators and students in higher education.* Sterling, VA: Stylus.

Constantine, M. C., Gloria, A. M., & Baron, A. (in press). Counseling Mexican American university students. In C. Lee (Ed.), *Multicultural issues in counseling: New approaches to diversity,* 3rd ed. Alexandria, VA: American Counseling Association.

Delgado-Romero, E. A., Flores, L., Gloria, A. M., Arredondo, P., & Castellanos, J. (2003). Developmental career challenges for Latino and Latina faculty in higher education. In J. Castellanos & L. Jones (Eds.), *The majority in the minority: Retaining Latina/o faculty, administrators and students in higher education* (pp. 257–283). Sterling, VA: Stylus.

Gloria, A.M., & Castellanos, J. (2003). Latino/a and African American students at predominantly White institutions: A psychosociocultural perspective of educational interactions and academic persistence. In J. Castellanos and L. Jones (Eds.), *The majority in the minority: Retaining Latina/o faculty, administrators, and students* (pp. 71–92). Sterling, VA: Stylus.

Gloria, A. M., & Pope-Davis, D. B. (1997). Cultural ambience: The importance of a culturally aware environment in the training and education of counselors. In D. B. Pope-Davis & H. L. K. Coleman (Eds.), *Multicultural counseling competencies: Assessment, education and training, and supervision* (pp. 242–259). Thousand Oaks, CA: Sage.

Gloria, A. M., & Rodriguez, E. R. (2000). Counseling Latino university students: Psychosociocultural issues for consideration. *Journal of Counseling and Development, 78,* 145–154.

Gloria, A. M., & Segura-Herrera, T. M. (2004). *Ambrocia* and *Omar* go to college: A psychosociocultural examination of Chicanos and Chicanas in higher education. In R. J. Velasquez, B. McNeill, & L. Arellano (Eds.), *Handbook of Chicana and Chicano psychology* (pp. 401–425). Mahwah, NJ: Lawrence Erlbaum.

Grijalva, C. A., & Holman Coombs, R. (1997). Latinas in medicine: Stressors, survival skills, and strengths. *Aztlan: A Journal of Chicano Studies, 22*(2), 67–88.

Gonzalez, K. P., Figueroa, M. A., Marin, P., Moreno, J. F., & Navia, C. N. (2002). Inside doctoral education in America: Voices of Latinas/os in pursuit of the Ph.D. *Journal of College Student Development, 43*(4), 540–557.

Herrera, R. (2003). Notes from a Latino graduate student at a predominantly White university. In J. Castellanos & L. Jones (Eds.), *The majority in the minority: Expanding the representation of Latina/o faculty, administrators and students in higher education* (pp. 111–125). Sterling, VA: Stylus.

Hodgson, C. S., & Simoni, J. M. (1995). Graduate student academic and psychological functioning. *Journal of College Student Development, 36*, 244–253.

Holmes, T. H., & Rahe, R. H. (1967). The Social Readjustment Rating Scale. *Journal of Psychosomatic Research, 11*, 213–218.

Hurtado, S. (1994). Graduate school racial climates and academic self-concept among minority graduate students in the 1970s. *American Journal of Education, 102*(3), 330–351.

Ibarra, R. (1996). *Enhancing the minority presence in graduate education VII: Latino experiences in graduate education: implications for change, A preliminary report* (Report No. HE029366). Washington, DC: Council of Graduate Schools.

Ibarra, R. A. (2001). *Beyond affirmative action: Reframing the context of higher education.* Madison, WI: The University of Wisconsin Press.

Levine, E. S., & Padilla, A. M. (1980). *Crossing cultures in therapy: Pluralistic counseling for the Hispanic.* Belmont, CA: Wadsworth.

Marín, G., & Triandis, H. C. (1985). Allocentrism as an important characteristic of the behavior of Latin Americans and Hispanics. In R. Diaz-Guerrero (Ed.), *Cross-cultural and national studies in social psychology* (pp. 85–104). Amsterdam: North Holland.

Marshall, H., & Jones, K. (1990). Childbearing sequence and the career development of women administrators in higher education. *Journal of College Student Development, 31*(6), 531–537.

Menchaca, V. D., Estrada, V. L., Cavazos, C., & Ramirez, D. (2000). *Challenging the face of educational leadership: A unique method of mentoring Hispanic doctoral students.* Washington, DC: U.S. Department of Education, Office of Research and Improvement.

Morales, E. (1996). Gender roles among Latino gay and bisexual men: Implications for family and couple relationships. In J. Laird & R. J. Green (Eds.), *Lesbians and gays in couples and families: A handbook for therapists* (p. 272–297). San Francisco, CA: Jossey Bass.

Nieves-Squires, S. (1991). *Hispanic women: Making their presence on campus less tenuous.* Washington, DC: Association of American Colleges, Project on the Status and Education of Women.

Poock, M. C. (1999). Students of color and doctoral programs: Factors influencing the application decision in higher education administration. *College & University, 74*(3), 2–7.

Roach-Singh, I. (1994). Perceived stress among graduate students: Development and validation of the Graduate Stress Inventory. *Educational and Psychological Measurement, 54,* 714–727.

Santiago-Rivera, A. L, Arredondo, P., & Gallardo-Cooper, M. (2002). *Counseling Latinos and la familia: A Practical Guide.* Thousand Oaks, CA: Sage Publications.

Sue, D. W., Arredondo, P., & McDavis, R. J. (1992). Multicultural counseling competencies and standards: A call to the profession. *Journal of Counseling and Development, 70,* 477–486.

Trevino, J. G. (1996). Worldview and change in cross-cultural counseling. *The Counseling Psychologist, 24*(2), 198–215.

Ülkü-Steiner, B., Kurtz-Costes, B., & Kinlaw, C. R. (2000). Doctoral student experiences in gender-balanced and male-dominated graduate programs. *Journal of Educational Psychology, 92*(2), 296-307.

Valverde, M. R., & Rodriguez, R. C. (2002). Increasing Mexican American doctoral degrees: The role of institutions of higher education. *Journal of Hispanic Higher Education, 1*(1), 51–58.

Williams, K. B. (2002). Minority and majority students' retrospective perceptions of social support in doctoral programs. *Perceptual and Motor Skills, 95*(1), 187–196.

PART THREE

APRENDIENDO DE LOS PASAJEROS (LEARNING FROM THE PASSENGERS)

II

FINDING MY WAY
Enculturation to the Ph.D.

Mark Kamimura

The Ph.D., for most students, regardless of ethnic identity, is a challenging experience. My doctoral program has introduced multiple challenges that confront my core cultural values. As a multiracial Ph.D. student (Okinawan-Chicano-White American), I bring to the doctoral experience different cultural norms from my White peers and from those of the university environment. Challenges embedded in the culture of the academy include the demand to understand, analyze, and create knowledge and scholarship regardless of the discipline. Although each program and discipline has different norms for doctoral student adherence, internalization of these values is essential for academic success. This chapter focuses on my enculturation process in the pursuit of a doctoral degree. In particular, I define enculturation and explore the environmental influences of my experience. Finally, I discuss the phases of my enculturation, drawing on personal experiences from my doctoral training.

Defining Enculturation

Enculturation is defined as a *process* of functioning within a given set of values and cultural norms needed to integrate into a new culture (Bernal & Knight, 1997). Process is primary to enculturation as it emphasizes how one experiences a new culture. When students enter a Ph.D. program, they engage an academic culture of specific values, behaviors, and perspectives. The culture and nuances of the academy have existed for generations, and learning the rules of engagement introduces a process of trial and error for some students. Familiarity with the academic culture varies for many Latina/os as they continue to be first-generation college students (Gloria & Castellanos, 2003). Some of the particular doctoral program values emphasize research, individuality, independence, challenge of perspectives, and the pursuit of power. In contrast, Latina/o cultures espouse values of family, reverence for and support of elders, interdependence, and community collaboration. The doctoral enculturation process introduces unique challenges for Latina/os who adhere to cultural values and mores that are in contrast to those of the university.

Overcoming the challenges presented by the Ph.D. enculturation process relies on one's individual abilities to negotiate internal value conflicts successfully (Bernal & Knight, 1997). Internal value conflicts can occur when core cultural values are challenged by the cultural values within Ph.D. programs. Developing the skills to negotiate these value conflicts is integral and can often be found in past experiences. Latina/o students come from diverse pre-college, undergraduate, and graduate experiences before entering Ph.D. programs, so they are prepared differently to address the value conflicts that arise in their programs (Solorzano, 1995, 1998). The impact of these earlier experiences is important: they are a source of what makes doctoral enculturation difficult and also a source of strength guiding students successfully through each situation.

The Impact of *Familia* and *Communidad*

My path, like that of many other Latina/o students, begins with my family history. My grandfather worked in the California farm fields with his brothers, raising themselves and struggling for the "American Dream." *Obisbio Jimenez* served our country as a captain in the U.S. Army, for which he received a shoebox full of medals, including a Purple Heart, all with a second-grade education. One of the most important lessons *mi abuelito* (my grandfather) taught me was finding value and meaning in all situations and experiences. For example, in college I learned about the experiences of farmworkers through books; however, their description of conditions did not match my *abuelito*'s stories. The stories I remembered were about freedom, family, and opportunity.

My cultural influences came from my immediate *familia* (family) and *comunidad* (community). Community for me has included the neighborhood (*barrio*) in which I grew up, the larger community of color, and the

Chicana/o/Latina/o *comunidad.* My neighborhood community reminds me of my history, which included navigating the influence of gangs, street violence, police brutality, and drugs. These negatives motivated me to find a way out—education has been the path to fulfilling my version of *mi abuelito*'s "American Dream." Following *mi abuelito*'s path, the *barrio* taught me how to navigate hostile environments, deal with individuals who do not want me to succeed, have a healthy respect for power, understand the importance of *familia*, and learn whom to trust. These skills are directly applicable to and highly useful in the academic environment, where I have encountered similar situations.

The second constituent of influence that I negotiate is the larger community of color and Latina/o *comunidad* within my institution. Some universities have Asian, Latina/o, African American, and Native American (ALAANA) organizations for graduate students. These organizations are cross-disciplinary and serve as retention systems for graduate students of color because of the support network developed through shared experiences. At the University of Michigan, I became heavily involved in an organization, called the Students of Color of Rackham, also known as SCOR. Involvement in the community of color as a Ph.D. student exposed me to a shared value system across racial and ethnic groups that included family, support, and community development. SCOR offered such supportive relationships as peer mentorship, advising, and common predoctoral experiences. For ALAANA and SCOR-like organizations to exist, one must commit time and energy to all of the individuals in the community of color to "bring up" each generation. I consider SCOR a lifeline and refer to it as my retention program. I am certain that the relationships established through SCOR will be my support network professionally and socially for the rest of my life.

Community connections provide me the focused support I need to succeed in my graduate program. At the same time, I am challenged by the responsibility and time commitment necessary to support the local and undergraduate communities. Although I am committed to these communities, the expectation that I would be involved is an additional commitment with which my White peers do not contend. My professors have told me directly to avoid commitments to my communities: "They will hold you back; you will fail if you continue on this path; they are not there for you." These comments clearly present a conflict in values for me as well as a lack of recognition and understanding by faculty of the needs, roles, and responsibilities that I encounter as a Chicano/Latino doctoral student.

The Phases of My Enculturation as a Chicano/Latino Doctoral Student

Reflecting on my experiences, challenges, and values as a Chicano/Latino doctoral student, I have grouped my enculturation experiences into six phases. For me, enculturation into a doctoral program means the development of a new social identity. I understand that doctoral programs produce scholars, researchers, critical thinkers, professors, and eventual experts on a specific topic within a field; however, doctoral program culture also influences social behaviors, political positioning, and socioeconomic status. As I reflected upon my experiences and those of other students of color around me, I realized that the process of enculturation to the culture of doctoral training could be equated to racial identity development (e.g., Cross, 1995; Helms, 1990)—each stage building on the previous in which different aspects of identity are developed, explored, and understood. Making meaning of my experiences and lending validation to others, I propose that my doctoral enculturation process includes the follows phases: *Open-mindedness and Self-awareness* (Phase 1); *Cultural Mismatch and Dissonance* (Phase 2); *Rebellion and Self-distancing* (Phase 3); *Self-reflection* (Phase 4); *Re-integration* (Phase 5); and *Navigation/Control/Power* (Phase 6).

I entered graduate school with an *open mind.* I was optimistic and open to learning the behaviors, values, and views of the discipline, my faculty, and my peers. At first, I accepted aspects of the culture that were in conflict with my personal values. For example, I tried to write my first paper from a viewpoint that did not reflect my perspective or my voice as a student of color, as I wanted to avoid being scrutinized by faculty because of my views on race, ethnicity, and culture. Without accounting for or using race as a component of the topic, the paper was by far the hardest assignment of my doctoral training to date. I attempted to assimilate into the university culture to appease the likes and dislikes of my faculty; it was difficult to complete the assignment, and I was intellectually distant from my interests, which ultimately benefited no one. At first, the compromises I made did not feel like a sacrifice, but I soon discovered that I was on a path far from my original reasons for earning a Ph.D.

Beyond the academic culture of the Ph.D. are the sociocultural aspects of graduate life. Some of these aspects for me included attending cohort functions, participating in faculty-initiated and program social events, exploring faculty mentoring relationships, and joining student organizations. Engaging in the social aspect of the Ph.D. was translated later into opportunities for leadership positions with professional organizations, funding, co-authoring articles, paper presentations, and mentoring. Watching other students have these experiences raised questions for me about why I was not engaged in the same opportunities. These questions included: Are they smarter than I? Did I miss something at orientation? Am I behind in my professional development? How could *I* get these opportunities? Do the faculty like me? These questions prompted *self-awareness*. As I tried to keep an open mind, I felt guilty and blamed myself for a lack of initiative. Seeing the unequal treatment of students, combined with these unanswered questions running through my mind, influenced my interactions with my classmates and the faculty in my department.

As the newness of the program wore off, my mind was no longer open to incorporating the academic culture without question, particularly as I realized that the culture was biased. For example, I realized there was a differential reward system for different students. For some, their faculty-student relationships developed into "friendships." It was this separation and disparate treatment among students that triggered me to enter the next phase, *Cultural Mismatch and Dissonance*. A critical incident for me was seeing White students glorified by professors as critical thinkers for addressing topics on race and ethnicity, yet being scrutinized as having biased perspectives, stating opinions instead of facts, and lacking multiple perspectives when *I* introduced the same issues. From this difference in treatment, I realized that I was dually enrolled in my program—as a Ph.D. student and as a Chicano/ Latino Ph.D. student, each of whom had distinctly different expectations.

The third phase, *Rebellion and Self-distancing*, refers to the frustration I experienced when navigating the academic value systems and my native cultural values. In managing my frustration, I began to separate myself from the social and academic aspects of the department. I separated from my program by increasing my community involvement, taking courses outside my discipline area, and seeking mentorship from faculty outside my department; I found myself detaching from the department altogether. The rationale behind this response was my rejection of the culture inherent to the department and my attempt to avoid the enculturation process.

I entered the rebellion stage early in my program and was "rebellious" for two of my first three years as a doctoral student. Unmotivated to perform in my courses, I committed much of my time to community of color service activities on- and off-campus—I had lost sight of why I had entered a Ph.D. program. To make matters worse, a professor indicated that my application and academic record were being re-examined because it could not be determined from my class performance how I would possibly be successful in my program. It was insinuated that I was only admitted because of affirmative action. According to the professor, "You may have gotten into this program, but you will be lucky to pass the CQE [comprehensive qualifying exam], and [you] may even graduate, but you will go nowhere in this field." These comments came at the beginning of my second year, making it extremely difficult for me to feel motivated to perform academically. For example, I lacked confidence in nearly every paper I wrote, because I knew it would be read from a biased perspective.

For me, the dangers of this phase include diminished quality of work, lack of participation in courses, and a distancing of relationships with professors in my department. If I had continued along this path for too long, I would have become an outsider to the doctoral culture and possibly even forgotten. The beginning of the end of this phase came with the unfortunate passing of my mother, *Melody Jiménez Kamimura*. For me, this event was a clear indicator of my need to re-evaluate my academic position to complete my program successfully.

A series of critical incidents during my rebelliousness and self-distancing prompted me to the *Self-reflection* phase. As I self-reflected, I realized how my rebellion was academically self-destructive. It was during this phase that I regrouped and recognized the importance of coming to terms with my values conflict. Moving through and beyond this phase depended on my re-evaluating my current behaviors and attitudes. I asked myself what I was doing that guided me toward my degree and what was keeping me from my goals. I found myself so busy with "other" commitments that my academic career was getting squeezed out. I was under extreme stress with the passing of my mom, while simultaneously managing the reality that I had failed to take the steps needed to move smoothly to candidacy, and my lack of investment in my department caught up with me. I lost an entire year of candidacy funding because of my educational decisions. Having been in the *Rebellious and Self-distancing* phase for so long, I was not prepared to situate myself academically to deal with major events (i.e., a new baby, marriage, death in the family, illness). Instead, I needed extended time away from school.

During this time of self-reflection I returned to my *barrio*, spent time with family, and frequented places I had visited with my mom. These places were important, because our conversations there had focused on my life goals, telling her about my desired accomplishments, and hearing her voice in my memory telling me how proud she was of me. During this reflection time, I came to terms with what I had already sacrificed to be in my program. I had spent the last three years of my mom's life away from her. I knew at that point I had invested more than I had anticipated, because if I had known she would pass, I never would have left home. This motivated me enough to get off my knees and start walking forward again.

The end of the *Self-Reflection* phase began with my developing a plan for *Re-integration*, the phase where I needed time to get back "on track." Unfortunately for Latina/os and students of color, this can be a challenging experience because of stereotypes linked to affirmative action, race, ethnicity, and gender. I had already performed poorly in some classes during my *Rebellion and Self-distancing* phase and had not developed a strong academic reputation. My actions and performance only supported the biased claims of professors looking for reasons to create obstacles for me. The situation I created for myself made the re-integration phase a challenge; I spent more than a month negotiating the terms of my fellowship to maintain health care, funding, and my status as a student. The key to my successful re-integration was finding a faculty member who mentored and advised me through this process, developing a short- and long-term plan that will lead me to graduation while limiting external commitments. Deciding to meet with my faculty was a critical step for me. I needed to ask for what I needed and to determine what I could do for myself. My immediate plan was to prepare for and pass my qualifying examinations. I now needed to focus on my next step— becoming a doctoral candidate.

The last phase is labeled *Navigation/Control/Power* to represent the skills developed through the enculturation process. I currently find myself transitioning from the *Re-integration* phase into this next developmental step of achieving candidacy. The navigation of the Ph.D. program has not been an easy or simple task considering the cultural conflict between my values and those of the academy. These factors will continue to influence my experiences as I reach the final stage of my doctoral training. I presented the phases of my doctoral enculturation to provide insights to help other Latina/o students navigate their doctoral training. I emphasize the importance of seeking guidance, carefully considering from whom to seek support, and trusting and acknowledging the dual expectations as a doctoral student and a Latina/o doctoral student. Although I cannot control the various factors influencing my educational path, I can control how I negotiate and contend with these factors.

The process of enculturation to the Ph.D. is a humbling and disempowering experience. The last component focuses on embracing the power I have as a Chicano/Latino doctoral student. The realization of this power is important because I know that my success has far-reaching implications for the academy, communities of color, and future generations of Latina/o Ph.D.s. I represent the struggles across my *familia* generations and serve as a role model for other Latina/o students. Unfortunately for me, I am only now beginning to understand this phase of my doctoral experience, but I hope to navigate this process by building on and learning from my past.

Recommendations for Students and Faculty

The enculturation process outlined in this chapter is primarily based on my personal experience, influenced by conversations with other Latina/o Ph.D. students across the country. The value of the enculturation phases for students, faculty, and staff is that they highlight my doctoral program experiences from a developmental perspective. Through these phases, students can develop negotiation strategies and faculty can implement retention efforts and support services that focus on the common issues Latina/o students, women, and other students of color may similarly encounter.

- Students should take notice of their feelings and their negative experiences and work through them to avoid academic self-destructive attitudes and behaviors.
- Students should develop at least one working relationship with a faculty member to whom they can turn for advisement and mentorship.
- Faculty should acknowledge and understand the specific issues of Latina/o and other students of color students in their programs. For example, learn how student organizations facilitate retention, peer-mentorship, support services, recruitment, advising, and professional networks for students.
- Academic programs should implement faculty enrichment programs that focus on diversity and the types of discriminatory situations that occur in doctoral programs. Implementing such efforts ensures that *all* faculty and students take responsibility for diversity issues.

References

Bernal, M. E., & Knight, G. P. (1997). Ethnic identity of Latino children. In J. G. Garcia & M. C. Zea (Eds.), *Psychological interventions and research with Latino populations* (pp. 15–38). Boston, MA: Allyn and Bacon.

Cross, W. E., Jr. (1995). The psychology of nigrescence: Revising the Cross model. In J. G. Ponterotto, J. M. Casas, L. A. Suzuki, & C. M. Alexander (Eds.), *Handbook of multicultural counseling* (pp. 93–122). Thousand Oaks, CA: Sage Publications.

Gloria, A., & Castellanos, J. (2003). Latina/o and African American students at predominantly White institutions: A psychosociocultural perspective of cultural congruity, campus climate, and academic persistence. In J. Castellanos & L. Jones (Eds.), *Majority in the minority: Expanding the representation of Latina/o faculty, administrators and students in higher education* (pp. 71–92). Sterling, VA: Stylus Publishing.

Helms, J. E. (1990). *Black and White racial identity: Theory, research, and practice.* New York: Greenwood Press.

Solorzano, D. (1995). The baccalaureate origins of Chicana and Chicano doctorates in the social sciences. *Hispanic Journal of Behavioral Sciences, 17*(1), 3–32.

Solorzano, D. (1998). Critical race theory, race and gender microaggressions, and the experience of Chicana and Chicano scholars. *Qualitative Studies in Education, 11*(1), 121–136.

Rocio Rosales

Rocio Rosales is a first-generation Mexican American raised in Santa Ana, California, by her mother, Evelia Meza, along with her two younger sisters, Dalia and Susan. Ms. Rosales graduated from the University of California-Irvine with a B.A. with honors in psychology, cum laude, and Phi Beta Kappa in 2002; she is currently a doctoral student in the Department of Education, School and Counseling Psychology at the University of Missouri-Columbia. Her primary research interests include psychosociocultural factors and the college student development of Latina/o and other racial and ethnic minorities in higher education. Other areas of research interest include academic achievement, academic motivation, cultural congruity, and identity development of Latina/Latinos and other racial/ethnic minorities. After completing her doctorate, Ms. Rosales plans to return to Southern California to reunite with her family, to give back to her community, and to follow in her mentor's footsteps by mentoring students of color in higher education.

12

MANTENIENDO NUESTRA CULTURA (SUSTAINING OUR CULTURE)

Cultural and Social Adjustments of Latina/os in Doctoral Programs

Rocio Rosales

In beginning graduate school, I expected to be intellectually challenged; however, I did not expect for my culture and identity to be challenged as well. I did not anticipate that my cultural values would serve as additional obstacles in my pursuit of a doctoral degree. Coming from Southern California, I expected to experience "culture shock" in moving to the rural Midwest; however, I did not envision culture shock as part of my doctoral experience. I expected to train with a cohort of doctoral students and faculty who would embrace and value diversity. Instead, I encountered feelings of alienation and isolation from my student colleagues and the program in general. Through all of this, I underestimated the role *mi familia* (my family), mentors, and friends would take to facilitate my survival and successful completion of graduate school.

As I continue my educational journey, I realize the immense personal growth and understanding that these experiences have engendered in me, while managing discrimination, tokenism, and marginalization. As I tell my story, this chapter presents factors that both hinder and facilitate my educational journey. In particular, this chapter addresses mentorship, familial support, and peers as they have facilitated my cultural and social adjustment in my graduate training. Sharing my experiences will potentially validate other doctoral Latina/o students' experiences and feelings and educate faculty and administrators on the importance of *cultura* (culture) in our educational pursuits. This story reflects my experiences in my first two years of graduate training in a doctoral program that I no longer attend. I have transferred to a new institution, where I am completing the final stages of my doctoral degree.

Mi Familia y Mi Cultura (My Family and My Culture)

Although I am the first in my family to graduate from college and pursue higher education, my mom was instrumental in teaching my sisters and me the value of education. My mom always emphasized that education can never be taken away despite the course of life—the knowledge that I would acquire will always remain with me. Just as important, she also reinforced the value of cultural roots—to know who we are and where we come from and to embrace our Mexican culture. Being raised as a first-generation Mexican American (born to Mexican immigrants), who grew up in a predominantly Mexican city (Santa Ana, California), my culture is paramount to who I am, the goals I set, and how I accomplish these goals.

In addition to reinforcing *cultura* as a backdrop for my educational pursuits, she provided me with unconditional emotional support, courage, motivation, and love, enabling me to seek opportunities and follow my dreams. Today, my *familia*'s support reinforces my inner strength to complete my doctoral degree. I believe that to truly understand any Latina/o, one must understand the importance of family. Family is difficult to separate from the individual, and without the family, my journey would not be complete.

Cultural Incongruity

In pursuing graduate education, I found myself in a context significantly different from my upbringing, culture, and home environment. I was at a predominantly White institution located in a rural town far away from home and in direct contrast to *mi cultura*. As a Latina graduate student with strong cultural values, I encountered unique challenges in learning how to navigate the environment. My experience is best described as a mismatch between my cultural values and those of the university environment. Growing up Mexican American, I was raised with core values of *familismo* (familism) and *collectivismo* (collectivism). *Familismo* is the value of maintaining close and reciprocal connections to *familia* (Santiago-Rivera, Arredondo, & Gallardo-Cooper, 2002; Falicov, 1998). Central to the value of *familismo* is a collectivist worldview in which individuals' primary focus is on the welfare of the group and individual needs are often secondary (Marín & Triandis, 1985).

As a result of the geographical distance from my family, I have found it tremendously difficult to preserve my family practices and frequency of contact. Graduate education requires time to study, conduct research, entertain original ideas, and develop scholarly skills, much of which is conducted individually and with great focus. However, this educational focus requires a complete immersion into academic culture that is individualistic and requires me to be "selfish" with my time. I am faced with choosing between being successful in graduate school or maintaining ongoing cultural balance and connections. I will not choose between the two, so I constantly struggle with learning how to balance these opposing worlds. I was experiencing what Rendón (1992) identified as having to chose between staying true to culture and succeeding in academia.

Initially, I experienced what Rendón (1992) describes as "academic shock" compounded by "ethnic and racial shock." I questioned from where these adjustment challenges came. It was not my level of academic preparation, as I had strong undergraduate training at a research institution. Instead, it was clear that my department environment invalidated and intimidated me and led to my feelings of cultural isolation and being misunderstood. Being in an environment where the faculty were primarily White and had minimal understanding of *mi cultura* contributed to my feelings of being marginalized and alienated. It is a complex task for faculty to understand Latina/o and other racial/ethnic minority students when they do not understand their own culture. For example, faculty and student peers in my department constantly complained that I isolated myself from the department and the other graduate students. But I never quite understood: How could I have been isolating myself when the department wasn't doing anything to help me feel included?

My isolation stemmed from multiple layers within my education context. First, at the university-wide level, there was no ethnic minority student representation, nor were there support programs. At the departmental level, the curriculum did not include racial and ethnic minority issues or practical relevancy to under-represented communities. The values inherent in the training were Eurocentric and invalidated my experiences and culture. Further affecting my alienation, the environment did not support my multicultural research interests and emergent research agenda. As a result, I began to question my role and fit within the department and university—I asked myself, "What am I doing here?"

Experiencing Racism and Discrimination

In the predominantly White, rural, small town where my program was located, I experienced overt racism that made me feel different and out of place. For example, when I entered a restaurant, I often saw people staring at me, and I received less prompt service than White customers. Although these overt acts of racism were unpleasant and made me feel inferior, they were easier to deal with because I expected them. What I did not expect, however, were similar racist interactions and comments from my professors. These acts were subtler as my research interests and projects were devalued, deemed not "good enough" or "not original" as they were perceived as simply replicating previous work with a new population. Having my professors dismiss me and my ideas was stressful; I was being asked to separate my culture from who I am and what I do. This invalidation, which served to isolate me even further, was detrimental to my educational training and development.

These feelings of marginalization and isolation constantly evoked self-doubt and forced me to question whether I should be in school. I have alternated between returning home and staying to complete my degree. I asked myself, "Is enduring the racism and discrimination of higher education worth having left my family and community?" Such questions are not easily answered; however, I have been fortunate to have the support of many individuals both inside and outside of academia, helping me to realize that the positive outcomes ultimately will outweigh the negative.

Coping Techniques: Family, Mentors, Peers, and Community

As a Latina in graduate school who feels culturally incongruent, I realized that I would need to learn to navigate the academic environment to complete my training. I developed coping skills that many of my White counterparts would not need. For example, we students needed to become accustomed to constant evaluation; however, I also had to contend with questions that challenged my academic competence as a Latina and my culture in general. I felt watched and examined even more than my White counterparts, which further affected my feelings of being out of place. In addition, I felt that my progress was used to assess the performance of other Latina/os as well—that I was representing Latina/os in general, rather than just myself.

Although my graduate school experiences have been negative at times, the support of family and mentors has helped me to make sense of events, negotiate my environment, and, ultimately, stay in school. First, my family provides me with the emotional support that I need when I have feelings of self-doubt and cultural isolation. My mom and sisters constantly reminded me of the *orgullo* (pride) they and the rest of my family felt because I was pursuing a graduate degree. Their encouragement and confidence gave me renewed strength to face the daily struggles and obstacles as well as to maintain my cultural and personal values—maintaining my relationships with them keeps me rooted in my culture. Finally, my mom helped me to realize and appreciate the struggles and hardships that she endured coming from Mexico, which provided me with the courage to honor her sacrifices.

Because I do not have family members who have earned a higher education, I needed to rely on my "academic family" to provide me the support and encouragement to achieve my academic goals. This academic family includes my mentors, Drs. Castellanos, Parham, and Cokley (my graduate advisor), who created a foundation for my self-efficacy and confidence by providing vital opportunities to facilitate and challenge my intellectual growth and potential. Knowing that they went through the same educational struggles yet ultimately succeeded helps me feel that I, too, can succeed. In particular, Dr. Cokley has affirmed my belief in cultural issues through cultural validation, his research agenda for racial/ethnic minorities, and serving as a bridge for me to the department. In our conversations, we processed my negative feelings and even joked about the disparities that racial/ethnic minorities and their White counterparts experience in their graduate careers. Equally important, Dr. Cokley presented me with opportunities that enhanced my graduate school experience, such as working on a multicultural research team, presenting at conferences, and introducing me to other scholars who had similar interests and a passion for work with racial/ethnic minorities.

Although I experienced cultural isolation in my department, I found comfort and validation from my good undergraduate friend, a Latina doctoral student at a different institution, who was going through similar experiences. We are fortunate to share stories, vent, and have someone with whom to connect. Although we were close friends during our undergraduate years, our struggles in graduate school strengthened our bond. At times we could not find the words to describe what we were experiencing, but no words were needed; we just knew. Because of her similar experiences, her support was different from others' in that she understood what I was going through and what I was talking about. We were able to share our frustrations and our feelings of loneliness and homesickness.

My long-distance support from family and friends is important; however, having connections with others on campus was imperative. There were few racial/ethnic minority students in my department, and I took advantage of connecting and forming friendships with these students. In particular, we had similar experiences that we shared, and we gave each other advice and support. Recognizing the overlap of experiences, I joined the Black Student Caucus, a group that allowed me to connect with other students who felt passionate about their culture and cultural issues. Seeing the commonalities of experience allowed me to make connections across disciplines and with others of different racial/ethnic minority backgrounds. Being able to relate to people from different cultural backgrounds in the same town and at the university allowed me to develop strong connections. We were experiencing the same unreceptive environment and the same cultural mismatch.

Establishing a connection with the Latina/o community was also critical in my cultural and social adjustment. Having a connection *con mi gente* (with my people), created a feeling of "home away from home." Although I did not know each of the community members individually, I felt a personal connection and a sense of *familismo*. They celebrated my successes and were proud of me because I represented the future opportunities for others in my community. Recreating the feelings of family and culture with the community renewed my determination to persist.

Recommendations for Latina/o Doctoral Students

Although graduate school is a long, hard road, full of struggles and obstacles, it is our time to rise to its many challenges. As we struggle and overcome these difficulties, we will enter into influential roles that will allow us to make changes that benefit the Latina/o community.

Moreover, I have learned that "academic success can be attained without total disconnection" (Rendón, 1992 p. 60). In other words, you do not have to change yourself completely or disconnect from your *cultura* (culture)— having strong connections to your culture and your cultural values will give you the inner strength and energy to be successful. Connections also come in the form of relationships with family, friends, and community.

- Remain close to what is most important to you as Latina/os: *familia y cultura*. Although your family may not understand or be able to relate to your educational experiences, do not let this stop you from talking to and keeping in touch with your loved ones. Use your family as a primary source of support, rather than distancing yourself and creating additional cultural barriers. They may not be able to offer you advice in the academic arena, but they will provide you with priceless *amor* (love), *cariño* (warmth), *valor* (courage), and *apoyo* (support) that only they can give.

- Seek out peers and colleagues, both inside and outside your department, who are experiencing similar educational struggles and difficulties. Although it might feel best to turn to other Latina/os, students from other cultures and backgrounds can be helpful in providing similar support.
- Address and implement your commitment to Latina/o and ethnic minority issues in your research. Although research that is community-based and provides some intervention for oppressed groups may be more difficult and time-consuming, in the end your work will be more meaningful and valuable because it has purpose and relevance. Along the same lines, become involved in extracurricular activities that address Latina/o issues and/or help younger Latina/os on campus. This work will motivate and sustain you in a department that may lack elements and opportunities for cultural connections (Herrera, 2003).
- Finally, be true to yourself and do not give in to your self-doubts. Although this is easier said than done, do not forget how hard you have worked or how hard others have worked to support you in your educational journey. Honor those who believe in you by believing in yourself as you continue to excel in your endeavors.

Recommendations for Individual Faculty and Training Programs

For Latina/o students, the value of role models and mentors cannot be overestimated (Castellanos & Jones, 2003). Recognize and value Latina/o and other faculty who provide critical support and mentorship for Latina/o students. Having faculty who take personal and professional interest in Latina/o students can often make the difference in keeping students connected and staying in school.

Be honest and fair with students. As noted by Herrera (2003), "be honest about what you can offer, who you are, and your limitations" (p. 123) as faculty, in training programs, and in understanding cultural issues in the field, classroom, and interactions. Honestly assess the degree to which your graduate program integrates and manifests multicultural competence. For example, assess how culture and multiculturalism are implemented in your curriculum, teaching style, teacher-student relationships, and research opportunities. Best stated by Rendón (1992), faculty and training programs "must consider past experience, language, and culture as strengths to be respected and woven into the fabric of knowledge production and dissemination, not as deficits that must be devalued, silenced, and overcome" (p. 62). Ultimately, integrating Latina/o students' culture (and those of other racial/ethnic minorities) is a means to increase their retention, positive training experiences, and graduation.

Recommendations for the University to Recruit and Retain Latina/o Students

Recognizing that Latina/o graduate students are often the "lonely only" in their graduate programs and departments, it is important for the university to sponsor culturally diverse programs, events, and workshops for them and for community members. Doing so can help students feel less intimidated, more welcomed, and an important part of the university environment.

My Journey Continues

My journey to the Ph.D. continues, and it is with the support of *mi familia* and my mentors that I have come to realize my ability and confidence and know I will succeed. My experiences are more than an educational success story. Mine is a cultural success story that reminds me of the importance of my family, my values, and my cultural identity within the context of education. ¡*Si Se Puede!* (Yes We Can!)

References

Castellanos, J., & Jones, L. (Eds.) (2003). *The majority in the minority: Expanding the representation of Latina/o faculty, administrators, and students in higher education.* Sterling, VA: Stylus.

Falicov, C. J. (1998). *Latino families in therapy: A guide to multicultural practice.* New York: Guilford.

Herrera, R. (2003). Notes from a Latino graduate student at a predominantly White university. In J. Castellanos & L. Jones (Eds.), *The majority in the minority: Expanding the representation of Latina/o faculty, administrators, and students in higher education* (pp. 179–206). Sterling, VA: Stylus.

Marín, G., & Triandis, H. C. (1985). Allocentrism as an important characteristic of the behavior of Latin Americans and Hispanics. In R. Diaz-Guerrero (Ed.), *Cross-cultural and national studies in social psychology* (pp. 85–104). Amsterdam: North Holland.

Rendón, L. I., (1992). From the barrio to the academy: Revelations of a Mexican American "scholarship girl." *New Directions for Community Colleges, 20,* 55–64.

Santiago-Rivera, A. L., Arredondo, P., & Gallardo-Cooper, M. (2002). *Counseling Latinos and la familia.* Thousand Oaks, CA: Sage.

Raul Ramirez

Raul Ramirez is an organizational behavior doctoral student from the Graduate School of Management, University of California-Irvine. His research interests include ethnic identity and social status within organizations, motivational perspectives of employees' reactions to organizational change, and development of human capital and human resource management systems. His teaching interests include organizational behavior and human resource management. Mr. Ramirez has more than five years of human resource experience serving as a generalist and specialist, including working for Frito-Lay, Inc., a division of PepsiCo, and Merck & Co.

13

MAINTAINING A STRONG LATINA/O IDENTITY WHILE BALANCING TRAILS

Raul Ramirez

Looking around my apartment, there are family pictures—especially of my 4-year-old niece—and my most cherished possession, a gold cross given to me by my grandmother, the matriarch of my father's family. Old concert tickets and CDs reveal my musical tastes, such as rock 'n' *español*, salsa, merengue, and mariachi. Art work and literature on display include Simon Silva's *"Un dia de campo"* (A Day in the Fields), Irene Carranza, a Spanish dictionary, biographies of Zapata and Villa. There is Aztec and Mayan artwork, such as paintings, a blanket, leather decorations, an Aztec calendar, and a beautifully colored green turkey made by my niece. As I begin and end my day as a doctoral student, these are my reflections, symbols of my ethnic identity, reminders of who I am and to whom I am connected. My ethnic identity connects me to my family and Latina/o community. It is a source of motivation, empowerment, and stability. Although it is helpful to have symbolic reminders in my apartment, it is quite another matter to maintain and reinforce my ethnic identity daily as I pursue my doctorate in organizational behavior.

In this narrative I share my view, a Latino's view, of maintaining a strong ethnic identity throughout my doctoral training. First, I begin with a brief history of my origins and how my values and identity were formed. My focus is on culture throughout the doctoral experience, and I specifically address issues of cultural resistance, congruity, trade-offs, and maintenance. I also discuss critical issues encountered during the course of my doctoral experience, including social status, collectivism, trade-offs given time demands of a Ph.D. program, family expectations, and cultural aspects of being humble. I conclude with recommendations for current and future students, faculty and program coordinators, and university personnel to support Latina/o students' maintenance of ethnic identity throughout their doctoral training.

As I began my quest for a Ph.D., I promised myself and others that I would not lose myself in the process. That is, I would maintain and even enhance the various identities that comprise my self-concept—most important my ethnic identity. I identify as a Latino and, more specifically, as a Mexican American male. My values have been passed down to me from family members who have endured far more obstacles than I can imagine, all in the name of making a better life for our family. At the core of these experiences are my grandparents' lives in the Mexican Revolution, their immigration to the United States, and the hardships of working in the fields and living in cramped housing with dirt floors. Through these trials and tribulations, my ancestors have been taught and passed on their values from one generation to the next—to my parents, to my sister, and to me. Through their example and consistency of involvement in cultural and family traditions, the central aspects of my identity, values, and beliefs include:

- knowing the importance of taking care of family;
- being proud of my heritage and celebrating it through traditions;
- having a strong sense of spirituality;
- giving back and being supportive of others in my community;
- understanding that education is a liberating mechanism through which an individual can have wide and deep impact on others;
- persisting in the face of self-doubt is as critical as intellectual ability to academic success;
- fighting for that in which I believe; and
- taking responsibility to change the negative aspects I see in the Latina/o community (e.g., dropout rates) and to be supportive of other Latino/as.

In addition to my family, my neighborhood provided me with valuable lessons on how to maintain a strong Latino identity amid an environment that was not supportive of my ethnicity. I was raised in Fontana, California, which today holds cultural events such as Latina/o art history shows. However, when I was a child, the city was a regional headquarters for the Ku Klux Klan. Although KKK parades and distribution of the group's fliers had stopped before I was born, racist attitudes and behaviors were still felt intensely in our community. Given my physical features I could not hide that

I was of Mexican descent—not that I would have wanted to, but it brought the issue of ethnic identity to the forefront. At an early age, I had to decide to walk either in shame or with pride in my community. As you can imagine, the environment limited my expression of my ethnic identity in unfamiliar settings. My upbringing, however, emphasized ignoring the negative influences and distractions of my environment and focusing instead on performing well in school to pursue a college education. It is interesting to note that coping with these early negative experiences equipped me with a valuable skill to use in an academic setting that often does not embrace my ethnicity fully. For me, being different from most other students makes my ethnic identity more salient and helps me gain a deeper understanding of that identity.

My life experiences have enriched my identity, enabling me to straddle the multiple worlds of family and community, corporate America, and academia. One world ties me to my Mexican heritage and grounds me among my family. A second acculturates me to this country and polishes my professional skills as I navigate corporate industry. A third allows me to roam the classrooms of a prestigious university. However, none of these worlds fully embraces who I am. Instead, I am pulled among them and am expected to embrace each separate world fully. I have come to realize that each world reinforces who I am—a Latino doctoral student on the journey to becoming Dr. Ramirez.

Before I began my Ph.D. program, I conducted a "values check," recording my thoughts in a journal so I could refer to them later. In this journal I documented the reasons why I wanted a Ph.D., many of which coincide with my ethnic identity. For example, a primary reason that I desire a Ph.D. is because I want to make a difference in my community. The community I refer to is not only the Latina/o community but also the surrounding community where I live. I believe that, with a doctoral degree, I will have the ability to have a positive impact on my community, and I will be able to take care of my family. I refer to this "values check" to remind me what matters most, especially during difficult times during my training program.

My cultural values and learning permeate my doctoral experience. For example, one issue that negatively influences my ethnic identity is that of status cues. I have studied how status cues (e.g., race, gender, education) serve as surrogates for an individual's level of respect during interpersonal interaction (Pearce, Ramirez, & Branyiczki, 2001). Given limited or no information about an individual (such as a Latino student like me) the majority of people use status cues to assess whether they should treat an individual with high or low status. Because I am a Latino, others often make mistaken assumptions about me—that I lack discipline, that I believe a woman's place is in the home, that machismo pride governs all my actions, or that I am uneducated. Based on such assumptions, I'm typically treated with lower status. People's reactions to me change once they learn that I am pursuing my Ph.D; they stare at me quizzically and often looked surprised. Based on my newly perceived status cues, my pursuit of a Ph.D. lessens or erases their negative expectations of me and makes me someone with whom they are more willing to interact. These encounters remind me how both non-Latina/os and Latina/os (including myself before starting graduate study) do not expect to meet Latina/os who are pursuing a Ph.D.

Contending with others' misguided and inaccurate assumptions is only one issue Latina/o doctoral students encounter. There is also a lack of receptivity about research related to ethnicity. In addition, I see resistance to attempts to raise ethnic issues in terms of the organization, such as poor efforts at recruiting minority candidates for the Ph.D. program. I am fortunate that the faculty members in my department are very open. Many of the senior female professors were among the few women in our discipline when they first entered the field, so they tend to have more empathy toward me as a minority in an academic setting. While I am fortunate to be in this situation, other Latina/os have had the opposite experience. I have also been fortunate in having supportive Latina/os in my department, which has helped to lessen the impact of a graduate student's social status within a Ph.D. program.

Another interesting issue that I encounter is a collectivistic dynamic that exists within the Latina/o community when I share with other Latina/os that I am a doctoral student. I have found that community members are extremely encouraging and full of praise for the achievement of being a Latino Ph.D. student. It is humbling, uplifting, yet challenging. For those I do not know, it is as if my earning a degree is like a member of their family earning a degree. If they have children, I hear remarks such as, "good to see that some day my daughter/son will have a Latina/o as a professor." It is as if when I receive my degree it will be conferred on the entire Latina/o community. At times it feels like a burden, having the community expect me to succeed—I do not want to let my community down. Although sometimes this expectation feels like a heavy burden, those times are rare and often are overridden by motivation and a sense of strength knowing that the community supports me.

A similar collective dynamic occurs within the academic setting with Latina/o colleagues (when you can find them in academia). I was fortunate that, when I entered my program, there were two senior Latina/o students and one Latina faculty member who were supportive of me and my graduate processes. These individuals were key in my transition from the corporate world to academia. The guidance they provided is invaluable, especially in helping me to navigate departmental politics. Even more important, we related beyond the professional level—we related on a personal level as people of similar ethnic backgrounds. If not for their interest and encouragement in conducting research related to ethnic issues, I most likely would have postponed my research interests in this area. I am grateful for their support, as my areas of research within the Latina/o community are avenues to enrich my Latino identity. For example, I am investigating ethnic identity in the workplace and how it is related to one's social status and organizational helping behaviors (Martinez & Ramirez, 2004). Also, I am examining the relevance of ethnic identity within the hospitality industry, particularly as this arena comprises primarily minorities, women, and immigrants. My areas of research have flourished, as has my sense of my ethnic identity. Although each of my three colleagues has moved on in his or her academic career, they are a permanent resource, network, and collaborative source for me.

Another area in which I have experienced a sense of collectivism is among other Latina/o doctoral students on campus. I diligently seek out Latina/o Ph.D. students in different departments, and I am always elated when I meet others of similar heritage, on a similar educational journey. Having others with whom to share experiences, challenges, and culturally specific support provides yet another means to strengthen my ethnic identity. As my schedule permits, I also provide career advice and discuss different career opportunities with Latina/o professionals and M.B.A. students, frequently raising the option of graduate school. Through this connection I am able to strengthen my ethnic identity by sharing the values of education, giving back to the community, and being supportive as a means of strengthening the Latina/o community. I anticipate that my mentorship will reach a broader audience as those I mentor provide mentoring to others. Through these collective interactions and connections to community, I am invigorated and motivated to work hard on my Ph.D. requirements, so my time in the community is time well spent.

Trade-offs of the Ph.D.

It is only natural that, with the time and energies I spend working toward the Ph.D., come trade-offs. Having less time to attend cultural events, with friends and family is perhaps the greatest disadvantage. Due to time constraints, I find that I need to be more selective about which cultural events I attend. Although I would like to attend more events to help reinforce my ethnic identity and enjoy the traditions, I just do not have the time.

Keeping in touch with friends becomes a matter of time management as well. My friends are respectful of my commitment to my studies, and we manage to keep in touch via e-mail. I miss reinforcing my sense of ethnic self with them; however, their words of pride and encouragement enrich me. One friend wrote the cherished words, "Do what you have to do to graduate, we'll have time to hang out when you're a professor making a difference in our community."

Perhaps most important is temporarily having less family time. For me, being Latino means being an active part of my family, but doing so is a challenge given the demands of a Ph.D. program. I distinctly recall having a difficult conversation with my mother before I began school about how my time with the family would be limited. The look on my mother's face was heartbreaking. Given that I live within driving distance, my parents would much prefer for me to visit and spend the night once a week, but that is not feasible given my program. While I attend far fewer family events than my family members would like, I make time to attend the important ones. Being supportive of my family translates from spending time with them into making daily progress toward my degree. On my office wall I have pictures of my niece, and visitors to my office jokingly say it is a memorial. She represents the future of my family, and it is for the future of my family that I put in the long hours. I remind myself that the lack of time with my family is only temporary.

Another aspect of family life that I have decided to put on hold for now is marriage and children. My grandmother, as well as my parents, has finally figured out that until I have completed my Ph.D. I am not getting married and giving her more great grandchildren. She has gone from greeting me with, "*Como estas*," (How are you?) to bypassing the small talk and asking me, "*¿Donde esta tu novia?*" (Where is your girlfriend?) to "*Cuando terminas la escuela*," (When will you finish school?) to "*Andele! Termina tu escuela mas rápido!*" (Come on, finish school quicker!) In terms of grandchildren for my parents, I'm fortunate that my niece was born in the second year of my program. Overwhelmed with the news of my sister's pregnancy, my mother blurted out with joy, "Thank goodness! We had given up on your sister and were counting on you" [for a grandchild]. The reassuring aspect to my ethnic identity is that my doctoral degree will help me take care of the family I will have some day.

Recommendations

As I reflect on my experiences of maintaining and strengthening my ethnic identity and keeping true to those lessons learned from my family and community, I offer the following recommendations to future and current doctoral students, faculty, and university personnel.

For Future and Current Doctoral Students

- Perform a values check before beginning, or while you are engaging in, your Ph.D. journey. Document your values and refer to them often. In one or two sentences or perhaps even a word or two, state clearly why you want a Ph.D. Refer to your own words during your most difficult moments to motivate you.
- Make a commitment to empower yourself by focusing on creating synergy with the constraints of your doctoral experience to maintain and even strengthen your ethnic identity.
- Establish Latina/o support groups and make a conscious effort to engage in activities that reinforce your ethnic identity. I am fortunate to be networked into the Ph.D. Project whose purpose is to increase the number of under-represented minority professors in the field of business. The Ph.D. Project has provided me access to other Latina/o students at the national level, a blessing I cannot begin to describe. They hold an annual conference for prospective Ph.D. students to inform them of the rewards and difficulties of attaining a Ph.D. and pursuing a career as a professor. I would highly recommend that those even remotely interested in obtaining a Ph.D. attend this conference (more information can be found at www.phdproject.com). However, such an organization may not exist for your discipline of interest, but you should make an effort to find those of similar mind and ethnicity.
- Realize that you may need to reach out to individuals in different disciplines. If you happen to be in a geographical area where there are few Latina/os, you may need to reach out via the Internet.
- Seek out mentors who are supportive of your research and your culture. They do not have to be of the same ethnicity as long as they are committed to helping you develop.
- Be prepared to cope with non-Latina/os', and even other Latina/os', stereotypes about Latina/os. Keep in mind your abilities and trust those who believe in you.

- Consider reading the book, *Getting What You Came For* by Robert Peters, a comprehensive guide to doctoral degrees in terms of deciding to pursue the degree, choosing and applying to a program, doing well throughout the process, and landing your ideal job. It is an absolute must-read for students and prospective students.
- Before accepting offers or even before applying to programs, visit the school and meet the faculty members to determine whether they exhibit a sense of openness to working with minorities and addressing minority issues. Also consider the number of minority students and faculty members at the school. More important, ask why there are not more or even any.

For Faculty

Strive to be a good mentor to doctoral students, maintain a sense of fairness, and keep the best interests of the student in mind. Extend yourself by understanding students in terms of their ethnic identity and be supportive of that identity. Be open to Latina/o students who have race- or ethnic-based research interests, which can serve to strengthen their own identity.

For University Personnel

Work closely with Latina/o doctoral students to understand their needs and establish activities that enhance their ethnic identity. Their needs will vary, depending on the students and the circumstances of the university. Publicize their success stories as milestones of accomplishment to which others can aspire. Universities in California for example, hold Raza graduation ceremonies and dinner receptions for undergraduates and their families. Such events are a natural fit where Ph.D. and master's candidates can be introduced as mentors and advisors for the graduating undergraduate class. Finally, provide funding and fellowship opportunities for Latina/o and other racial and ethnic minority students who conduct research related to ethnic identity or building awareness of racial and ethnic issues. Doing so supports their personal enrichment and contributes to the academic and general community's awareness of ethnic issues.

In closing, I cannot emphasize enough the importance of maintaining and strengthening ethnic identity throughout one's doctoral program. A strong ethnic identity can help you form closer connections with family and community and serve as a source of motivation, empowerment, and stability in successfully navigating the doctoral process. Although each of our paths will be different, I hope my narrative helps others know that this educational journey is possible. In the words of poet and writer Antonio Machado (1875–1939) (which hang on my office wall), *"Caminante no hay camino, se hace el camino al andar"* (Traveler there is no trail, you blaze the trail as you go).

References

Martinez, P. G., & Ramirez, R. R. (2004). *An empirical examination of employees' ethnic identity and ethnic citizenship behaviors in organizations.* Unpublished manuscript.

Pearce, J. L., Ramirez, R. R., & Branyiczki, I. (2001). Leadership and the pursuit of status: Effects of globalization and economic transformation. *Advances in Global Leadership, 2,* 153–178.

Theresa A. Segura-Herrera

A native of Chicago, Illinois, Theresa A. Segura-Herrera earned her bachelor's and master's degrees at Loyola University-Chicago. She is currently a doctoral student in counseling psychology at the University of Wisconsin-Madison, with research interests in educational and mental health issues affecting Latina/o communities. Some of her specific research activities include examining the educational experiences of racial and ethnic minority students attending predominantly White universities, understanding the psychological help-seeking behaviors of Latina college students, investigating ethnic pride and prejudice in Mayan-descent children in Guatemala, and exploring the psychological experience of ethnicity for Mexican American youth.

14

QUERER ES PODER: MAINTAINING AND CREATING *FAMILIA* AS A DOCTORAL STUDENT

Theresa A. Segura-Herrera

Querer es poder, or to want something is to be empowered to attain it, is a *dicho* (saying) frequently used by my parents for as long as I can remember. My optimistic and hard-working parents emigrated from Guanajuato, Mexico, to the north side of Chicago with hopes for a better life. They reiterated and emulated the essence of this and other *dichos* to my younger sister and me to remind us that our very *ganas* (desire) to attain a life goal fuels us to achieve it. They firmly believed that an education would provide us with the empowering access to resources and choices denied to them. They would say, *"Por eso* tienes *que estudiar"* (That is why you *must* study), and that is what I did. Hence in this chapter I share the more salient aspects of my journey to the Ph.D. and include how my initial shock and disbelief at being on this journey transformed to a newfound sense of understanding and hope. I highlight the wise *dichos* used by my parents because they have served to uplift me during the difficult treks along my journey. My wish is that by sharing my process along this journey, especially as it relates to experiences of maintaining and creating *familia,* some of the light of hope that has illuminated *mi camino* (my path) toward the Ph.D. may radiate the paths of others.

Shock

As I reflect back on my first year in the doctoral program, I must admit that it was filled with a pervasive sense of shock and disbelief for having been accepted! Here I was, a second-generation Mexican American woman from the inner city of Chicago, of working-class background, and the first in my family (of origin, creation, extended) to make it this far educationally. It was unbelievable to have applied and received flattering offers from my top-pick programs, while simultaneously planning and working overtime to pay for my big, fat Mexican wedding. The evidence of my credentials and acceptance letters *should* have been sufficient indication that I had earned my entrance into doctoral studies, but I felt a powerful disbelief in knowing that *I* was realizing *my* educational dream.

The sense of shock and disbelief deepened due to numerous life transitions. It was surreal and tumultuous to manage the concurrent and multiple levels of shock as I had to adjust to my new roles and identities of being married (e.g., consistent with my parents' traditional Mexican cultural values) and a doctoral student who is female and of color (e.g., also consistent with my parents' expectations, yet also facing the challenges of academic rigor, imposter syndrome) in a large, prestigious, White university located in a relatively small and segregated city. I felt blessed to have married my supportive soul mate who chose to leave the warmth of his loving family and a stable, well-paid position to accompany *me* in pursuit of *my* educational journey. It was unusual enough within the context of my community for a female to pursue doctoral studies, but for one's husband to leave the stability of his career and family for that of his wife was all the more atypical. It opened the door for lots of *chisme* (gossip). Simultaneously I feared failing in all of my new roles (e.g., not meeting the program's academic expectations, not completing my studies, not being emotionally available to my husband). Overall, I feared that my journey to the Ph.D. might jeopardize being happily married and that being happily married decreased the likelihood of completing the program. Last, I couldn't understand why these highly desired events caused so much joy, pride, and excitement, but why they also caused much emptiness, sadness, pain, and isolation. I would ask myself, "I should just be happy with all of this, right?" It was later that I came to better understand the roots of these feelings.

Empezando a Comprender/Beginning to Understand with *La Facultad*

With time and exposure to the inspirational writings of Gloria Anzaldúa, *que en paz descanse* (may she rest in peace), I came to realize that my sense of shock was much more multilayered and complex. She eloquently described *la facultad* (the faculty), as "the capacity to see in surface phenomena the meaning of deeper realities" (Anzaldúa, 1999, p. 60). My process of becoming aware of *la facultad* and how it serves as a powerful inner tool was among the most empowering experiences of my journey.

With *la facultad* and tear-filled dialogues with *mi pareja* (my partner), my advisor, and select friends, it became clear that the combined feelings of *angustía* (angst), shock, isolation, and living what felt like contradictions made sense. The reality of not quite fitting into the multiple contexts of my reality, namely dominant, mainstream, academic, and traditional Mexican cultures, left me to deal painfully with the implications of being in, living within, and straddling the borderlands, or the paradoxical/ambiguous psychological spaces described so powerfully by Anzaldúa. Before the awareness brought on by *la facultad*, I did not feel fully accepted by the multiple cultural contexts of which I was a part. For instance, interactions within academic contexts felt cautionary and unwelcoming, whereas interactions within familial and traditional Mexican culture were unconstrained. I was married (thankfully, according to this context), but time demands (e.g., coursework, research projects) did not allow me to fulfill my cultural expectations of being more physically present and attentive within my home. I was beginning to understand the complexity and fluidity of belonging to multiple contexts, however, and the accompanying identities, roles, and expectations, within these contexts. The self-awareness gained from Anzaldúa's *facultad* helped me to reclaim the beauty, diversity, and richness of emulating what is *both* congruent *and* seemingly at odds within each cultural context. I began feeling at peace and harmony with my decision to pursue doctoral studies and the way in which I was doing it (e.g., both culturally traditional, by entering married life consistent with the values of Mexican Catholicism, *and* nontraditional, with the challenges of what others in our community thought about our relocation in pursuit of my studies, putting off children). I realized that *my* educational journey was living, breathing proof of "*Querer es poder,*" because I was empowered to attain my degree.

With time came further clarity. I learned that my reactions stemmed from a combination of explicit and implicit mixed messages that I internalized from my earliest to my most recent educational experiences. Senders of these resonant messages were authority figures in my life (e.g., parents, uncles, aunts, *madrinas* (godmothers), elementary and high school teachers, counselors, college professors) with primarily three radically opposed messages. Negative stereotypes perpetuated by outlets of pop mainstream culture (e.g., media) comprised the first message. This message sadly reduced Mexican American females like me to sexual objects who did not belong in academic settings *unless* our role was that of custodian. Being in the role of custodian would ensure that I would be able to support myself and the numerous children that I am expected to have at a young age and not burden the welfare system. The second message was from the dark side of old world *marianismo*. Gil and Vasquez (1996) fluently described that old-world *marianismo* as the socialization of and adherence to female gender roles based on traditional Mexican/Latina/o cultural values whereby women are expected to emulate the sanctity of Catholicism's Virgin Mary, including examples such as not forgetting a woman's place, not forsaking traditions, not striving for a career outside of the home. The third message, however, was the strongest and most protective. It fostered a sense of resilience and empowerment that fueled my motivation to overcome the previous two because it was from *mis padres* (my parents), and a *small* number of teachers and professors who told me that I *did* belong in academic settings and in the role that I chose. This message shouted loudly and told me, *si se puede* (yes, I *can*) purse my academic aspirations, even in the face of many obstacles.

Uprooted

I was beginning to better understand my journey with *la facultad*, but the initial shock that I experienced was intensified by the feeling of being uprooted. While I was aware, through their vivid stories, what my parents and *suegros* (mother and father-in-law) experienced when they emigrated from Mexico to Chicago (e.g., experiences with discrimination, limited access to job opportunities, especially a sense of displacement), I knew that I felt extremely displaced in my journey toward the Ph.D. and, to an extremely lesser degree, I was re-experiencing what my family members had in their journey from Mexico to Chicago. I had never heard it described and labeled as a physical, cultural, and social uprooting until I was exposed to Falicov (1998). My family members, like many immigrant *familias*, overcame the sadness and grief of *physical* distance from the warm familiarity of home, the *social* disconnection of not having the safety of a supportive community, and the *cultural* struggle of straddling two opposing cultures (e.g., Mexican and mainstream Anglo). I fully acknowledge that, unlike my immigrant family members, I had an excellent command of the English language, a strong educational background, and their solid moral support. However, similar to them, I experienced the physical, social, and cultural uprooting and subsequent implantation in the foreign, individualistic, and competitive culture of academia, even with exposure to academia as an undergraduate. I was *physically* apart from the comfort of those who make home safe and familiar and *socially* and *culturally* disconnected.

The feelings of being uprooted affected several realms of my life. I physically hurt and felt ill from being so homesick and from having few social connections through my program, much less the university. Although I did have the protection and support of family members who believed in my ability to succeed, I was coming to believe that the negative image of Latina/os meant that I did not have the academic ability and potential to succeed. I felt distracted by my distress and unable to focus wholeheartedly on my studies. I wondered whether systems of the past (e.g., disempowering teachers and high school counselor) were right in discouraging me from pursuing higher education. This spiraled to a staggeringly low sense of self-confidence in my academic abilities. Further, these feelings of hopelessness were intensified by my and my husband's experience with both overt (e.g., inferior service at shopping centers, false and blatant accusations of stealing) and covert (e.g., unaccompanied White women ensuring that their handbags were farthest from where my husband and I were) discrimination. The passion, pride, and *ganas* that I once felt about pursing a Ph.D. were leached out of me. I barely had the energy and motivation to show up to class. I was nearly convinced that I did not belong in the Ph.D. program and that perhaps it would be better to return to Chicago. I was regularly miserable and ready to pack our things.

Luz de Esperanza (Light of Hope) in Coping with Uprootedness

Traversing the space of wanting to leave the program to committing to persist until completion happened due a combination of events. It was during these most difficult times that my parents and their wise words gave me hope, even in my despair. They reminded me of a less used *dicho*, "*Tienen que haber piedras en el camino*" (There must be rocks/barriers along the path/road). Although this did not offer direct consolation, I slowly realized that I had the obligation to own my reactions and reclaim my existence of what *I* wanted to emulate in my borderlands/multiple contexts. Knowing that *mis padres* valiantly sacrificed so much to pave an educational path for their children and for future generations helped me to more fully appreciate their experience of being uprooted. My parents and their experiences inspired me to move forward on my path because reaching my final destination—a Ph.D.—represented *their and my* compensation for all of their sacrifice.

I replaced thoughts of packing my bags with a commitment to stay, plant, and cultivate seeds of friendship. These processes lead to the creation of an extended academic *familia* and helped to minimize the effects of the rocks along my path. Further, *mi pareja y yo* (my partner and I) worked even harder to support one another by deciding to spend more time with friends from the university. This translated into making the hard decision to spend less time with family in Chicago. We initially tried to maintain the sense of warmth and comfort of family connections with weekly attendance at family gatherings (e.g., *bodas* [weddings], birthdays, dinners). We realized that these driving trips meant time away from my studies, which contributed significantly to my stress and feelings of low self-efficacy, and missed opportunities to build new friendships with the handful of students who displayed genuine interest in getting to know us. Our choice to connect with and nurture our budding friendships made in the university setting was also difficult because it meant not fulfilling the cultural expectations and sense of obligation to attend family functions.

It was an openness and commitment to the process of doctoral training (no matter how bumpy the route to self-awareness may be) that has allowed me to receive the support of family members, old and new friends, and an incredibly empowering advisor/mentor and to persist. The inspiration and regular reminders of my parents' experiences and *dichos* (e.g., how those pesky *piedras* affect our trajectories) have allowed me to gain new understanding of and meaning from my journey. It became clear that too many current and ancestral generations of *nuestra raza* (our race) have had *piedras* that completely obstruct *any* educational path. Getting in touch with all of these, as well as my reasons for pursuing doctoral studies, nurturing new relationships, and maintaining previous ones, slowly revitalized me. A sense of responsibility to myself and to those (especially my parents) who have been blocked from such a path and/or who worked to build the very path on which I traveled became evident. The attractive option of leaving my studies lost its luster, thanks to the arduous process I have described.

In hindsight, two aspects of nearly leaving the program were most striking. One was the unconditional kindness, safety, and acceptance displayed by my immediate *familia*, advisor/mentor, and friends from the program to whom I entertained the possibility of leaving my studies. None of them wanted me to leave, but each told me that I would still be a person worthy of love, *respeto* (respect), and acceptance. The second striking aspect was my feeling for the first time that advising/mentoring relationships and friendships may recapitulate the loving, comforting, and warm sense of *familia*. More specifically, I began to realize that the love and sense of attachment I felt toward blood relatives, godchildren, and *comadres* (co-parents), *can* be repeated and re-created by the reciprocity of genuine relationships. I discovered that, with the support of my academic *familia*, I could face the struggle of straddling multiple borderlands and contexts and wanting to build community. Hence, my sense of *familia*—who comprises it and how I experience it—evolved to a more complex and inclusive understanding. Even though it may appear that my realization and new notions of family came overnight and all lived happily ever after, it is important to convey that I still asked myself nearly daily: "What do we do when these *piedras* feel like insurmountable boulders?"

Other Forms of Coping and Implicit Recommendations

I plowed forward by creatively using these rocks of different shapes and sizes to construct my path and a safe refuge within the foreign and intimidating world of academia. It was during these loneliest of times that I became actively involved in working with faculty on research projects. The following may sound absurd, but it was my involvement in research that helped me to plod through these challenging times. For instance, active involvement in research projects with my mentor to understand the educational experiences of Latina/os at predominantly White universities was an opportunity to seek and build connections with other students of color on campus. My experience in this and other research projects allowed me finally to find my reflection, be a reflection for others, eventually build beautiful academic *compadrazgos* (spiritual relationships) between co-parents (e.g., to our educational endeavors in this context), and create the sense of *familia* for which I was so homesick. Further, the two faculty members whom I consider mentors became more like *padrinos* (godparents) of sorts. These professional and personal relationships allowed me to receive continuous mentorship and support and, most important, a safe refuge to be me—regardless of how frazzled, sad, confused, angry, or stressed I might be. Last, the benefits of active involvement in research were not only interpersonally therapeutic, but they also led to being published as well as attending and presenting at conferences for the first time in my life. It was really incredible for me, my husband, and my family to see our name in print! Overall, my research experiences provided so many wonderful opportunities for me to be in relationships with others and to feel the emotional warmth, connection, and sense of belonging that only a sense of *familia* offers.

Explicit Recommendations to Students

Based on these glimpses of my journey, I have the following recommendations. I have learned, heard these along the way, and/or would have appreciated knowing them early on to better maintain and create the sense of *familia* (and sanity). *Ahí van* (Here they go).

Time for Self-Reflection

Graduate school is often a psychologically taxing experience because of the multiple and qualitatively different academic and cultural demands on us, compared to our mainstream counterparts. Graduate school often becomes a time to face our demons (e.g., insecurities, increased self-awareness). Make time for self-reflection, and take personal inventory of your value system as it relates to family. This will allow you to determine your and your *familia*'s needs based on your life roles (e.g., doctoral student, mother, life partner) and other realities (e.g., geographic distance, difficulty of coursework). Remember that because both academic demands and life roles are not static, we often need to revisit these several times during our journey (e.g., every academic semester or year). In this way, when events emerge, you will have some sense of what you will or will not do (e.g., attending some family events over others to manage the *chisme* you elicit by trying to be all things to all of the people in your life). It is critical to empower yourself to manage, find balance, and live out your multiple life roles, including that of doctoral student, in a personally, culturally, and spiritually congruent way. Be creative with how you re-create the sense of *familia* (e.g., peers, faculty, advisory-mentorship relationships, having *tía*'s infamous *salsita* in the freezer, cooking your favorite dishes with friends, having books and music handy) to elicit inspiration and motivation when times are hard.

Keep Familia *Emotionally Close and Involved*

Remember that your *familia* often will not understand why you are not visiting, calling more often, and/or not attending all of the family functions. Because we may already feel isolated as students, not seeing family as often as we may want to can be very difficult. Find reasonable ways to expose your *familia* to your world and help them understand what you are doing in school. This can help to decrease your feeling of being viewed as disloyal (not to mention avoiding the *chisme*) by *la familia*.

Reach Out to Others When You Feel Safe to Do So

Reach out to those who seem supportive and who want to understand you and your subjective experience as a Latina/o pursing a Ph.D. Often, even caring people get caught up in the hustle and bustle of academia and may be unaware of what you are experiencing. Open up to those who want to know how you are *really* doing.

Reach Out to Others Outside of Your Program

Try not to over-rely on your department as your primary source of support. Take the time to get to know other students and faculty (especially those of color both inside and outside your program). Chances are, if you feel isolated, they may feel or have felt the same at some point. Remember that this is how extended academic *familias* are formed. Seek connections with other undergraduate and graduate students and organizations on-and off-campus to expand your *familia* even further. Venting and exchanging "war" stories with others can be cathartic.

Reach Out Beyond the Ivory Tower

Do not forget that there is a whole world beyond the privileged ivory tower of the university we find ourselves in. It is too easy to become self-absorbed in academics and overly self-reflective. We do not need to go too far to find communities in need off-campus. Give back and get involved in volunteer opportunities (e.g., tutoring/teaching youth, mentoring, English-as-a-second-language programs) and practicum/internships (e.g., community mental health clinics, community colleges, alternative high schools).

Recommendations to University Personnel/Faculty

Become Informed

Read all of the student narratives and other sections of this book to begin understanding the complexities of being a Latina/o on this journey. Resources like this book bring an understanding of the importance of maintaining our cultural values such as *familismo*. In this way you will be better prepared to offer Latina/o students the support they need.

Become Informed of the World Outside of Your Department and *the Ivory Tower*

Know about the university (e.g., student services, organizations, faculty of color to serve as mentors) *and* the surrounding community (e.g., Latina/o, other racial/ethnic community centers, health/mental health clinics, places of worship in town and neighboring towns). These resources may provide

Latina/o students with culturally familiar and meaningful resources of social support to access through attending, volunteering, interning, and possible mentorship opportunities.

Offer a Welcoming and Warm Environment

Strive to provide a welcoming, supportive, and warm climate for all students to feel safe enough to open up and be themselves. Demonstrating genuine support, acceptance, and an open-door policy goes a long way.

Do Not Be Afraid to Ask

Do not be so afraid to ask, "How are you *really* doing?" (if you really can't handle it, then don't). The few university personnel who have asked me this question have demonstrated a genuine desire to know about my true experience and not the sugar-coated response, with a forced smile, "Everything is fine."

　　In conclusion, much hope now lightens my journey. My hope is that this narrative will provide others on similar journeys with some hope as well. It is important to remember that *querer es poder*, or to want something is to be empowered to attain it, with *piedras* and all. Also, a wise academic *comadre* once said that, if we remember that even in the darkest and loneliest of times on this treacherous, yet rewarding path, "we are reflections of one another, and when one of us succeeds, we all succeed," just as when one of us falls we all should try to reach back. Just like our *familias* of origin, we will always be reflected in and interconnected by this journey, regardless of where we may be within it. To me, that is the beauty of it . . . the stabilizing consistency of familial interrelatedness, interdependency, and reciprocity. I feel that this will continue to invigorate and inspire me and infuse me with a sense of purpose to persist so that I may be a stabilizing and uplifting force that reaches back in return—for that *is* what *la familia* is all about.

Acknowledgments

This chapter is dedicated to each member of my beautiful *familia* whose unending love and support inspires me daily, particularly *mi pareja*, Jaime; our little *hijito*, Jaime Alejandro Herrera; and my sister and our parents, Denise, Daniel, and Teresa Segura. I also want to give many thanks to my academic *comadre*, Cecilia A. Nepomuceno, for her heartfelt comments in the writing of this chapter.

References

Anzaldúa, G. (1999). *Borderlands/La Frontera: The new mestiza.* San Francisco: Aunt Lute Books.

Falicov, C. J. (1998). *Latino families in therapy: A guide to multicultural practice.* New York: Guilford Press.

Gil, R. M., & Vazquez, C. I. (1996). *The Maria paradox.* New York: Perigee.

Claudio Gabriel Vera Sanchez

Claudio Gabriel Vera Sanchez received his A.A. degree from Cerritos College in Norwalk, California, his bachelor's degree in psychology at California State University, Long Beach, and his master's degree in criminal justice at the University of Illinois at Chicago. He is currently working on his Ph.D. at the University of Illinois at Chicago in criminal justice. His interests include the relationship between the police and Latina/o communities, with a specific focus on adolescents. In addition, he is interested in how the political economy, education, and participation in the workforce facilitate contexts that create gangs within Mexican communities.

15

JUGGLING INTELLECTUALITY AND LATINO MASCULINITY

La Calle, Mi Familia, y la Escuela
(The Streets, My Family, and School)

Claudio Gabriel Vera Sanchez

If I had been asked eight years ago to write a chapter on my educational experiences, I would have laughed at the idea. Never did I imagine that I would attend college; instead, I thought a higher education would be nothing more than a dream deferred. If not for my mother, who never gave up on me, and all the wonderful individuals who offered me a helping hand, this essay would not exist.

In this chapter I provide an overview of my experiences as a Latino in graduate school. More specifically, I highlight the challenges I encountered in the long pursuit of my educational journey. Emphasized are my transition from Mexico to the United States, the challenge of not having residency and legal status, my struggle with the education system, and the unique barriers faced in the context of a lower socioeconomic environment by a Latino forming a masculine identity. I also address the influence of the environment, peers, family, and teachers and describe the means to overcome challenges on the road to the Ph.D.

Schooling in Mexico

My mother has been instrumental in my educational training since I was a young boy. I was born in Mexico City, where I lived until I was 10 years old. I lived in a serene environment, spending my time swimming at the recreation center, playing with my friends, and snacking on Mexican candy.

However, I had always been a reluctant student; I would rather ride my bike or search for rare specimens by the lake. Although my mother was an English teacher in Mexico, I struggled to learn the letters of the alphabet with my mother's phonetic techniques. The funny sounds of the letters made me laugh so hard that I eventually learned English. I remember the tiresome hours of studying and my mother pestering me until my homework was completed. The many hours of dedication and consistent motivation taught me the importance of education for my family. My mother, a teacher, felt education was the vehicle to advancement; she learned this from my grandmother, a single parent in the early 1940s who worked hard to educate her ten children.

When my mother left to go to the United States without me, I experienced an intimidating fear of education. My mother temporarily left me in Mexico with nuns at a Catholic school, because my father failed to sign my custody documents. The nuns taught me to read and write through repetition and used physical punishment and intimidation tactics to get me to finish my homework and learn. In addition, the nuns beat the children as a disciplinary measure. They never laid a hand a hand on me, but, in retrospect, the other kids were orphans. I, on the other hand, was a devious child, always tripping girls in the hallways but never reprimanded because I had a mother and family.

My father's refusal to sign my child custody documents and his absence from my life were the two significant negative factors in my development. Yet, my mother's love and persistence to provide me a good life overshadowed his limited involvement. Because my father did not sign my papers and was never present, my mother brought me to the United States illegally. Specifically, I crossed the river through Tijuana with great trepidation, not knowing what to expect, but the people who brought me over (*los coyotes*) were good and honest. I was thrilled to be reunited with my mother. In the States, my mother never spoke negatively about my father and always emphasized his intelligence, since he was a lawyer in Mexico and later a *gobernador* (governor). In hope to maintain a connection with my father, in fact, I even remember aspiring to become a lawyer when I grew up.

Schooling in the United States

Elementary school in the States made me feel alienated. My feeling of isolation came as a result of our finances, my limited English abilities, and my inability to engage with other boys in sports and other masculine activities.

To improve the situation, I transferred to another school, yet my distance from the other boys remained evident, and the social skills to engage in sports and other physical activities were beyond my reach. My quietness and disconnection from others resulted in numerous fights (in and out of school) and perpetuated my fear. Without having a positive environment and strong connections, I wondered, how can society expect Latino kids to learn and develop positive masculinities in these dire conditions?

My performance in junior high school was just average, but I soon enjoyed the experience. My English-as-a-second-language teacher was caring, and I developed solidarity with other kids who could not speak English. Although my mother was an English teacher in Mexico, I still did not have English proficiency. Socially, while I enjoyed some of my classroom experiences, my junior high years still included bullies picking on my cheap "Payless" shoes and some boring teachers. Yet, I adjusted, made some friends, and had some positive experiences along the way.

High school meant additional challenges for me as a Latino male in a tough neighborhood struggling to make friends and be socially integrated. I only read three books in high school because the educational system was inadequate and it was never masculine to be intelligent. The three books I read were Aldous Huxley's *Brave New World*, Ray Bradbury's *Fahrenheit 451*, and *Night* by Elie Wiesel. I remember these books clearly because they were all taught in the same class and I enjoyed them. However, I could not allow my friends to see me carrying books, so I would hide them in my locker or in my pocket since baggy pants were common in those days. I remember the occasional embarrassment when teachers read grades out loud and I earned 90% or higher. After all, boys in marginalized contexts gain respect by being tough in the streets, not by being intelligent. In general, I did a good job of concealing any mental acumen and had everyone believing that I was a mediocre student. When asked to ditch, I would falsely claim that I was on probation, and that my teachers were keeping close tabs on me. Again, you must understand that no matter how much I enjoyed school, I could never allow other boys to know; I imagine that in middle- and upper-class communities it is masculine not only to play sports, but to be intelligent or even to quote Shakespeare. I will never know this for sure; however, the only certainty is that being a male in my environment did not facilitate learning.

Immigration Impediments to Education

I had done the best I could scholastically within the confines of my context and poor schooling, but I was unaware that my immigration status would be an obstacle. A college counselor rudely told me that I could not attend college because I did not possess a green card. I became extremely melancholic and felt lied to, frustrated, angry, and, deep inside, disappointed. I asked myself, "I did everything I could so far, why am I deprived of an education— simply because I was not born in the United States?" I had never felt so dismayed in my life, but I reasoned that a higher education was not in my destiny.

Since a college education was beyond my reach, I began working at various odd jobs. I worked in a water company lifting bottles, a steel factory, and at a temporary agency that accepted fake Social Security numbers. The temporary agency received most of the money, while we made $4.25 an hour. I hated these jobs. I would clean warehouses, put labels on barrels, move furniture, and do other menial jobs. I prayed to God every morning as I walked to work at 4 a.m. and pleaded with Him to give me another direction (i.e., go to school). I cried inside many times, but there was nothing I could do.

Part-time work and school did not create proper masculinity in my neighborhood. Instead, hanging out in the streets and fighting earned one a great deal of respect. I would only work occasionally, therefore, so I had plenty of time to hang out with my homeboys. We did many things of which I am not proud. In some ways, I thought I would pay the world for what it had done to me. We would often beat up other youngsters and take their money and personal belongings (e.g., pagers). There is no way to justify what we did, yet this was the only way we knew at the time to feel like men. Undoubtedly, these situations brought us a healthy number of beatings from the police. I often wonder how I survived despite all the times we were shot at. In addition, all of these events were associated with occasional visits to jail. Again, I wonder why I was chosen to write this essay while others took a different path (e.g., gangs, prison), falling before my eyes. Why are so many of my people in these predicaments, while I was fortunate enough to attend college?

Shortly after the various rumbles and police encounters, getting a job that paid well became my only goal in life. I landed a job at a steel company, where I was paid $10 an hour. An 18-year-old making that kind of money in 1994 was quite an accomplishment. I would finally create a masculinity based on something other than the streets (i.e., a hard-working man). However, my early prayers were answered unexpectedly when a 400-pound steel bin fell on my foot and broke it into pieces. The doctors had to perform two surgeries and put metal pins in my foot. In addition, the doctors claimed that I would never walk correctly again. I was 19 years old and had permanent damage to my body. I became depressed and hated the world once more. What had I done to deserve such fate?

Parental, Social, and Professors' Support

Throughout the time when I was defining my masculinity, surviving the streets, and managing my depression as I struggled with my newly acquired disability, my mother's perseverance and tenacity never subsided. She always nagged me about going to college and said that she knew of a way to circumvent the green card problem. But, I did not want to go to school anymore; I hated school, and I wanted nothing to do with it. One day, however, my mother lied to me and asked me to accompany her to an errand. When she revealed that the errand was a visit to Cerritos College, I said I was not ready. She did not listen and had made an appointment with Stephanie Rodriguez, a college counselor. I was fearful of school and did not believe that I could be successful. Part of my trepidation was based on the fact that no one in college was similar to me; they were all preppy-looking Latina/os, Whites, and some Asians. I was a six-foot-tall Latino, who had a shaved head, wore baggy pants, and spoke vernacular. To my surprise, everyone I met accepted me with open arms. Maybe I was a novelty, or maybe they liked me, but their positive response to me ruled out my first hypothesis.

The support networks that I built catalyzed my success, and for the first time intelligence became a masculine trait. I became involved in college clubs, student government, research programs, and other activities, and I did not have to hide my books anymore. In fact, the more I knew, the more I was praised. My fellow students asked me to read their papers and comment on them; I had never felt so important in my life. Today, my teachers, my counselors, and all of the wonderful students I met throughout the years remain in my mind wherever I go. Most important, though, is the fact that a Latino male could be masculine, even if he was not getting his hands dirty or working 60 hours per week.

Graduate School Experience

The thought of graduate school riddled me with fear because I would be leaving my family. Initially I had agreed to attend Ohio State University, but the professors at Chicago convinced me otherwise. My mother suggested, "Go where they really want you," and going to Chicago has been the best decision of my life. The professors became my surrogate family. I can go into my advisor's office whenever I need guidance, one of my other professors called my mother and told her that he would "look out" for me, and others are friendly enough to take me to lunch. As a result of these warm encounters, I know that being in Chicago I am not alone. My anxiety was never rooted in any insecurity about my academic ability. In fact, I knew that my teachers had taught me well. Anything from defusing group conflict, to speaking to large groups of people, to writing an academic essay was possible. In retrospect, it was my relationships and interactions with my professors that made all the difference in my transition to graduate school.

Unfortunately, my experiences with the students, especially the White students, were not as positive as those with my advisor and the other professors. In fact, my peer encounters were racially charged. For example, I recall a number of White students asking, "Did you get kiss up points for that presentation?" "Are you sure that you are in the Ph.D. program?" I find these statements comical. I know that these students fear that I can outread and outperform them, and that I can generate unique theories and concepts. I see the fear in their eyes, a subtle fear, similar to the one that I instilled when I caused trouble in the streets. I would like to believe that their racial/ethnic background has nothing to do with their stupidity. After all, it was my White professors and Latina/o mentors who facilitated my success.

I was asked to write about my graduate school experiences in this essay, but I feel that my toughest challenges are in the past. I believe that the negative events in my life have already occurred, and the present and future are bright. I love graduate school; it is a thousand times better than the odd jobs I used to do. I have the opportunity to write, create, and think; I have these privileges that many do not have. Graduate school is challenging but absolutely feasible. The workload is heavy, but if you learn how to manage your time well, there should not be a problem. I enjoy traveling to conferences, talking to groups of scholars, and being asked for my opinion on prestigious projects. The only pressures are those associated with academic careers (publishing, writing, etc.). Essentially, graduate school is the best experience of my life and I do not regret for even a second where I am.

Recommendations for Teachers and Administrators, Professors, and Latina/o Students

There are numerous points to be made in directing Latina/o paths toward the Ph.D. I question my qualifications to provide this guidance, but perhaps my background, hardships, and unique journey offer this privilege.

Teachers and Administrators

Every teacher who expected the best from me, and every counselor who lent a helping hand during my college years, made a difference. I thrive in graduate school because I know there are people here who care about me. The key is to help Latina/os by giving them the same support you give White students. Help them to attain the necessary academic skills, socialize into networks that can aid them in the future, and train them in how to be successful in the everyday world (e.g. public speaking abilities, how to work with people, etc.).

Professors

The warm embrace I received from my advisor and my department facilitated my transition to Chicago and graduate school. It is essential to offer a welcoming environment to Latina/o students when many of us are leaving our families and relocating to another state for our graduate studies. Beyond the warm welcome, it is essential to build a relationship with your students to help them gain confidence in their abilities and understand the system. As Latina/o graduate students, we have the capacity and motivation to conceptualize, examine and develop theory, and make substantial contributions. Yet, good mentorship and guidance are essential for any student to flourish. Hence, while a comfortable social environment is essential, a stimulating and acceptable intellectual environment is just as imperative for a high-quality graduate experience.

Students

First, I want to emphasize that one's experiences, such as the ones I describe here, are important. Your past helps you build on your present and your future. Don't take your time lightly, and do recognize that each life event has a lesson. Grow from your experiences, no matter how unfair, overbearing, or negative they may seem at the time. Take the initiative in deciding your life choices.

Second, my mother taught me never to be mediocre, always strive to be my best. If a professor asks for 15 references, work harder by giving 30. If you are to read three chapters for class, read and type up notes to ensure your understanding of the materials. If have a paper due, finish it early so you will have time to review and revise it. As a minority student, you cannot afford to do the minimum because others will believe you are in graduate school because of your race. Demonstrate your capacity and be proactive in your studies.

Third, do not overemphasize grades in graduate school. You have been indoctrinated throughout your life to care about getting an A or B, but the goal in graduate school is to learn, think critically, and perform to the best of your capacity. Focus on gaining the most from your readings, projects, and group activities. In the process, learn how to write proficiently, to conceptualize abstract concepts, and apply theory. Your job after graduate school will focus on your acquired skills, not solely on your academic transcript.

Fourth, recognize that class is only one forum for learning. Your main purpose as a graduate student is to generate knowledge. Attend colloquiums, symposiums, and workshops, and do not limit yourself to the offered curriculum. Instead, be innovative in complementing your educational training outside the classroom by participating in scholarly dialogues, creating scholarly networks, and fostering strong social supports that will enhance your experience in graduate school and stimulate your learning.

Last, do not be afraid to take risks. In social science, and even in natural science, we are simultaneously right and wrong. Do not be afraid to think differently because you might be wrong. Spend your time thinking, imagining, and pushing your theories to another level. Do not limit yourself based on previous theories or parameters. Be innovative, introspective, and daring by constructing knowledge, not just learning from it.

In retrospect, I am amazed to be in graduate school, when I never even envisioned attending college. I still cannot fully understand what led me here. I would like to believe in free will, and that I accomplished this educational success on my own accord, but that would be a lie. My mother's unconditional support and the teachers who provided me with the necessary academic skills to be successful, as well as their mentorship, are the two consistent themes in my life. Based on these experiences, it is not a mystery why I want to become a professor; people often want to be like those we admire. Therefore, it is my hope to return one day all that has been given to me by motivating, training, and inspiring a generation of future Latina/os and other scholars.

Marisa Garcia

Marisa Garcia, an engineering doctoral student at UC-Irvine, was born in Orange, California, where her parents and sisters live. Ms. Garcia graduated from Saddleback High School in Santa Ana in 1997 and considers this her hometown. In 2002, she received a B.S. in mechanical engineering from UC-Riverside and she received a masters of science in biomedical engineering from UC-Irvine in 2004. Currently pursuing her Ph.D. in the same field, she is the first in her family to attend college and pursue an advanced degree.

Ms. Garcia's interest in pursuing research in the field of cardiovascular biomechanics is motivated by her fascination with cardiovascular disease. Her research focuses on the mechanical properties of coronary arteries to understand the biomechanics and adaptation mechanisms of the coronary circulation system and predict its response to conditions such as hypertension and hypertrophy.

16

THE BROWN DIAMOND

A Latina in the Sciences

Marisa Garcia

In the diamond industry, the category of brown is used broadly to denote a wide range of hues and color tones. Such are Latinas, who embody an eclectic range of cultural roots. I am of Mexican descent and grew up in Santa Ana, a predominantly Latina/o Southern California city. I attended schools where the student population consisted mainly of Latina/os. I went on to pursue a bachelor's in mechanical engineering from the University of California-Riverside (UCR) and a master's in biomedical engineering from the University of California-Irvine (UCI), where I am currently working toward a Ph.D. It was not until my college years that I realized my earlier classmates and friends were not on the same educational path as I was. In my first two years of college, I took general courses where, even though minorities were scarce, the presence of women was not negligible. As the curriculum became more focused on engineering, I became one of the few women and the only Latina in my classes. This trend, which continues through graduate school, emphasizes for me that women in the sciences are like diamonds, and Latinas are the rarest form of this precious jewel.

Colored Diamonds Are Truly Rare

The science, technology, engineering, and mathematics (STEM) fields are known historically to be male-dominated. With limited representation in the field at the graduate level, Latinas must navigate a seemingly new world. Of course, before entering graduate school, I prepared as much as possible by completing all of the prerequisites. I also attended workshops and seminars, spoke with counselors, and joined organizations geared toward helping minorities pursue a postbaccalaureate. Although the seminars and organizations undoubtedly helped me to achieve my goal, they did not prepare me completely for what I would encounter in graduate school.

Because I am a Latina in a STEM field, people have presumptions about my gender and culture. In this chapter, I introduce how my culture helps me negotiate the stereotypes Latinas face. I also address how my gender and culture influence my personal and professional interactions and relationship dynamics. Finally, I share my experiences and challenges to help Latinas navigate their own way through graduate school in the sciences.

Latina Stereotypes

Influential heroes in history have demonstrated Latinos' potential to be leaders. The strong Latinas who have made a major impact in history include Eva "Evita" Peron, the fearless activist; Frida Kahlo, the infamous Mexican painter; and my favorite, the great poetic nun, Sor Juana Inés de la Cruz. Among many others, these women are influential icons whose notable achievements have changed the way women are viewed. They possessed the courage and wisdom I wish I could emulate, but their stories seemed mythical and I never seem to be able to relate to them completely; I am not like them. Even though Latina role models in the technical fields have slowly emerged, such as Ellen Ochoa (the first Latina to become an astronaut), they are still too scarce for me to say that Latinas have role models in the sciences. The absence of women in these fields, I believe, is a major reason why our stereotypes have not changed significantly.

The few role models, coupled with media and societal stereotypes, shape the negative assumptions about Latina gender and culture. Latinas are perceived as dependent, submissive, and unintelligent without regard for their inner strength, resiliency, and ability to work collaboratively (Lopez, 2001). Being considered the least likely of any group of women to complete a bachelor's degree may lend insight to questioning Latinas' intellect (American Association of University Women, 2000). Unequal access, less financial support, and limited degree achievement, however, are systemic aspects that hinder the educational process for Latinas, in addition to familial, cultural, peer, and media pressure. A critical stereotype that plagues Latinas is that of being natural mothers who bear children at an early age. Because of this stereotype, Latinas' roles in higher education are questioned, further limiting what others might invest in their educational journeys and raising questions about whether they have a place in higher education. Consequently, Latinas, and their abilities and qualifications, are questioned throughout their college years and are often perceived as "having slipped through the cracks of admissions" and treated as a novelty or an admissions quota. These damaging perceptions often linger and ultimately hinder Latinas' overall educational experiences. Reflecting on my own friends and family, only one did not attend college due to pregnancy. Further, my older sister, who is a single parent, has returned to school because she realized that having a family is not her only life's purpose.

I wonder what effects these stereotypes have had on Latinas' efficacy and culture and gender ideologies. What assumptions do Latinas make about other Latinas or, more important, about themselves? If a Latina internalizes these stereotypes, will she deny her interests or potential for something different (e.g., engineering or math)? Will she attribute other Latinas' successes to extraordinary genius, detaching her from possible role models? I can only speculate on the limits that have been set unconsciously.

Perseverance and Resilience: Internal and External Infrastructures

Resilience through Cultura: *My Foundation*

My resilience in graduate school is rooted in my *cultura* and childhood experiences. In many Latina/o cultures, Latinas start working in the home at an early age. Among other things, I remember washing dishes with my sister at age five and learning how to lay tile with my father a few years later; these tasks taught me how to work well with my hands. In Mexico, my grandmother taught me how to make cheese from scratch, reminding me about what I miss when I take shortcuts: the experience. My cousins taught me how to ride horses, which made me more adventurous. And, when I began riding sheep, which were like small bulls with no horns, I knew I was not afraid to face new challenges. These experiences not only helped me build strong ties with family, they also helped me gain confidence, a sense of fearlessness, patience, and insight.

Additional significant childhood experiences include my parents, their attitudes, and *consejos* (advice). For example, I lived in a household where only Spanish was spoken. My parents worked hard at adjusting, acclimating, and striving toward their American dream. However, when my parents struggled, I also recall my aunts and uncles always providing support and sustenance; this taught me the meaning of family, which would later become part of my support system for encouragement. Last, my mother's sayings run in my mind constantly and have become my most important stress relievers. Her tenacious attitude lives through me as I recall her saying, "There's always time for everything," reminding me that there is always room for improvement.

Other challenges include the financial burdens that the majority of my college peers did not have to face when my family struggled to help me through school. Again, my cultural teachings to be tenacious and resilient offered me the strength to search for scholarships, loans, and work. In addition, an internalized added pressure of not having someone to fall back on if I do not succeed (to not be a burden on *la familia*) forced me to keep focused on my work.

Overall, my family's determination to succeed helped me to build stamina, while making the hard work required of engineering seem less threatening. Engineering fields demand intelligence as well as substantial vigor and endurance. For example, the toughest professors did not compare to the stern Mexican men with whom I was raised and continue to encounter. My strong religious beliefs provided the faith that keeps me optimistic, even when taking multiple exams in one day after having stayed up all night to study. My culture has inadvertently prepared me for my educational challenges. Moreover, being a child of struggling immigrant parents, I feel a certain responsibility toward them to show my gratitude and appreciation by persevering in life.

Persistence and External Structures

College-prep organizations, various summer programs, and specific gifted programs also helped me counter the negative societal stereotypes, limited faculty expectations, and few role models that provided limited entry to higher education. In particular, college-prep organizations helped relieve the pressures I encountered and offered opportunities to learn about various educational options. Moreover, specific programs such as Upward Bound and Mathematics Intensive Summer Session (MISS) directed me to pursue an advanced degree. These programs provided educational resources and various guidance counselors and role models who countered the multiple messages that I did not belong in higher education and belonged even less in a STEM field.

Diamonds in the Rough

Personal and Professional Interactions in Engineering

According to Weinberg's (2004) review of 2000 U.S. Census Bureau statistics, women make on average only three-quarters of the salaries men do. Examining specific figures, in the same year, college-educated women earned just $5,000 more a year than male high school graduates did. The female sector of general industry and the academy simply is not as respected, in terms of pay and position, as males are. Further affecting this trend, in 2002, women earned 10% of the degrees in the STEM sciences, and a dismal 16% of these were engineering degrees (Student Effort and Education Progress, 2004). The minimal reward system and under-representation of women in academia and the STEM fields creates a challenging environment for women to navigate.

Communication Differences and Embedded Biases

The relationships I encounter as a female engineer differ from those of my male peers and faculty/professionals—these differences are primarily evident in our interactions. For example, I have observed that males hide their inefficiencies, whether it is by covering them up or not taking responsibility for their faults. Women, on the other hand, tend to acknowledge their mistakes; this leads us to be perceived as weak and uninformed. Similarly, men are more direct when they communicate. By speaking this way, false or misleading statements are not questioned. Moreover, by being more direct, they are establishing their positions (Vikesland, 1998). In contrast, women mainly carry conversations to establish relationships or aim to create equality between the two in conversation. As a result of such gender-based interactions, I continuously catch myself giving my power away by couching statements as if they were questions. This way of interacting has inaccurately made me seem less of a threat among my peers.

Knowing that others misinterpret my qualities and undermine my abilities as a result of gender dynamics, I consciously look for ways to gain position and respect. To gain their respect, I have had to outdo my male counterparts on assignments and tests. I can see their attitudes change when they get stuck on a problem and *I* help them solve it. My male friends seem to overstate the obvious when explaining concepts to me more often than they do with each other. To prove to them that I am smarter than they think, I started finishing their sentences, which makes them laugh but also lets them see what they are doing. Dealing with my peers has pushed me to try harder, and I appreciate their giving me that extra nudge.

With professors, it has been my experience that, although they may not perceive me as an equal, they have treated me equally. For example, after my preliminary exam, which determined whether I would advance into the Ph.D. program, one of the three professors who sat on my oral exams confessed he was *surprised* that I "did better than everyone [he] tested." He had a look on his face that seemed to say he has been wrong about me. Although he had an embedded and perhaps subconscious biased belief that I would not outperform my male counterparts, I respected him more based on his acknowledgment and the respect he offered me as a result of my perform-ance. Moreover, while such encounters often remind me of the traditional male-dominated views in the field, changing attitudes establish hope and re-inforce my position. Similarly, resistant male-dominated viewpoints also mo-tivate and remind me of the importance to persist for change.

Other Unique Challenges

Although communication differences and gender biases limited female ad-vancement, the male-dominated environment in the STEM fields also intro-duces female engineering students to particularly challenging situations. Such unique female challenges include exclusion from male-dominated cir-cles, or, when we are included, being seen primarily in terms of our sexuality and not being taken seriously in our profession. For example, I vividly recall being stared at by numerous men in the field during research presentations at conferences. Following these encounters, I always tried to convince myself that their glaring stares were isolated occurrences. The key for me, however, was to remain strong even when I felt I had limited control because of the circumstances.

Specific techniques I implement to minimize awkward gender dynamics in academia include dressing conservatively, limiting my social encounters with men to a professional setting, and preparing the best I can so the audi-ence doesn't stare at me when I stumble over my words or search for my materials. Pointing at the presentation board, standing behind the podium, and even dimming the lights are other means of keeping the audience from watching me directly; however, these techniques often remind me of the lim-ited control I feel with the audience and how stifling it can feel to present to a male-dominated audience. Other means of navigating such encounters include taking some time to reflect on the situations as opposed to reacting in the moment. Many times I have to remind myself of my ultimate educa-tional goals and assess best options to alleviate the circumstance while still preserving my dignity as a Latina student in higher education.

Diamonds Require Polishing: The Importance of Mentorship

Only recently did I find a role model who has replaced the imaginary person I had been modeling myself after for most of my educational career. I did not think such a role model existed, but I knew who I wanted to be and kept that person alive in my mind. I realized the importance of a guide when I decided that I wanted to excel in my field. I needed someone whose footsteps I could follow and who could help me understand what my future was going to be like. Although I did not have anyone who encompassed *all* the characteristics I was looking for, I did find pieces of these characteristics in various individuals around me. I had a couple of teachers and counselors who gave me great advice and influenced my decisions. Although this was helpful, I still needed someone who could relate to my experiences and whose guidance was more specific—a mentor who could warn me of potential pitfalls and reveal the opportunities that I would never have known otherwise. The qualities I sought I found in my principal investigator (PI), who later became my role model and mentor.

A PI in graduate school, known as your advisor, is the person whose lab you choose to join to do your research. My advisor's personality and character are very welcoming, although you may not think it from his rugged looks. His sense of humor keeps reminding me of how important it is to do what I love and have fun while I work. His wisdom is intimidating at times, but it gains him endless respect. His tenacious attitude toward work keeps me motivated; when I question his presence in the lab on the weekends, he smiles and replies, "A good leader always leads by example." His high expectations ensure that his students are well prepared when they leave his lab. In addition to research skills, my advisor has taught me about the secret politics in academia, including those of my and other graduate programs and the fellowship and grant process. Although I find myself working through weekends, I am extremely grateful and hope to make him proud.

Being male and not a Latino, I believe my PI could never truly understand my experiences and the added pressures of my gender and culture. It is easier to relate to his culture than his gender because he experienced a similar upbringing. He did not grow up in a privileged home; his success is a direct result of his hard work. I do not believe, however, that he has the same familial pressures. My biggest obligation as a Latina is that I am expected to take care of *la familia* financially as soon as I am able. As a woman, my experiences are undoubtedly different. Males in any profession probably never need to choose between a career and a family; males may not need to put their careers on hold, whether temporarily or permanently, to have children. I wonder what choices I will need to make as a professional Latina in engineering. Fortunately, I believe my PI is aware of the differences, and he offers guidance in all the areas that he can. As a mentor, he is the type of person I strive to be.

Recommendations

In light of the discrimination, harassment, and pay inequality that females face in the STEM fields, why pursue scientific careers? It is because of these challenges that women, Latinas in particular, *must* pursue these degrees. Women cannot afford to wait until the system has changed. In fact, the environment may never be positive until women are more represented and begin to influence their circumstances. Moreover, the differences that are slowly appearing demonstrate that there is hope. For example, practices that reinforce assimilation are being eliminated in classrooms where teachers say "she/he" instead of the traditional "he," and an increasing number of women are being hired in top managerial positions. The growing numbers in the various fields and the slow-but-growing number of females and Latinas in top leadership positions (in both industry and academia) help me to picture a better environment in the future. Moreover, I will take the responsibility of trying to change it for the Latina scholars who follow me.

Directions for Fellow Students

- **Pick a mentor early.** Imaginary role models count as well. Realize that a role model and mentor do not have to be one person, and that they may come from anywhere, including home. In the future, you may be the one who encompasses all of the mentor traits for someone else.
- **Find a support system.** Whether it is friends, a religious group, a teacher, or family, find someone or a group that will assist you in addressing your challenges and discussing your encounters. Talk with these individuals, share your experiences, and help them to understand your situation. Be assured that you are not alone, and that many are rooting for your success.
- **Create a stress outlet.** Many times you will be frustrated, angry, and disenchanted with your circumstances, and stress outlets will help you to channel your energy positively. Specific techniques that may be helpful include exercise, yoga and meditation courses, karate, or self-defense courses. These avenues help you to clear your mind and be more productive.
- **Don't change who you are but be able to add complementary behaviors.** Be an advocate for yourselves by emphasizing your strengths—such as being persistent, hardworking, detail-oriented, and nurturing—while also being expressive and communicative. Hence, you do not have to be like a male to get ahead in engineering; you have to be a strong woman instead (Sagario, 2003).

Recommendations for the University in General

Gender is a subset of diversity that universities have overlooked for too long. Latinas are America's fastest-growing minority population, and schools, at all levels, need to meet their educational needs. To recruit and retain Latina students to graduation, I recommend the following:

- **Create female-based programs.** Create outreach programs such as Project MISS (Fullerton, California) that are designed to enhance the mathematics skills of young women from different communities. These programs should help offset at least part of the cost of their education while providing the extra educational support they need.
- **Work with existing organizations.** Ask for assistance from organizations like the National Science Foundation (NSF) that recognize the problem and are working to rectify it. Recognizing the importance of science and technology competence in the workforce, the NSF is committed to the recruitment and retention of women and girls in science, engineering, and mathematics studies and careers (Vikesland, 1998). The NSF has provided financial support for a variety of programs that address educational issues, from grade school through graduate school. Organizations like the NSF might be able to provide the support institutions need to start a new program.
- **Develop youth outreach.** Create summer school programs that reach our girls as early as the elementary level. Too many females are unaware of their options, and we need to reach them before the negative influences do. Without knowing about the possibility of a higher education, how can we expect them to get there? Early exposure and encouragement will help change stereotypes.
- **Recruit and train Latina faculty.** Latinas need to be seen in different roles to accustom society to our new status. Latinas are a growing minority in academia, and higher education should make an effort to recruit these women into the professoriate. In such capacities, they can serve as role models for women in academia directly. If you do not feel that the Latinas you are interviewing are qualified, maybe you have to re-evaluate your search, but do not simplify your task by saying no Latina Ph.D.s met your qualifications. Broaden your search, attend Latina/o specific conferences for recruitment, place your ad in Latina/o professional list servs, and target ethnic-specific academic publications.

Advice for Individual Faculty and Doctoral Training Programs

Know that most, if not all, Latinas in the sciences never had a technical role model, someone in whose footsteps they could follow. Most do not have anyone on the "inside" who can relate tips or share personal experiences. When surrounded by peers whose parents are professionals, Latinas may feel intimidated. Listen and help guide them. To support and mentor Latina students to succeed, I recommend the following:

- **Organize and support workshops.**
  - For retention, provide the essential information that Latinas need to understand their environment. Expose them to an early support system that could assist them during their transition. In addition, provide female role models and Latina/o leaders who will help them deal with their insecurities while increasing their self-esteem.
  - Address any sexual static in your department among students, students and faculty, and even faculty and faculty. Provide informational seminars on gender issues, gender communication, and gender stereotypes. These dialogues and educational seminars will help men and women understand each other by allowing them to voice their opinions.
- **Understand the Latina/o culture.** Understand that the Latina/o culture values family first, above all. Faculty must deal meaningfully with such Latina/o stereotypes and gender-specific biases as Latina teen pregnancy in association with school performance. Also recognize that being a young Latina mother and a student does not mean this individual has competing values. Her education is essential for her future and the future of her family. Offer the support needed (child care, alternative scheduling, counseling) to allow this growing student population to excel in higher education. Also, recall that not all Latina students are mothers or females who want to bear children at an early age. As Latinas, we are a diverse group with various backgrounds, strengths, and experiences.

Importance of Diversity

As a Latina doctoral student in engineering, I have had shocking and astoundingly uplifting experiences on the journey toward my future. I still have a couple of years to go before I complete my educational journey, but my struggle to succeed has made me stronger and has given me the confidence to handle whatever lies ahead. My expedition continually reminds me about the importance of gender and cultural issues. Our color and gender used to prevent us from advancement; are we using it now to beat the competition? Did racism and sexism reverse? I do not think so; we are not even near the catch-up mark. Latinas have been and remain an untapped resource for communities and organizations. I am happy with the decisions I have made and excited to see where they will lead me. I wish I could say that there would be no other unexpected and unwelcome experiences for Latinas preparing to pave their own paths through graduate school, but just like the brown diamond is unique in creation, each Latina will have a unique experience as she shines. The key, however, is to shine despite the multiple challenges, always keeping in mind the asset you are for society, your community, and other future Latina students in the STEM fields.

References

American Association of University Women (2000). *Gender equity in education research*. Retrieved March 14, 2005 from http://www1.minn.net/~aauwmn/research.htm.

Lopez, J. (2001, January 27). *Should something be done about the Latino stereotypes?* Rosa Parks Research Paper. Available at http://web.uccs.edu/ethnicstudies/site/Rosa%20Parks/Previous/2001/rosaparkswinners.htm.

Sagario, D. (2003, December). Put down powder puff, grab weapons of success. *Des Moines Register*.

U.S. Census Bureau (March 1, 2005). Available at http://www.census.gov/.

Vikesland, G. (1998). *Communication 101: Supervising men*. Available at http://www.employer-employee.com/comm101.htm.

Weinberg, D. (2004, May). *Evidence from Census 2000 about earning by detailed occupation for men and women*. Retrieved March 14, 2005, from http://www.census.gov/prod/2004pubs/censr-15.pdf.

David Alberto Quijada

Dr. David Alberto Quijada is assistant professor in education, culture, and society and in ethnic studies at the University of Utah. He has a Ph.D. in sociocultural studies in education, with a designated emphasis in feminist theory and research from the University of California, Davis (2002). He was awarded a Chancellor's Postdoctoral Fellowship for Academic Diversity at the University of California, Berkeley (2002–04). Dr. Quijada has taught mathematics in public school, worked as a gang alternative specialist, and co-created "A World Acting with Respect and Equality" (AWARE). His research interests and areas of specialization include inter-cultural/interethnic youth alliances and identity formations; community coalition-building projects that develop across race, class, and gender; feminist ethnographic method; and critical discourse analysis. His research interests emerge from his experiences working with youth as a community activist, teacher, and researcher. He is committed to becoming a better ally to youth by working directly with youth. Dr. Quijada believes in teaching and research that are interdisciplinary and that seek to ask questions and reorient assumptions about our lives and the lives of others and how we are positioned in society.

17

COLLEGIAL ALLIANCES?

Exploring One Chicano's Perspective on Mentoring in Research and Academia

David Alberto Quijada

> It is crucial that those among us who resist and rebel, who survive and succeed, speak openly and honestly about our lives and the nature of our personal struggles, the means by which we resolve and reconcile contradictions. This is no easy task. Within the educational institutions where we learn to develop and strengthen our writing and analytical skills, we also learn to think, write, and talk in a manner that shifts attention away from personal experience. Yet if we are to reach our people and all people, if we are to remain connected (especially those of us whose familial backgrounds are poor and working class), we must understand that the telling of one's personal story provides a meaningful example, a way for folks to identify and connect. (hooks, 1993, p. 103)

In the spirit of hooks's call for us to speak openly and honestly about our struggles to resolve and reconcile contradictions in our professional lives, in this chapter I examine my personal journey of being mentored in graduate school. I experienced that journey as fragmented and disjointed in many ways; therefore I follow the example of feminist and other postmodern scholars whose writing is intentionally constructed to reflect experience (Anzaldúa, 1987; Trinh, 1989; Moraga & Anzaldúa, 1983). They strategically use discontinuous narratives and other violations of academic genres to call attention to taken-for-granted institutional and interpersonal hierarchies and oppression. In my case, I use asterisks rather than subsection headings between narratives to signal my talking back to the assumption that experience can be condensed into a phrase. The quotations that frame some sections are guides to how the sections are to be read and often represent readings and ideas that influenced me as I thought through the issues I address here. As will become clear, my experience has led me to conceive of mentoring as reciprocal collegial alliances that emerge from conflict and coalition between faculty and students united by shared goals.

*   *   *

As I watched the snowfall through the airplane window as the crew de-iced the aircraft before takeoff, I wondered how I would share this trip with friends and family. How would I describe my job talk, the dinners, the meetings, the campus, the snow, the faculty, the questions I was asked, and my feelings about the possibility of leaving California? My first academic interview did more than challenge my training, scholarship, and research; it forced me to confront my vulnerabilities.

Once again the Chicano child of yesterday emerged, reminding me that I hadn't worked hard enough, published enough, asked the right questions, or delved deeply enough theoretically and methodologically. This familiar script I had internalized reminded me that there was always one more thing to prepare and always a better way to write, explain, and "be." How easily I slipped into deception and became the imposter who graduated from the university with a Ph.D., was on a postdoctoral fellowship at UC-Berkeley, and was now in the job market. I was consumed with fear, falsely creating stories that faculty at the institution where I had interviewed would catch their mistake and realize they had interviewed the wrong candidate.

Flying 30,000 miles above the ground, the pilot announced that the airplane had reached a safe altitude and we could unfasten our seat belts. With this announcement I noticed that the airplane was empty, the overhead lights were off, and we had departed. Overwhelmed by my interview experience, I still could not believe that this new institution valued my research and teaching. In that moment I began to cry, and this is what I wrote in my journal: *They want ME; they made themselves available to ME; and now I have to believe in ME!* As I wrote in my journal, fear blended with excitement as I thought about my future possibilities of becoming a professor in a research institution, a dream I would realize sooner than I had imagined.

*   *   *

Graduate school was as much a struggle over issues of identity as it was an opportunity to confront and explore learning as a source of transformation and contribution to social justice issues. I learned to question my experience and commitments to education. In this capacity I sought to transform inequities in school contexts that I experienced as a Chicano student, as a mathematics teacher in the public schools, and as a counselor in a nonprofit, gang alternative program.

Unlike most graduate students, I entered graduate school fully funded and recruited by a tenured faculty person of color who wanted to mentor me. I still remember my mother's excitement as she enthusiastically relayed a message to me from the professor who was to be my advisor. I answered the phone at work, and before I could say hello, my mother began[1]: *¡Chavelo la profesora/el profesor te hablo de la universidad! ¡Hijo estoy tan orgullosa de tí—te aceptaron y que te van a dar una beca. Ella/El era tan amable y hablaba muy bien el español!* (Chavelo [nickname], the professor called you from the university! Son, I'm so proud of you—they accepted you, and they're going to give you a scholarship. She/he was so nice and spoke very good Spanish!)

Overwhelmed with feelings of happiness, fear, and excitement, I could not believe that I was about to become a graduate student in a Ph.D. program. I had never known a graduate student personally, and other than the brief office hour visits I had had with professors, I had not talked to anyone with a Ph.D. The reality of pursuing a graduate degree was before me, and still I doubted myself as I asked, "Why did they choose me?" Clearly they made a mistake and picked the wrong candidate.

*   *   *

My first weeks in graduate school had me rethinking why I had given up my secure teaching job. The whole experience seemed surreal. People were speaking an alien language and arguing over seemingly meaningless problems at the same time *real* people were struggling with *real* problems. I was reminded that for many children, school is not a *real* place. (Ladson-Billings, 1997, p. 55)

As a graduate student I delved deeply into coursework and readings, began working as a research assistant, and desperately tried to understand what a literature review, research question, and theoretical framework meant. Despite my efforts I often felt without skills or language to articulate my position on education. I noticed how other graduate students smoothly navigated through seminars, easily accessing language not only to introduce and present themselves and their views, but also to describe their research interests. Many expertly discussed and researched educational issues that affected marginalized communities like the one in which I was raised. However, what was written and discussed did not connect with my experiences, and, in fact, it was in opposition to the oppression I and others had been subjected to or had worked to dismantle.

While other students framed their educational concerns through research questions that grappled with theory and methods, I needed to understand people's relationship to education by listening to their experiences and

---

[1] I've purposefully made this narrative gender-neutral to protect the identity of the professor.

questioning my own assumptions. Discussions felt detached and removed from the real-life experiences of people who were struggling, like me, with identity and issues of race and class. Rather than incorporating feeling, empathy, or even a personal commitment to and relationship with education, I found discussions in seminars and hallways solely focused on educational outcomes, generalizability, and quick-fix solutions. Like the communities we were researching, where participants openly confessed their educational experiences, I wanted students and faculty to share why they did research and how it contributed to their lives and the lives of others.

Of course, there were those rare occasions when someone brought up the difficulties of doing research. That's when it was okay to talk about research subjects (participants) and their relationship to research. I listened intently, believing discussion might shift toward recognizing the problem of the unequal power relationships associated with research. Rather than acknowledge their biases and privileges by discussing their research relationships with participants and community, or what I later learned to call my "researcher positionality," seminar members quickly shifted and began to complain about the difficulty of doing research and to justify our research and practice sites. However problematic, these passing anecdotes about research left me wanting to hear more. I wanted to discuss research relationships as central and not just as a point of reference or a social category of analysis.

I was frustrated and discontented because I found myself immersed in a type of learning I disagreed with and to which I felt no connection. Yet, the more I questioned its process, and compared my participation to others', the easier it became for me to blame myself for not working hard enough or not reading enough. It seemed like there was never enough time to read and synthesize my arguments, much less develop an argument to discuss in class or examine in research. Yet others seemed to do it, and do it well—or so I believed.

*   *   *

When my father died in a car accident during my first year of graduate school, I was not encouraged by professors or staff to take the quarter off, nor did I know that doing so was an option. Instead I went home for two weeks, buried my father, cried with my family, and returned to graduate school to finish the quarter. I fell behind in my work, and I was scared to admit that I couldn't make it, so I ended my first year of graduate school with three "incompletes" and a letter from the dean of graduate studies telling me that I was on academic probation. My first-year evaluation from my advisor reprimanded my slow progress and threatened to pull my fellowship if I didn't finish my incompletes quickly.

I missed my father. I felt alone, inept, and out of place, but still I persisted and remained a graduate student. I delved even deeper into my studies, but this time I sought to locate my personal experience in the theories we discussed. The juxtaposition of home and community struggles and suffering with the required detachment of both research-created knowledge and the university as an institution from home and community in the name of "objectivity" brought me to a new realization—that education and knowledge also emerge in everyday interactions that include family and friends. We and our communities own that knowledge, and it is grounded in experience and practice. I began to question and challenge: Where am I and the people we research in the texts we read and discuss? In seminars I took notice of who was speaking, who was not present, and whose voice was heard.

I read across disciplines and took courses outside of education, in women's studies, Chicana/o studies, anthropology, and sociology. I immersed myself in feminist theory, critical discourse analysis, and feminist ethnography, applying an interdisciplinary approach to education that gave me a new language to engage, critique, and extend education. I remember almost begging my advisor to let me take a course that recognized "the novel as research" that was cross-listed in Chicana/o studies and critical theory. I couldn't believe it, a graduate seminar offering readings by the same feminists of color whose works I was already reading, such as Anzaldúa, hooks, Moraga, and Collins. Without acknowledging the theoretical significance of such a course, my advisor agreed to let me take it because, "In graduate school it's good to have entertaining courses—I'm hoping it will help you focus."

I was excited by the courses I took outside of my department because I now had a language in which to discuss education. I read works by authors who empowered me to rethink my position in the world by questioning my relationship to others. I recognized how interactions invested in conflict and coalition become important educational moments to engage marginalization and identity as a source of learning, with the potential for social transformation.

Eager to engage these new ideas, I now spoke up in education seminars. To my surprise, graduate students, faculty, and my advisor responded to my questions and contributions with critique and cynicism. Under the guise of a sociocultural strand in education (my area), most faculty and coursework in my department framed educational issues as psychological and quantitative variables of analysis. Rather than engage interdisciplinary education, they privileged their area of study, constraining educational issues, reform, methods, and findings through disciplinary terminology that did not acknowledge epistemological differences.

While others spoke freely in seminars, I had to translate well-researched feminist and critical theories to defend my positions and engage my ideas. As a learner I felt put in place for "not knowing." I quickly learned that I had crossed an unspoken border that, because I had not yet negotiated the required rites of passage, meant I could not critique the established order of education or what faculty in my department policed. I learned the irony of the academy that encourages us to create new knowledge provided we stay within a presumed paradigm. I was still in coursework, without a qualifying exam committee and nowhere near being "All But Dissertation." Once again I felt alone, confused, and now an imposter to my own learning.

*   *   *

During my first year in graduate school, I naively learned that research could transform how we live if we just asked the right questions—or rather, the types of questions most faculty in my department asked. In this capacity, I confronted how power and privilege operate and are cloaked by graduate education, bestowing privilege only on some faculty, coursework, and research while constraining how and why we learn in graduate school. I quickly learned that, in part, my retention in graduate school was determined by the faculty relationships I developed, the institutional structures and types of research that faculty supported, and, of course, the financial assistance they ensured.

The more strained my departmental relationships became, the more aware I was of the cultural politics that frame graduate education. In fact, the very same power differentials I began investigating within youth-adult relationships that constrain learning, agency, and education were operating in my graduate education. My mentoring relationships promoted a linear approach to learning, sustaining my position as novice graduate student and my mentor as expert professor. I realized this type of mentoring replicated conservative teacher/learner positions and did little to rethink the academy despite its sincere attempts to get me through the program. Feeling constrained, I began to question, What is learning? Learning for what? Learning for whom? I brought theoretical questions close to home, reminding myself that educational inequities are not just about other people's lives but include my own life as well—forcing me to confront my own socialization into the academy via the mentoring relationships I was in.

Awakened by the realities of graduate education, I was confused about how to proceed in graduate school. Like others, I had been recruited through a Ph.D. pipeline that offered open, direct passage via an under-my-wing mentoring approach that outlined my coursework, determined my research questions, and defined best methods and theoretical frameworks. Smothered within a research trajectory that did not match what I set out to do, I wondered, "Did my advisor read my statement of purpose?" And finally I asked, "Where am I in this research?"

*   *   *

. . . all genuine hope has to go through the fire of despair. (West, 1997, p. 57)

In my search for graduate education, I learned that institutionalized education was not just about differing commitments to social justice, theoretical orientations, and research agendas. The broad implications of my social awareness revealed how internalized oppression operates to silence critical thinking while institutions sustain this process. My initial advisor, as I see it, adhered to the positivistic research agenda that upheld the department's dominant paradigms, constraining how I and others engaged the academy through our research and teaching. An easily identifiable solution would be to change advisors, which I did in the third year of my Ph.D. studies. But even as I changed advisors, I wondered how we transform inequities in the academy or foster better support and mentoring for Latina/o graduate students to succeed and graduate.

As I considered switching advisors my current advisor suddenly told me that my funding was being terminated at the end of the month. In other words, my advisor unjustly fired me as a research assistant. Jeopardizing my funding was one attempt to prevent me from continuing my area of study. At the time a small group of concerned graduate students, including myself, rallied against the dismantling of sociocultural studies in education. We also sought to disseminate faculty power across all areas of study. Our position in the department was met unfavorably by some faculty, including my advisor, who retaliated by ending my research assistant position. When I filed a formal grievance with Graduate Studies (which was successful, and my funding reinstated), I realized I needed help. I could no longer do graduate school alone. I needed a community of scholars to engage with my writing, to discuss and read research. Most faculty in my department discredited my research, and a large number of graduate students, although for the most part encouraging, talked with me cautiously and never mentioned departmental politics for fear of losing status in the department. Doors to my graduate education were closing quickly. In a department where news circulates quickly and power is unevenly distributed, I felt alone and vulnerable.

Although difficult, isolating, and emotionally painful, switching advisors greatly transformed my learning and education and increased my commitment to social justice. I sought direction from professors who had taught courses that had transformed my thinking. To my surprise, I was not alone. Other faculty and graduate students shared similar experiences, influencing how we discussed research and asked questions. Personal testimony now blended with theory and practice, which helped me to reconceptionalize my relationship to research.

I still remember how excited I felt after my first meeting with a professor in my department who, though now emerita, continues to be a strong influence in my learning. This professor sincerely asked, "What would you like to study and why?" We spent the next hour sharing our childhood memories of learning with family and in schools. It was the first time in my graduate career that I was asked, "Why did you choose graduate school?" Our conversation, and the many that followed, both included and prioritized "everyday life" and did not assume that graduate school chose me. I recall how this same professor compared graduate education to preschool, reminding me how much I enjoyed learning to play, share, and explore new ideas in relationships with others.

At about this same time, I was struggling with how to locate a research site for the ethnographic methods course I was enrolled in. The professor of the course, who later became my new advisor, talked me through my research dilemma after class. I was surprised that, instead of asking how I was negotiating a research site, this professor sought to learn more about my commitments to a "community learning center" that other activists and I had initiated in East Oakland, California.

We spent the next hour discussing the coalition-building efforts of activists, locating new literacy in their commitments to transform education. I excitedly described how educational theory came alive through my community participation, which I did on the weekends. Through our conversation, I realized how my activist involvement could no longer be kept separate from my graduate education, but in fact could inform my research. By engaging my commitments to social justice, this professor transformed my relationship to research, practice, and theory by reconstituting "education" as a site of liberation.

In addition to engaging my research questions and consulting my expert knowledge, the faculty I now work with inspire critical thinking by personally sharing dilemmas they experience in the academy. They offer insights into their research that go beyond outcomes but inspire collective participation toward rethinking our privileged positions in society. They create opportunities for collective participation beyond the classroom by organizing critical reading and writing groups where research and theory merge with everyday life. These new learning relationships challenge me to ask questions, re-orient assumptions, and think critically about our lives, the lives of others, and how we are positioned in society. I have learned that it is okay to approach "education" as a co-constructive process, situated within relationships we form as a community of learners. I have also learned that sites of struggle afford opportunities to form learning alliances, only to be reconstituted within deeper, more engaged, and complex struggles from which we can collectively learn.

*   *   *

> [T]he future of higher education and of our nation, must be the forging of ways to feel, think, and teach together. It is our responsibility to continue the complex task of understanding our conflicting and painful stories, to help our nation value not only democracy but also the critical thinking and action that allow democracy to thrive. (Butler, 2000, p. 28)

> What if mentoring were conceived not just as the dispensing of advice or as empathetic listening but also as the reimagining of self and place in a new context? (Gunning, 1999, p. 180)

Where I had struggled alone, tackling graduate education as an isolated event, I now recognize and experience learning in collegial relationships, characterized by struggles over the equal sharing of authority. I understand "education" to be a situated and subjective process that is not a neutral act. If graduate education is about the production of new knowledge, then it must also address the cultural politics and differences in power that frame mentorship.

Mentorship requires "redoing the academy" by "undoing power inequities" through the telling of our stories, vulnerably taking apart our lives in relationship to others and putting them back together by forming respectful and reciprocal learning relationships across differences to engage social justice. Mentorship also engages our disparate subjectivities, not by upholding dominant paradigms and epistemology, but by collectively rethinking our positions and acknowledging how our biases and privileges can constrain learning. For example, faculty and students must interrogate categories that position expert and novice relationships by questioning when and why we uphold these categories to inform learning and by understanding that learning relationships can be collectively explored and formed when we confront such questions.

I envision a graduate education that dismantles political hierarchy by engaging our individual commitments to becoming better allies in addressing marginalization. In other words, if we collectively (in)form academia through our research, teaching, and service, then why not challenge ourselves as students, faculty, and the institutions that oversee our work to collectively ask:

- How does scholarship engage our commitments to social justice and create opportunities to dismantle oppression?
- How can we reorient our positions by questioning our affiliations and by acknowledging learning in conflict and coalition?
- How can our contradictions and struggles within marginalization re-create rather than reproduce "education"?

I believe that we in the university must engage these questions if we are to seek ways to support, recruit, and retain Latina/os and other marginalized groups in graduate school. In addressing these questions, we understand learning as a site of transformation that is equally invested in maintaining hierarchy through unequal power relationships. We locate marginalization as a source of learning that demonstrates agency, awareness, and resistance. And last, as Gunning (1999) powerfully states, we "recognize that [our] presumed naturalized access to authority, and indeed, the very construction of knowledge, and research methodology [we] have often taken for granted are distinct, historicized products forged in earlier moments of exclusion within the profession" (p. 182).

Two years before I graduated, I became the graduate student assistant to the dean of Graduate Studies and to the chancellor. A group of four concerned graduate students, including myself, sought to understand the above questions by developing "The Graduate Coalition for Diversity." We founded a project, the Graduate Academic Achievement & Advocacy Program (GAAP) for the "Recruitment, Retention, Development and Advocacy of Graduate Students of Color." Discontent with how the university, departments, and faculty grappled with our graduate education, we wrote a proposal (Gutekunst et al. 2001) that funded us $38,000 to implement our own efforts.

We informed our practice by investigating the climate of the university and by synthesizing local research and executive reports specific to our campus (see Delgado & Stefancic, 2000; Lewis, 2000; West, 1999, 2000). We acquired space on campus for our graduate student project from the Student Recruitment and Retention Center, the first graduate student group ever to house such a project. We hired two graduate students to organize retreats and events, develop a graduate student handbook, and enforce the Graduate Council's "Mentoring Guidelines."

Although our collective efforts made real experiences come alive by grounding them in the local politics of our institution, we could not sustain our efforts alone. Our unified response as graduate students remained just "one voice" and could not inspire university, department, or faculty alliances. I have learned that individual efforts quickly become entangled and subsumed in "power" relationships, requiring more than one party to stretch and commit time, energy, and work. I recommend a coalition-building approach to support, recruit, retain, and mentor graduate students. In this way alliances can be formed across and within positions of power, questioning how marginalization operates and sustains conventional "mentoring" despite our collective efforts to transform it.

This process is no simple task, but it can begin with more dialogue about what is mentoring and what is an ally. This dialogue should begin immediately affording faculty and students opportunities to discuss how we write, research, and teach together. It should address our individual and collective concerns. Like the process it sets out to discuss, it should be done in coalition with other graduate students and faculty across disciplines affording opportunities to rethink and share our academic affiliations across campus. It should have institutional support and be recognized as a valuable contribution toward building a more diverse and equitable campus climate.

Now, as I move from a postdoctoral fellowship into my first academic position as an assistant professor, I seek guidance on how to be in alliance. I ask, how do I critically self-reflect upon my positions and cross boundaries of exclusion to rethink my academic affiliations in an effort to redo the academy in coalition with others? I begin this process by addressing mentoring as a source of concern. I engage feminist interdisciplinary research and teaching that locates power (individual, including my own, and institutional) as a valuable social category of analysis. I seek the guidance of past and present mentors who individually and collectively inform my practice, whether working within the academy or outside of it (community activists, family members, friends, and colleagues). I also seek to locate and build new networks of communication to sustain the potential of such mentoring. In this capacity I will confront my personal biases collectively through collegial relationships that endure conflict with coalition as a viable source of mentoring.

References

Anzaldúa, G. (1987). *Borderlands/La Frontera: The new mestiza.* San Francisco: Aunt Lute Books.

Butler, J. E. (2000). Reflections on borderlands and the color line. In S. G.-L. Lim & M. Herrera-Sobek (Eds.), *Power, race, and gender in academe: Strangers in the tower?* (pp. 8–31). New York: Modern Language Association of America.

Delgado, R., & Stefancic, J. (2000). California's racial history and constitutional rationales for race-conscious decision making in higher education. *UCLA Law Review, 47*(6), 1521–1614.

Gunning, S. (1999). Now that they have us, what's the point? The challenge of hiring to create diversity. In S. G.-L. Lim & M. Herrera-Sobek (Eds.), *Power, race, and gender in academe: Strangers in the tower?* (pp. 171–182). New York: Modern Language Association of America.

Gutekunst, L., Medina, H., Quijada, D., & Rabaud, N. (2001). *Project for the recruitment, retention, development and advocacy of graduate students of color.* Davis: University of California-Davis.

hooks, b. (1993). Keeping close to home: Class and education. In M. M. Tokarezyk & E. A. Fay (Eds.), *Working-class women in the academy: Laboreres in the knowledge factory* (pp. 99–111). Amherst: University of Massachusetts Press.

Ladson-Billings, G. (1997). For colored girls who have considered suicide when the academy's not enough: Reflections of an African American woman scholar. In A. Neumann & P. L. Peterson (Eds.), *Learning from our lives: Women, research, and autobiography in education* (pp. 52–70). New York: Teachers College Press.

Lewis, J. (2000). *The experiences of underrepresented minority graduate students at the University of California, Davis.* Davis: University of California-Davis.

Moraga, C., & Anzaldúa, G. (Eds.) (1983). *This bridge called my back: Writings by radical women of color.* New York: Kitchen Table: Women of Color Press.

Trinh, M. H. (1989). *Woman, native, other.* New York: Routledge.

West, C. (1997). *Restoring hope: Conversations on the future of Black America.* Boston: Beacon Press.

West, M. (1999). *1998 goals for hiring faculty of color-UC Davis.* Davis: University of California-Davis.

West, M. (2000). Faculty women's struggle for equality at UC Davis. *UCLA Women's Law Journal, 259,* 10.

Petra Guerra

Dr. Petra Guerra earned her B.A. at the University of Texas-Pan American in political science, an M.A. in communications, and her Ph.D. in individual interdisciplinary studies at Washington State University. She is currently an assistant professor in the Department of Communication at the University of Texas-Pan American, in the field of journalism–public relations. A longtime activist, Dr. Guerra is interested in creating a safe and conducive space for students of color to appreciate and fulfill their educational dreams.

18

BEING LATINA AND ABD

Cuando Terminas Mujer?! (When Will You Finish?!)

Petra Guerra

Throughout my educational journey, my determination and inner strength to succeed have been primary. From my early educational experiences to my struggle to complete my dissertation, it is with focus, connection, and belief in something greater that I have succeeded and continue to succeed educationally. This chapter is a story of those educational experiences and the personal and cultural aspects that influenced completing my dissertation. In particular, my story highlights my childhood education, identifies key events in my undergraduate education, and details my experiences with the final requirement of earning my doctoral degree, completing my dissertation.

My Context and Early Educational Experiences

I am a Chicana/Mexicana, from the Rio Grande Valley in Texas. I come from a migrant family, and I worked in the agricultural fields until I was 21. My family and I picked grapes in California, thinned sugar beets in Idaho, picked cotton in Texas, and eventually made our way down to the Rio Grande Valley. The Valley, as we called it, was home to most of the farmworkers of my generation. This is where our parents bought land and built a small home.

Education for those of my generation, especially children of migrant laborers, was not an easy task. In March we followed the crops north, and we returned home in either November or December. As we traveled for work and went to school along the way, we were usually segregated from White students, and our education was not of equal quality. Regardless of grade level, as migrant students we were grouped together in a single classroom. In one instance, our classroom was an abandoned building, and a retired teacher taught us. When we returned to the Valley, however, we continued to be segregated from the nonmigrant students.

As I reflect on my experience, I realize that I never had a teacher take an interest in me, and that I always felt invisible. In total, I had about 12 months of schooling by the time I stopped going to school at the age of 10. When I did not return to school, no one came looking for me—no one asked why I did not return to school.

At 16, I married and had two children. By the time I was 19 years old, I was divorced and raising a daughter and son on my own, along with two of my younger siblings. At 21 I stopped working as a migrant laborer and became involved with the Utah Migrant Council, advocating for migrants' rights. This was the start of my activism—a role that held great importance for me and for which I was getting paid.

Transition to Academia

As I continued my activist work, I later took a position with the Idaho Migrant Council developing migrant Head Start centers throughout the state. During this time, *Teatro Mal Queridos* came to town. Through its plays it delivered messages of social change for Latina/os, messages that I wanted to deliver as well. I immediately decided that I wanted to join the theater group and be part of its advocacy work. However, to do so I had to be a college student at *Colegio Jacinto Treviño,* the institution that sponsored the theater group. This college's mission was to develop students who had political consciousness, who could give voice and lend advocacy to Latina/o communities. In line with my advocacy and social justice needs, I moved to Texas, registered for school, and joined the theater group. What I didn't know at the time was that I was transitioning into academia.

The beginning of my undergraduate career was filled with difficulties. When reviewing my student file, the academic personnel assistant recognized that my high school diploma was missing. Because I did not have one, the assistant asked me for a copy of my GED, which I did not have. So I earned my GED and then began attending classes and conducting theater presentations throughout the state. Unfortunately, the college closed abruptly a few months later due to structural and governance issues.

I had tasted higher education, and I wanted to continue it, along with my activism. If not promoting social justice through theater, I felt the next best thing was to become a lawyer. Within many migrant communities, health and justice were among those human needs that were all too rare. If I were to become a lawyer, I could help promote access and opportunities for migrant communities.

But like most of my personal and educational endeavors, I did not have advising or mentoring on the way to earning my undergraduate degree. In fact, by the time I graduated, I had enough credits for two degrees. I worked full time and had several part-time jobs to support my family and siblings as well as to pay for my education. Through it all, I had the courage and persistence to get through college.

Following my plan to help migrant communities, I applied and was admitted to law school. In the end I did not attend because I was uncertain about how I would fund my education. Although I did not attend law school, I quickly realized the importance of earning an advanced degree. For example, my co-workers with master's degrees got paid more for the same job I was doing with a bachelor's degree. At the time I was involved in film and video production for different Latina/o communities. I was fascinated by the impact telling community stories had in calling attention to people's needs. Film and video production was also another means for me to maintain my advocacy role of informing others about different Latina/o issues and needs. I had found yet another avenue to give back to my community through studying documentaries. I again realized my need to earn an advanced degree, and even though I didn't have the money, I had a strong drive to go back to school.

Entering Graduate School

Project 1000 (www.asu.edu/project1000) was my stepping-stone to graduate education. Founded in 1989 at Arizona State University, Project 1000 aimed to recruit "home-grown Latina/os" especially Chicana/os and Puerto Ricans for college (Rodriguez, 1996). The program encouraged me to attend graduate school and sent (at no cost) a formal and intensive application to the selected schools to which I wanted to apply. The program opened the door between me and the university, by putting me in contact with graduate school recruiters, who, in turn, connected me with the graduate programs where I wanted to study. As I had no previous information on colleges and did not know what to expect from graduate school, Project 1000 was central to my getting the information I needed and having access to graduate school in a way I never thought imaginable. Although Project 1000's involvement was seminal to my process of exploring and applying to graduate school, once I was accepted, my ties to the program ended.

What I Found in Graduate School

Undergraduate education did not prepare me for the different educational, social, and cultural aspects of graduate school. I decided that my best option financially was to live in the dormitories; however, I was an older student who had never experienced residential hall living, and I was surrounded by young White students. My dorm mates assumed that I, an older Latina, was the janitor. Being asked for toilet paper, trash bags, and other cleaning supplies was an unfortunate part of my residence hall experiences. To my dismay, my academic experiences were all too similar. In particular, there were no faculty of color and only a handful of students of color in my program and department and this was also the case on campus in general. Although I had encountered this situation before, it had not bothered me. It was different now as I was on my own—I did not know anyone, and I had no family with me. To manage this situation, I became active within the different organizations that represented students of color to help me manage my doctoral experience—at least until I had completed all my degree requirements with the exception of my dissertation (also known as "all but dissertation," or ABD).

Working to Complete the Dissertation

I had survived the requirements of my doctoral program, albeit in the face of substantial challenges and difficulties. I had yet to complete the final phase of my degree, however—the dissertation. This process included the practical aspects of conducting a study (e.g., funding, project approval, data gathering), along with all of the psychological and contextual issues (e.g., loneliness, mentors, connections to family and friends) of my dissertation.

Deciding on a topic for my dissertation was not a problem. I was certain and passionate about examining an issue that would lend insight into and provide information about individuals. In particular, my study investigated abstinence programs, television programming, and adolescents' sexual behavior, along with how this affected sexually transmitted diseases and HIV prevention. Although I had a topic, my first obstacle was finding funding. Dissertation money was not available through my department or university, so I had to rely on my own source of funding. I did qualify for tuition exemption if I was a teaching assistant (TA), but this meant that I would need to register as a full-time student and teach at least two classes each semester. To support myself while working on my dissertation, I accepted the TA position, which imposed time restrictions and prevented me from meeting with the school district personnel to coordinate my data collection. Incongruent with my cultural style of interaction and means by which I had hoped to conduct my study, I communicated with the schools via e-mail and by telephone.

Project Approval

Another challenge was gaining Institutional Review Board (IRB) approval to conduct my study. The sensitive nature of my topic made it difficult to obtain IRB approval. After working diligently to meet the board's parameters, my project was not approved until the end of the semester, which meant that it was too late to collect data at the high schools for that academic year. From this difficult and time-consuming process, I realized the importance of being passionate about my project.

Data Gathering

Collecting data was no less challenging than finally securing approval had been. Superintendents and high school principals did not find this topic acceptable, so it was challenging to negotiate schools' participation. I knew the importance of my research, but based on experience, I also felt that being Latina affected others' perceptions of my competence and, ultimately, the credibility of my research. This was made evident to me when the same school administrators responded favorably to requests for time or information from a White colleague, who took it upon herself to help me get the data I needed. Despite my efforts to help school district superintendents see the value of my research, I was faced with daily rejections of my research requests, rejections that I took personally. I held on to my belief regarding the importance of my study as I managed the intensity of these rejections.

Analyzing and Writing the Dissertation

Although I had taken both undergraduate and graduate courses in statistics, I was not prepared to analyze my data (once I finally had secured them). As a hands-on learner, I am certain that, if I had had the opportunity to work consistently with a faculty member on research (applying what I had learned in the classroom), I would have been better prepared for my data analyses. My faculty advisor would review my work step by step, pointing me in the right direction. I was on my own, however, to figure out the specifics of what I needed to do. I spent every spare hour of my day in the computer lab analyzing my data and/or writing my dissertation. There were days and evenings when either computers or computer technicians were not available. I was dependent on this computer lab, because it was the only place where I could print out the numerous drafts of my dissertation. I spent many long and lonely evenings in that lab.

Connecting with Others to Complete the Dissertation

Being ABD can be a lonely and isolating experience. Because time was of the essence (I needed to have my dissertation completed within a time line imposed by both my program and university), and because I was consumed with completing the project, I needed to protect my time in a way that I was not used to. I no longer had time to be an active member of the university and Latina/o community—the places from which I gained my greatest support and encouragement. What a contradiction! While being ABD I needed the most support and connections with others, but it was difficult to maintain them due to time constraints. Also, as I was no longer taking classes, I did not have the camaraderie of my peers and no formalized avenues for me to discuss or brainstorm how to approach the challenges of my dissertation or gain support for my difficult experiences. It was clear that I had to create and/or consciously maintain my connections with others to help me address the practical, cultural, psychological, and social aspects of completing my dissertation.

First and foremost, my connection to my family was of great help. They all were proud that I was pursuing an education, but my mom was my biggest supporter. It was because of her that during my early years I had achieved a fourth-grade education. Although my family did not understand all that my dissertation entailed, they were consistent in their belief that I would succeed.

My friends also supported me and kept me sane. It was from my close friends that I was able to get practical help as well as emotional support. For example, in my times of need, someone would lend me a dollar or hold my hand when I felt the world around me was falling apart. I also had friends working in the school district with whose advocacy I eventually gained approval from schools to conduct my study. Another friend convinced her children's school principal of the benefits of my study and he, too, agreed to participate.

I was not the only graduate student who was facing challenges. A handful of graduate students of color organized a peer group to critique and provide feedback about each other's work and dissertation studies. We were fortunate to have a faculty member, the only Chicana professor on campus, who gave of herself and her time. She understood our concerns and validated our experiences. Our group would discuss issues that were affecting our educational pursuits, such as challenges with faculty and difficulties of accessibility to agencies or schools (as was my case) to collect dissertation data.

In addition to my relationship with our faculty group leader, I established a relationship with a Latina on campus who believed in my abilities. Elsa was an undergraduate advisor who had had similar educational struggles and had secured a position with the university. She understood me culturally, helped me find answers to my questions and solutions to my problems, steered me away from racist professors, identified teaching opportunities, advocated for me for scholarships within my department, and introduced me to other Latina/os on campus and in the community. With Elsa's genuine support, I had someone who addressed my personal and professional concerns as a Latina graduate student who was ABD. With her I could reveal my feelings and not be criticized or perceived as weak; with her my experiences were validated. Ultimately it was with her help that I completed my dissertation within the required time.

It was also the support of my dissertation advisor and those professional Latina/os in the community that helped me manage my process. While I was writing my dissertation, I also wrote and presented four papers related to my dissertation at Chicana/Latina conferences. My work was appreciated, and I felt validated by academically well-known Chicana/Latina professors. It was difficult to return to the campus after attending conferences when it seemed that the only person who was genuinely interested in the research was my dissertation advisor. Nonetheless, his consistent feedback at each stage of the process was instrumental.

Recommendations

My story is that of a Latina who came from the fields and entered academia, armed with courage, passion, and the support of my mother. Throughout my life my educational experiences have been difficult, but they have not been insurmountable. In reflecting on these events, I offer the following recommendations to those Latina/os who are ABD and to those who are working to ensure that they do not become ABD.

- Pick a topic that you are passionate about and willing to follow through. Also, be realistic in the selection of your topic and think through the practical aspects of accessibility to study participants.
- Seek advice and mentorship from your dissertation chair. If this relationship does not yield the kind of advice you need, find others (e.g., peer dissertation support group, other faculty mentor) from whom you can gain support.
- Maintain connections with family, friends, peer colleagues, and mentors despite time constraints. Be careful not to isolate yourself as you work on your dissertation. Open yourself to supportive assistance from others to validate you and keep you on task.
- Stay true to your belief in the value of your work. Even though some may not consider it valuable, remember the individuals and communities who will benefit from having their voice and needs addressed.

A few recommendations for university faculty and staff in working with their ABD graduate students include the following:

- Provide hands-on opportunities for students to become familiar with practical aspects of data management, analyses, and writing.
- Work to provide program, department, and university-wide funds and fellowships for ABD graduate students. Monetary awards, no matter how large, are financially and emotionally helpful because they provide validation and encouragement for students.
- Develop and implement supportive venues for ABD students to discuss their research progress. Also, consider the specific needs of graduate students of color when developing the programming (e.g., support groups run by programs or university counseling centers).

I have celebrated many days with my family, friends, and mentors—the day that I completed my data analyses, printed the final version of my dissertation, defended my dissertation, and was hooded at graduation. I was set for yet another transition into academia—my first position as an assistant professor. May the force, la *Virgin de Guadalupe*, or your mom (as in my case), be with you.

Reference

Rodriguez, R. (1996). . . . 3,000 and counting. *Black Issues in Higher Education, 13,* 10.

19

ENDEREZANDO EL CAMINO/ STRAIGHTENING THE PATH

Dispelling Myths and Providing Directions for Latina/o Doctoral Students

Jeanett Castellanos, Alberta M. Gloria, and Mark Kamimura

The U.S. demography shift has introduced substantial changes for the kindergarten through college (K–16) student population. This change demands that school systems and officials evaluate the experiences of a newly growing student population to ensure the means for quality education. The limited understanding of the educational process for Latina/o students poses a challenge to the nation's goal of developing a diverse set of leaders with different linguistic backgrounds, cultural values, and worldviews (Carnevale, 1999).

This book addresses the educational disparities and inequalities encountered by Latina/o students throughout their educational journeys. Using a psychosociocultural (PSC) approach (Gloria & Rodriguez, 2000) specifically for Latina/o doctoral students, the authors present the successes and challenges within the education system (e.g., poor quality of education) necessary to overcome to pursue a college education (i.e., baccalaureate, master's, and doctoral degree). In particular, the authors highlight the path to a quality educational experience and present specific directions for improving the historical undereducation epidemic of Latina/os.

To meet this call, the purpose of this chapter is threefold: (1) to identify and synthesize themes expressed in the book's student narrative while highlighting the interrelationships of their different dimensions; (2) to dispel myths of the educational process for Latina/o doctoral students; and (3) to provide macro and micro directions relevant for students, families, communities, and universities. More specifically, the first section provides a brief overview of the most salient themes within the students' educational experiences with specific examples. Next, we present four prominent myths repeatedly experienced by Latina/o doctoral students. Each myth is followed by directions for university official and students to ensure quality doctoral training experiences.

Narrative Synthesis: Consistent Patterns in Latina/o Doctoral Experiences

In reviewing and assessing eight Latina/o doctoral student narratives (see chapters 11–18), six main themes emerged: (1) negotiation and context of the training environment; (2) discrimination based on gender stereotypes; (3) management of resulting affect—loneliness, alienation; (4) solidification of ethnic identity; (5) realization that family comes in different forms and fashions; and (6) taking care of business—self-care. A brief description of each theme follows, including examples that characterize Latina/os' academic experiences. Considering the interrelationship of the various themes, coping strategies for negative experiences are present in more than one category.

Negotiation and Context of the Training Environment

Latina/o students described the importance of navigating the educational environment during their doctoral training. In particular, students identified an academic culture that did not parallel their perspectives and values (e.g., Guerra, Rosales). The environment invalidated Latina/o student experiences and created tension for the student. Describing their environment as "hostile and scrutinizing," students faced faculty and students who reinforced conforming and cultural assimilation to the department's norms and adjusting to the context despite cultural conflict (e.g., Garcia, Quijada). Additional challenges included tokenism and others' perspective that these students were "special admits" or a result of affirmative action (e.g., Kamimura).

Discrimination Based on Gender Stereotypes

Students also reported being marginalized by department peers (Vera Sanchez) and being excluded from projects that could enhance their research and critical thinking skills, ultimately limiting their scholarship. Similar to Ibarra (2001), faculty were noted to "devalue" work related to Latina/o issues and considered such work unoriginal (e.g., Quijada, Rosales). Last, the impact of limited role models and the importance of positioning oneself to disprove or dilute gender stereotypes for both Latinas and Latinos were emphasized. Specifically, Latinas' stereotypes included being perceived as dependent and submissive, while Latinos' marginalized context was perceived as being tough. Unfortunately, students reported having their competence questioned or intelligence challenged (Garcia, Ramirez, Vera Sanchez).

The student narratives implemented specific techniques of persistence throughout their programs. These techniques included reevaluating their purpose in graduate school, developing peer groups to discuss similar experiences, communicating among students and faculty advisors, returning home to visit, balancing home and schoolwork, connecting with local community, redefining and reshaping gender roles, self-reflecting, and distancing from their programs to stay strong in their abilities.

Management of Resulting Affect

Coupling the hostile environment experiences and the uprooting of some students to join doctoral programs, feelings of alienation, loneliness, and displacement emerged (e.g., Guerra, Segura-Herrera). Feelings of intimidation by the process accompanied with shock regarding social and role adjustment were experienced. In fact, students had had physical and internal pain when leaving their families (e.g., Vera Sanchez) and experienced discomfort as a result of limited interaction with students of similar cultural backgrounds (e.g., Rosales). Other emotions reported included anger, frustration, stress, and emerging thoughts of self-doubt resulting from negative encounters that invalidated Latina/o students' admission, experiences, perceptions, and contributions (e.g., Garcia, Kamimura, Quijada).

Students countered their negative affect by educating their peers about cultural biases, becoming accustomed to being evaluated constantly (both by faculty and peers), contending with self-doubt and securing confidence, and seeking peer and social support (i.e., mentorship) to rebuild strength and renew energy. Others instilled cultural values of *aguantarse* (endurance) and *ganas* (desire) to overcome obstacles and were inspired by the *orgullo familiar* (familial pride) and cultural resilience evident in their parents' and family history (e.g., Kamimura, Rosales, Segura-Herrera).

Solidification of Ethnic Identity

Enculturation is a socialization process that requires Latina/o students to adjust to a new environment with different values and norms (e.g., Kamimura). With a goal of scholarship development, doctoral training requires a transformative process for students to achieve their degree (Ibarra, 2001). This transformation is evident as each student narrative indirectly discusses the role of ethnic identity in his or her doctoral training. The authors describe how they experienced cultural incongruity between their native values and the surrounding academic culture and how they learned to balance these two elements (e.g., Guerra, Kamimura, Quijada). While creating discomfort, self-questioning, and marginalization, cultural conflict also prompted students to learn about their culture, reinforce their cultural practices, and solidify their ethnic identity.

Specific academic values that countered the students' native values included individuality vs. collectivism, independence vs. interdependence, challenge of perspectives vs. deference to authority, and pursuit of power vs. communal ownership. Assisting the navigation of academic culture included cultural values of *familismo*, the importance of *comunidad*, and community responsibility. For example, students surrounded themselves with external artifacts (e.g., pictures) to remind themselves of history (e.g., Ramirez), called home to share their experiences (e.g., Rosales), and reached out to the university community to interact with other Latina/o students (e.g., Guerra, Kamimura, Ramirez). In addition to person-specific initiatives, students identified department-related activities to counter their negative affect. Identifying role models and establishing healthy mentoring relationships with individuals of similar ethnicity and parallel research interests were additional means of establishing a solid ethnic identity.

Family Comes in Different Forms and Fashions

The underlying theme of family was evident in each doctoral student narrative. As the students expressed their adjustment to being away from home, many identified means to establish a university family (e.g., Segura-Herrera). University families were created with other Latina/o and students of color who encountered similar collegiate experiences. The practice of coming together, sharing time, and developing group cohesion was emphasized (e.g., Guerra, Rosales). Similarly, mentors and inspirational advisement during difficult experiences was highly valued. Students also found value in joining racial and ethnic minority student groups for peer support, social networks, peer mentorship, and advisement (e.g., Kamimura, Guerra). Common academic experiences validated students' realities and created a support system for navigation.

In addition, the value of e-mail access to other Latina/os was emphasized; these interactions helped reinforce the sense of connection and maintenance of ties to neighborhood peers and local community friends (e.g., Ramirez). At later stages of the doctoral program, students valued conferences that addressed race and ethnicity issues in their respective fields and social events that presented venues to connect with other Latina/o scholars and professionals. Overall, the effort to preserve family ties and community connection reinforced the value of collectivism and student community connection and their contribution for group social advancement of future generations.

Taking Care of Business—Self-care

Self-care, the final theme, played a strong role throughout the student experiences. Although students encountered racism, prejudice, cultural incongruity, and social adjustment challenges, many recognized the importance of developing a balance between personal and professional roles (e.g., Quijada, Ramirez, Rosales). Students emphasized the importance of spending time with family, creating cultural resurgence opportunities with peers and community, and attending to one's needs.

Specific coping techniques in balancing personal and professional roles included maintaining cultural values, involving family in graduate school activities, integrating into the Latina/o local and university community (e.g., Ramirez), and self-reflection and distancing (e.g., Kamimura). Openness to change and degree commitment (e.g., Segura-Herrera) facilitated the balancing of earning a doctoral degree and having a personal life. Also, creating outlets for stress was emphasized (e.g., through yoga, spirituality, exercise) (e.g., Garcia).

The six main themes in the narratives emphasize the roles of academic environments, ethnic identity, and family and the importance of balancing all three. In addition, the chapters' authors underscore the value of mentorship, constructive research opportunities, and quality support systems. As university officials, department deans, and faculty strive to recruit and retain Latina/o doctoral students, a critical mindfulness to cultivate a culturally inclusive doctoral training experience is warranted. These narratives also pose a framework from which other Latina/o doctoral students can find validation.

Myths and Directives for Students and University Personnel

The overview of Latina/o graduate students in doctoral programs underscores the multiple challenges students must overcome to persist and ultimately graduate. More specifically, the student authors document how graduate training programs fall short in providing culturally inclusive opportunities, ethnic-based research training, and a positive training environment for scholarship development. In an attempt to increase the representation and improve the educational experiences of Latina/o doctoral students, this section discuses four prominent myths in academic culture that are evident in Latina/o doctoral students' personal, social, and cultural encounters. Directives for institutions to deconstruct these damaging and misguided perspectives are provided and Latina/o student navigational strategies are recommended.

Myths and Directives

Myth 1: Latina/o doctoral students need to strip themselves of cultural identity and values in their training programs.

Too often faculty and university personnel foster and nurture Eurocentric values on university campuses, reinforcing environments that promote assimilation for school adjustment. Such environments alienate Latina/o doctoral students and affect their satisfaction and persistence.

University Directive 1: Recognize that cultural differences are not deviance but, instead, broaden and deepen perspectives and application of concepts.

As the United States becomes more diverse and universities serve changing student body needs, the role of culture must be considered in developing a more sensitive curriculum, campus culture, and faculty pool. Multicultural directives must be at the forefront of university initiatives to ensure a culturally inclusive experience that promotes the value of diversity and cultural awareness across the campus.

University and department chairs must have specific diversity goals and initiatives to recruit and retain Latina/o students while exemplifying cultural awareness, the value of diversity, and integration of perspectives. Specific programs include diversity awareness workshops and dialogues for all faculty, staff, and administrative assistants; a biannual cultural assessment conducted by outside diversity consultants of campus climate that assesses all departments; and the inclusion of items addressing faculty's cultural integration in class evaluations. Such efforts reinforce the perspective of theory in academic disciplines and enhance the relevance to theory application.

Student Directive 1: Honor your cultural rituals, tradiciones y celebraciones *(traditions and celebrations) in your personal, professional, and doctoral training interactions.*

The mindset that graduate studies force students to dismiss cultural beliefs, values, and practices creates anxiety and distress for Latina/o students. Do not devote all your time to your studies. Instead, dedicate some time to reinforce your cultural foundations and understanding. In the short term, you will be more productive. Over the long term, devoting time only to your studies may introduce psychological and social consequences that create internal guilt and distress. For example, establish opportunities on- and off-campus to practice your cultural rituals and traditions; involve yourself with the university Latina/o cultural center, participate in *Mes de La Raza* or *Semana de La Familia* and do not pass up cultural opportunities. Other forms of cultural resilience include forming an educational family with your peers, making ongoing arrangements to go home, visiting a neighboring Latina/o community to develop a local cultural support system, and remaining connected to your *gente* (people) (e.g., cooking cultural foods, going to Mass, e-mailing friends).

Myth 2: Equal training opportunities are available to all students.

Latina/o doctoral students have different experiences from their White counterparts in graduate education. Many times first-generation Latina/o students do not know what financial opportunities and faculty advisory benefits are available. In particular, Latina/os are unaware of fellowships and various assistantships (e.g., research, teaching, staff, and counseling) to fund a graduate degree.

University Directive 2: Graduate deans, department deans, faculty, and student recruiters must take the initiative to inform Latina/o students about fellowships and assistantship opportunities.

Differential treatment is not necessarily discrimination as many Latina/o students are not familiar with their rights and roles as graduate students to seek out and ask for assistance. Too often, departments complain about limited minority applicants or extend only a few offers to Latina/o students and, as a result, have few acceptances. Latina/o doctoral students will be recruited by institutions that are seriously committed to increasing diversity by offering a comprehensive financial packet. Invest in your diversity initiatives; be prepared to help Latina/o students to fund their training if there are means to decrease their educational expenses. Latina/o doctoral students may not know about the available resources, deadlines, and benefits of different funding. Inform students and provide opportunities for true, equal access. Also, be prepared for students to resent funded Latina/o students when funding is limited. When funding is scarce, Latina/o students are labeled special initiative efforts or affirmative action admits.

Student Directive 2: Recognize that your doctoral training experiences and access to opportunities may be different from those of others in your program.

Many Latina/o students experience different social and academic integration patterns from their White peers. Early on, Latina/o students witness other student colleagues' involvement with research and departmental activities that are different from their experiences. For example, White peers often have academic fellowships or research assistantships, while Latina/o students have limited means to pay their tuition (e.g., on-campus hourly jobs for tuition wavers or off-campus employment). As a result, Latina/o students may inadvertently dedicate less time to their studies and research projects.

For enhanced integration, seek out information from faculty advisors and departmental secretaries about fellowship and assistantship opportunities. Apply for all educational scholarships to decrease the need for multiple jobs to pay your bills. Getting a fellowship or employment on campus in your department is most recommended; this allows students to have more faculty contact and department socialization. If you do obtain funding, be cautious with whom you share your funding circumstances; too many Latina/o students experience *peer envy* when receiving limited funding within the department. In relation to research opportunities, identify your faculty's interests and pursue involvement on their research teams. Become an integral member of a faculty's research team by collecting and analyzing data, writing for publication, and presenting at national conferences.

Myth 3: It is Latina/o students' role to teach others about "all things cultural" and to bring up cultural issues in classroom and discussion settings.

While most university campuses are predominantly White and are located in rural towns, cultural diversity issues often are not addressed and occasionally are overtly devalued. These restricted cultural interactions stem from limited diversity awareness, knowledge, and skills. As a result, university campus officials and faculty often rely on racial and ethnic students to lead the university community in its diversity initiatives. Similarly, these students are given the responsibility to work with the university to address ethnic community issues. For example, Latina/o doctoral students are expected to be willing recruiters of other Latina/o doctoral students despite their experiences.

Latina/o doctoral students are also expected to be the cultural experts of their *gente* (people) and other minority communities. Often asked to speak on behalf of racial minority communities in the classroom, these students become more alienated.

University Directive 3: It is the role and responsibility of the university (e.g., faculty, instructors, administrators) to be knowledgeable and effectively conversant about diversity and not rely on Latina/o students to teach them and other students about cultural-diversity issues.

Universities should bear the responsibility to foster relations with local under-represented communities, student-of-color organizations, and individual students. Although the opportunity to connect with the community is essential for Latina/o students, requiring such time- and energy-consuming tasks of students limits their study time, on-campus activities, research projects, and faculty interactions. If student involvement is needed, have numerous students on the project and provide reasonable time lines for the various tasks. Similarly, present varied opportunities beyond Latina/o-centered initiatives to ensure multidimensional development. Assess the university's commitment to diversity and local communities by requiring top-ranked officials to address diversity as a frontline issue. Introduce a community relations university professional to establish a community-university relations plan for recruitment and retention. Finally, disseminate information about increased university-community relations and interactions (e.g., Spanish-language university quarterly newsletter, quarterly community luncheons, community day).

Relative to faculty instructors, expecting that Latina/o students will represent their community or other minority communities when discussing diversity in the classroom diverts responsibility from the instructor and the other students. It is the responsibility of the doctoral faculty to model the intricacies of diversity interactions by respectfully engaging in dialogues that enhance students' understanding of diversity, promoting constructive diversity discussions in the classroom, reconfiguring misconceptions, integrating multiculturalism into the curriculum, and enacting the role of a cultural diversity advocate.

Because Latina/os are often exploring their role in research of Latina/os (which is generally taught in higher education), deans, department chairs, and faculty have the responsibility to offer research opportunities that address diversity within the discipline. Consequently, Latina/o students may feel alienated and disconnected from a research process that addresses general issues not inclusive of diversity and cultural variables. Ensure a variety of on- and off-campus opportunities for students to conduct research on diversity issues. At the same time, do not place all the responsibility on them to become experts on a topic without direction and faculty supervision. Along with cultural expertise at the department level, develop a lecture series enabling Latina/o researchers, scholars, and fellows to showcase their research.

Student Directive 3: Do not assume that doctoral students and faculty are culturally savvy and have the ability to engage in difficult cultural dialogues.

Despite being top scholars in their respective fields, faculty may have biased cultural assumptions and inaccurate diversity knowledge. As one of few minorities in one's cohort and classroom setting, Latina/os may be called on to voice their opinions about Latina/o community issues. Although Latina/o students are expected to voice their perspectives on Latina/o community issues, they often are not encouraged to address general academic issues. Do not fall into the primary role of the cultural voice (speaking only on diversity issues) while the role of a comprehensive learner becomes secondary. As a well-prepared student, engage in all class discussions and encourage others to address diversity issues, removing the responsibility from a single person.

Tokenism and unique expectations of Latina/o students create additional educational barriers in the graduate education process. To maintain cultural sanity, find others with whom you can have confidential and meaningful discussions about diversity, experiences of campus/departmental marginalization, and feelings of alienation. Form a support group to manage discrimination from faculty and empower yourself throughout the experience. Other means include writing about your doctoral experiences for a campus anthology and developing Latina/o-specific campus-wide or discipline-wide (e.g., Latina/o counseling psychology) list servs and chat rooms for open dialogue. Last, attend professional conferences to meet other graduate students in similar situations who can affirm your experience and decrease your sense of normlessness.

Myth 4: Staying true to your community means always discussing cultural issues, regardless of the cost.

Latina/o students often feel responsible to represent and protect their communities throughout their graduate studies. The battle to defend a culture, explain cultural differences, educate a group, and even protest against injustice takes energy, time, and investment. Although students need and gain gratification from cultural advocacy, it is important to recognize when to engage in self-care, and allow others to represent the community. Extensive community involvement is invigorating, but in the long term it is costly to doctoral studies.

University Directive 4: Attend and integrate psychological, social, and cultural elements within doctoral programs to ensure Latina/os' academic retention and success.

University officials must cultivate an educational environment that addresses the psychological, social, and cultural aspects of Latina/o doctoral experiences. In particular, campus and department environments should value diversity by providing educational and social opportunities for cultural inclusion (e.g., cultural conferences and diversity months, diversity in the curriculum, and diversity representation across campus). Administrators must assess the cultural context (e.g., values and work assumptions) for understanding the social influences (e.g., peer and family support, faculty and student relations, mentorship opportunities, campus climate) on the students' psychological well-being.

Specific social support systems must be implemented to ensure overall adjustment, academic satisfaction, and retention. For example, facilitate Latina/o graduate support groups, make available list servs and chat rooms for Latina/o students in the program and across campus; extend Web privileges to allow students to create Web pages addressing school adjustment; provide conference funding to promote social and cultural networking; and create space for Latina/o families to visit, learn about the university, and become comfortable in the setting. For example, *Noche Cultural* (Cultural Night), a play about Latina/o student life and educational challenges, may serve as a vehicle for family cohesion while enhancing parental understanding of the education process. Other efforts include showcasing Latina/o graduate students in the local newspapers—explaining their area of study and its benefits, describing their graduate experiences and responsibilities, and identifying their career aspirations. Highlighting student academics assists with the integration of both systems (school and family).

Student Directive 4: Stay true to your cultural commitments while maintaining self-care.

A part of being in graduate school is learning the professional and cultural savvy of protecting yourself. For example, know when you have to decline requests from family and community. As a graduate student, it is critical to understand the value of self-care and well-being. As students aim to become masters in their education, they should also aim to become masters of themselves (e.g., attend to inner feelings, pressures, and challenges). Dismissing stress and minimizing any episodes of incongruity, discomfort, and cultural conflict can introduce negative effects to your self-identity, motivation, and life satisfaction.

Balance your school and personal demands. Recognize the value of social support, develop a plan to address your personal needs, and establish a social network and connection with peers, family, and neighborhood friends. Remain connected to the community while ensuring that interactions create a balance to ground you. Assess what is too much to balance and what is too little to sustain you culturally. Similarly, find a mentor who can help you find a balance and reinforce your values and cultural experiences. A mentor does not have to be Latina/o but he or she should have cultural knowledge and understanding of Latina/os and their struggles. Finally, be attentive to your health, personal satisfaction, and overall well-being. Too often, Latina/o students spend their time and effort balancing academia and family while dismissing personal needs. Take time to relax, read empowering literature, find a positive escape to release anxiety and academic pressures, and develop opportunities to bridge your psychological, social, and cultural needs, both professionally and personally. As trailblazers of educational success, you are tomorrow's leaders and open pathways for future Latina/o doctoral students.

References

Carnevale, A. P. (1999). *Education = success: Empowering Hispanic youth and adults.* Princeton, NJ: Educational Testing Service.

Gloria, A. M., & Rodriguez, E. R. (2000). Counseling Latino university students: Psychosociocultural issues for consideration. *Journal of Counseling & Development, 78,* 145–154.

Ibarra, R. A. (2001). *Beyond affirmative action: Reframing the context of higher education.* Madison, WI: University of Wisconsin Press.

Jeanett Castellanos

Jeanett Castellanos currently serves as the director for the Social Science Academic Resource Center in the School of Social Sciences at the University of California, Irvine. Dr. Castellanos is responsible for coordinating many functions within the Social Science Academic Resource Center, including the Social Science Internship Program, Post Baccalaureate Opportunities Program, Research Liaison Program, and Graduate School Preparation services. She also serves as a lecturer for the Department of Social Sciences and the Chicano/Latino Studies Program. In this capacity, she has taught classes such as racial ethnic minorities in higher education, Chicano/Latino families, and research methods. In addition, she has served as a consultant for various higher education institutions in the area of cultural competency.

Dr. Castellanos holds a baccalaureate degree from the University of California, Irvine, a master's of education in counseling psychology and a Ph.D. in education from Washington State University. She also completed a summer postdoctoral fellowship at Indiana University–Bloomington. Her research focuses on the college experience of racial and ethnic minority students and the psychosociocultural factors that affect their retention. Other research interests include cultural competency in university settings, the underutilization of psychotherapy among ethnic minority college students, and coping strategies leading to resilience among Cuban refugees. Dr. Castellanos is a member of the American Psychological Association, actively participating in Division 17 (Society of Counseling Psychology) as programming chair for the Section on Ethnic and Racial Diversity. She also serves as the Student and Professional Development Officer for the National Latina/o Psychological Association (NLPA) and the California Latina/o Psychological Association (CLPA).

Alberta M. Gloria

Alberta M. Gloria received her doctorate in counseling psychology from Arizona State University and is a professor in the Department of Counseling

Psychology and Adjunct Faculty with the Chicana/Latina Studies Program at the University of Wisconsin-Madison. Her primary research interests include psychosociocultural factors for Latina/o and other racial and ethnic students in higher education. Addressing issues of cultural congruity, educational and social coping supports, and academic well-being, her work has appeared in journals such as *Cultural Diversity and Ethnic Minority Psychology*, *Hispanic Journal of Behavioral Sciences*, and *Journal of College Student Development*. An active member of the American Psychological Association, Dr. Gloria is currently chair for the Section on Ethnic and Racial Diversity for Division 17 (Society of Counseling Psychology) and member-at-large for Division 45 (Society for the Psychological Study of Ethnic Minority Issues). She was awarded the 2002 Emerging Professional Award from Division 45 of the APA for outstanding early career contributions in promoting ethnic minority issues in the field of psychology. More recently, Dr. Gloria received the 2003 Kenneth and Mamie Clark Award from the American Psychological Association of Graduate Students for her contributions to the professional development of ethnic minority graduate students.

Mark Kamimura

Mark A. Kamimura is a Ph.D. candidate in the Center for the Study of Higher and Postsecondary Education at the University of Michigan, with a concentration in public policy and administration. He has served as the political action chair and president of the Students of Color of Rackham (SCOR), a member of the Horace Rackham Graduate School Executive Board, graduate researcher on the Diverse Democracy Project, and program coordinator for the Office of Multicultural Student Affairs. Before coming to the Uniuversity of Michigan, Mr. Kamimura served as director of the Knowledge and Social Responsibility Program at the University of California, Irvine, and program specialist for the Intercultural Resource Center at Columbia University. Currently he is a graduate coordinator for the King/Chavez/Parks College Days program, facilitator for the Dialogues on Diversity program, chair of the National SCOR Conference, and serves on various campus-wide committees.

Mr. Kamimura is a Rackham Merit Fellow and Edward Ginsberg Fellow. He has an M.A. in organization and leadership from Teachers College, Columbia University, and a B.A. in social science from the University of California, Irvine.

INDEX

A

academic achievement. *see also* barriers to
academic achievement; degrees
factors associated with in high school,
28–31
and guilt, 128, 141, 172, 174
Mexican-origin student pathways to,
97–100
parent/school relationships, 10–11, 29–30
and resistance strategies, 129
role of cultural values in promoting, 10–11,
162–166, 282–283
role of faculty in, 85, 103–104, 142–143,
173–174, 177–178
role of parents in, 30, 59, 151, 162–165
stimulating in Latina/os, 92–93
academic achievement gap. *see also* barriers to
academic achievement; dropout rates
behaviors associated with, 9
and cultural deficit model, 7, 9–10, 12, 27,
149–150
educational attainment of full-time, first-
time freshmen by ethnic group, 47*t*
high school graduations/college
enrollments, compared to Whites,
41–42, 41*t*, 46
K–16, factors associated with, 3, 5–8, 11,
25–26, 27
Latina/o pipeline, ninth grade through
earned degree, by ethnic group, 41*t*
academic administrators. *see also* dean-based
leadership; recommendations for
retention and recruitment
impact on minority students, 105–106
Latina/o representation, 84, 106, 107*t*
role in increasing minority participation
in higher education, 80, 83–86
academic apprenticeships, 104
academic aspirations

of college students, 58–59
and faculty role models, 103, 142–143,
173–174, 177–178
and gender, 97, 162–165
academic culture
adjustment to college, studies of, 62–64
in doctoral programs, personal experience
of, 193–197, 202–203, 204–206, 237–238
in graduate programs, personal experience
of, 224–225, 245–249
myths regarding, 282–288
negotiating, 60–61, 171, 282–284, 285–286,
289–290
sense of belonging, factors associated with,
62–64
academic environments
balancing demands of, 60–61, 171,
176–177, 215–216, 221–224, 281,
289–290
multicultural directives for, 282–288
organizations and diversity, 104, 143–144
support of diversity at the doctoral level,
139–140
support of diversity at the graduate level,
83–85, 264–265, 272
academic fellowships, seeking, 284
academic performance and dropping out of
college, 58–59
academic shock, 203
acculturation, 138
Achor, Shirley, 129
action plan for academic/graduate deans,
86–87
administrators, academic. *see* academic
administrators
advanced degree attainment. *see* degrees;
doctoral level enrollments; graduate
schools; master's-level enrollments
Advisory Commission on Education

methodology, 151–155
respondent sample characteristics, 153*t*, 154*t*
results of Latina study, 155–159
similarities in educational pathways for Latina/os, 162–166
Hurtado, Sylvia, 56, 108

I

Ibarra, Robert A., 83
identity. *see also* narratives, personal
balancing personal and professional, 60–61, 171–173, 176–177, 217–218, 222–223, 281, 289–290
challenges to, in graduate school, 282–283
conflict, ethnic, 128–129, 138, 140–141, 175, 192
development, 135–137, 145, 194
framework, 144–145
importance of mentoring to, 139, 142–143
maintaining a strong ethnic, 213–214, 219–220, 282–283
masculine, 235, 237
immigrants
illegal, experiences of in U.S. schools, 233–236, 237–238
student, and persistence, 21
income
family, and dropout rates, 26
median, by educational level, xii
indebtedness as barrier to degree completion, 101
Independent School District v. Salvatierra (1930, 1931), xxviii
institutional barriers. *see* barriers to academic achievement
institutional programs, importance of, 166
institutions
elite private, 99
of higher education (IHEs), 106, 108, 167
non-selective, 97
selective, 98–99
instrumental knowledge, 166, 171
integration, social, and persistence in college students, 60
intelligence and masculinity, stereotypes regarding, 235, 237

intolerance. *see* discrimination
isolation, experiencing in graduate school, 176, 201, 203–204

J

jobs, as a factor in student persistence, 26, 44, 58, 107
Jordan, W.J., 27
junior colleges. *see* community colleges

K

K–8 schools. *see* schools, K–16
K–8 U.S. Public School Enrollment by Race/Ethnicity, 2000, 5t
Kahlo, Frida, 244
Kamimura, Mark A., 290, xxxiii
Kellogg, W.K. Foundation, xv, xvii
Kiyana, A., 30
knowledge, Latina/o student's, failure to recognize value of, 3, 9

L

Lang, D., 61
language barriers, 6, 26, 92. *see also* barriers to academic achievement
Lara, Juan F., 27, 105
later-life entry to graduate school, 83
Latina/o Faculty Members in the United States by Race/Ethnicity, Academic Rank, Fall 1999, 105*t*
Latina/o K–8 School Enrollment by Percentage and Total Number in Five Southwestern States, 4t
Latina/o Pipeline—Ninth Grade through Earned Degree, 41t
Latina/os. *see also* culture, Latina/o; demographics; families
college enrollments, compared to Whites, 46, 47*t*
complexity of defining, 81, xxiv
demands, unique academic, 179
educational pipeline, by ethnic group, 41–42, 41*t*, 47*t*
faculty and administrators, 84, 85, 101, 103, 105, 105t
gender dynamics in educational attainment, 113